MAJOR POEMS OF THE HEBREW BIBLE

Volume I: Ex. 15, Deut. 32, and Job 3

STUDIA SEMITICA NEERLANDICA

Prof. dr. W.J. van Bekkum
Prof. dr. W.A.M. Beuken s.j.
Prof. dr. H. Daiber
Dr. C.H.J. de Geus
Prof. dr. J. Hoftijzer
Prof. dr. T. Muraoka
Prof. dr. K.A.D. Smelik
Prof. dr. K. van der Toorn
Prof. dr. K.R. Veenhof

For publications in the series see page 207

Submission of manuscripts

- Manuscripts should be submitted to the senior editor of Van Gorcum Publishers, P.O. Box 43, 9400 AA Assen, The Netherlands.
  E-Mail: assen@vgorcum.nl

- Each manuscript submitted is reviewed by two reviewers.

- The reviewers will not be identified to the authors.

J.P. Fokkelman

MAJOR POEMS
OF THE HEBREW BIBLE

at the Interface of Hermeneutics and Structural Analysis

Volume I: Ex. 15, Deut. 32, and Job 3

1998
Van Gorcum

© 1998, Van Gorcum & Comp. B.V., PO Box 43, 9400 AA Assen, The Netherlands

All rights reserved. No part of this publication may be reproduced, stored in a retrieval system, or transmitted in any form or by any means, electronic, mechanical, photocopying, recording, or otherwise, without the prior permission of the Publisher.

ISBN 90 232 3367 0

Printed by: Van Gorcum, Assen, The Netherlands

Contents

Preface

                                                                                               page

Chapter One: Introduction to the study of
        classical Hebrew poetry   1

    A. Hierarchical text models
        The poet and his language
    B. The poem under the rule of prosody
        A finger exercise on Psalm 113
        Note on pre-Masoretic syllables
    C. The relations between syntax and the higher prosodic units
    D. Hermeneutics interacting with structural analysis

Chapter Two: A full description of Exodus 15   24

    § 1. The key to the poem: textural units
    § 2. Structures and contours:
        a description of strophes and stanzas
    § 3. Proportions

Chapter Three: A comprehensive description
        of Deuteronomy 32 as a work of art   54

    Text
    Introduction
    § 1. The first section: one stanza, three strophes (vv.1-6)
    § 2. The second section: four stanzas, eight strophes (vv.7-18)
    § 3. The third section: four stanzas, ten strophes (vv.19-35)
    § 4. The fourth section: two stanzas, six strophes (vv.36-43)

Chapter Four: The Song of Moses in Deut.32 as a whole   133

    § 1. The argumentative structure at three levels
    § 2. Patterns and proportions
        Strophes and strophe structure
        The structure of the strophes
        The structure of the L-strophes
        Figures for the eleven stanzas

Chapter Five: The poem of Job 3:   150
        its structure and numerical perfection

    § 1. Job 3 according to its various forms of regularity
    § 2. Structural analysis of strophes and stanzas
    § 3. Final remarks

Appendices: 179

    a) the Hebrew text of Ex.15 plus two tables
    b) the Hebrew text of Deut.32 plus four tables
    c) the Hebrew text of Job 3 plus two tables

Abbreviations   198
Selected Bibliography   200
Subject Index   203

Preface

A competent reading of the poetry in the Hebrew Bible brings about a transformation from latent to patent semantic richness. This transition from the unread text to the text as read and understood is called 'interpretation'. An analysis of the poem which patiently tries to trace all the poet's aesthetic decisions in order to re-enact them and gauge their consequences is hermeneutics in action.

The mastery of form shown at every level by the classical poets already commanded my respect when I was still a student, which is why I have waited a long time before venturing to express myself in print about their poetry. Since 1980, I have published two series of stylistic and structural analyses of poems. The first series can be found in my four-volume study of the books of Samuel, also published by Van Gorcum (Assen 1981-1993), and covers medium-length poems such as the Song of Hannah and David's dirge, the long psalm of thanksgiving by the established King David (II Sam.22), and a few shorter poems such as the lament for Abner and Samuel's prophecy of doom to Saul.

The other series consists of structural descriptions *cum* interpretation, published in various places, of the overture to Deutero-Isaiah (1981) and his Oracle to Cyrus (1997), plus two very difficult texts, Psalm 68 and Jud.5. A difficult text is clearly more enlightening with respect to the poetics I aim for than a transparent one. This consideration prompted me to make Deut.32 the *pièce de résistance* of this book.

To the birth of this study two people have made essential contributions, and I am grateful not only for their hard work and keen observations, but also for their friendship. Ineke Smit (Leiden) made the English translation. Aart Schippers (Amsterdam) checked all references to Bible verses in the Dutch manuscript and together with me went through the English proofs with meticulous care.

Leiden, March 1998

Chapter One

Introduction

Style, structure, and prosody:
from poetry to poetics

The texts created by classical Hebrew poetry are highly complex, and adequate study of these poems consequently cannot be a simple matter. In this book I continue to work on a comprehensive approach which combines the right principles and techniques and takes into account their relative importance.

The contribution I hope to make to Hebrew poetics starts from the conviction that poems with a high level of difficulty tell us a lot more about classical poetics than poems whose structure seems transparent. A reader with some experience in these matters soon notices that Psalm 114 consists of two halves which mirror each other, and that each of those halves may again be divided in two. He decides on a consistently binary structure: this one poem has two stanzas, four strophes, eight verses and sixteen cola. If, however, we turn to a text which does not reveal its structure so easily, or presents us with the problem of an outright tricky textual tradition and a highly uncertain translation, we are confronted by an object of study which is not only a big challenge, but will also prove to be far more productive and revealing, once we have managed to transform a lot of patience and trouble into a successful structural analysis. At those moments, an extremely intricate poem proves to have a transparent structure after all, and the process of detecting this transparency yields a surplus of various insights into the art of verse, strophe, and stanza structure. If our analysis manages to convince the expert reader, poetics has gained a lot. This has always been my point of departure in earlier days when I aimed at an exhaustive description of style and structure of demanding, sometimes very long poems, and it still is my starting point at this moment.[1] The texts of Ex.15 and Job 3

---

[1] The principles and analyses of this book are extensions of earlier work I have done. Some titles:
- Stylistic Analysis of Isaiah 40:1-11, OTS xxii (1981), pp.68-90;
- The Structure of Psalm 68, OTS xxvi, 1990, pp.72-83;
- The Song of Deborah and Barak: Its Prosodic Levels and Structure, pp.595-628 of *Pomegranates and Golden Bells*, Studies in Biblical, Jewish, and Near Eastern Ritual, Law, and Literature in Honor of Jacob Milgrom (edited by David P. Wright, David Noel Freedman, and Avi Hurvitz), Winona Lake, Indiana, 1995;
- The Cyrus Oracle (Is.44:24-45:7) from the Perspectives of Syntax, Versification and Structure, in: M. Vervenne & J.T.A.M. van Ruiten (eds.), *Festschrift* W.A.M. Beuken, pp. 303-323, BEThL cxxii, 1997, Leuven;

should not be underestimated, and the poem in Deut.32 is such a pinnacle of complexity that I have not been able to find a single satisfactory description of it above strophe level.

A. *Hierarchical text models.*
When dealing with the narrative prose of the Hebrew Bible I have found a linguistics-inspired text model very useful. This is a scale or ladder which in twelve steps ascends from the smallest to the largest linguistic and textual units. The first six levels are those of texture, comprising, in my definition, all language elements up to and including the level of the full sentence. This happens to be exactly the field of traditional grammar, which at the syntax stage did not go beyond the sentence. In a literary sense, texture is also the domain of stylistics. I define 'style' as everything which from the viewpoints of art and communication qualifies as relevant use of language, through to sentence level.

This century has seen the arrival of discourse analysis and text grammar. These new disciplines are concerned with the levels above that of the sentence, and formulate rules and characteristics which apply to texts and text sections. This range is covered by the second half of the model; here, too, at least six levels may be distinguished.

The model shows that the various levels within a text are arranged in a hierarchical order, which may be represented as a ladder. In the diagram below I have placed the two halves next to each other. This is a productive model for prose texts such as Genesis, Samuel or Kings:[2]

texture	*composition*
6. sentences	12. book
5. clauses	11. section (group of Acts)
4. phrases	10. Act (group of stories)
3. words	9. story
2. syllables	8. scenes
1. sounds	7. sequences/speeches

- in my tetralogy on Samuel (NAPS, Assen 1981-93) I have given extensive analyses of the Song of Hannah (I Sam.2:1-10), David's lament for Saul and Jonathan (II Sam.1:18-27), and the great Song of Thanksgiving of the established King David (II Sam.22).

[2] I have discussed this model in more detail in the introductory chapter to NAPS II. It stops at twelve, but whoever wants to may climb further. For instance, the Torah becomes level 13 in relation to a book such as Genesis, and the so-called Deuteronomistic History is level 13 in relation to Samuel or Kings. Level 14 belongs to the all-encompassing design which comprises Genesis through to Kings.

The stories in the Torah and the Early Prophets are never isolated, but have been arranged in groups which I call Acts. The books of Samuel, including I Kings 1-2, comprise more than ninety literary units (among which some strategically placed poems) grouped into fifteen of these Acts. They have been divided over four sections.³

For a well-written newspaper article, occupying an entire page, levels 7-10 would be: paragraph (7), section (8), chapter (9), the entire essay (10). In a narrative literary unit from the Hebrew Bible, not all levels are always present or necessary. The compound sentence occurs far less frequently than the simple sentence or clause. Short stories skip level 8. At level 7, in terms of written text, we get the paragraph. This covers what in narration is called the sequence: a cluster of actions reported in narrator's text which as a sequence forms a specific logical or narrative unit.⁴ The alternative for that level, in the case of direct discourse, is any speech of reasonable size.⁵ Long stories consist of parts which are often called scenes, for instance the nine elements of I Kings 1 or the six of Gen.27.⁶

The various levels deserve attention for their own sake: they should be listened to and sounded out in terms of their relative independence, their own structure and their own devices. This stage of analysing the separate levels is only a part of the whole, and in practice the reader inevitably carries an image of the whole which guides him and on the one hand can inspire him (lead him to new facts and discoveries), but on the other hand always threatens to become a form of foreclosure and thus a trap. What is necessary for the sub-analyses, which skim off layer after layer, and what justifies them in the final instance, is a synthesis which probes and mirrors the collaboration and coherence of the various

---

3   The four sections of the books of Samuel: I 1-12, I 13 - II Sam.1, II Sam.2-8 plus 21-24, and II 9-20 plus I Kings 1-2; see NAPS for a detailed account. These four large units, together with the sections containing the material from Joshua, Judges and Kings form the single grand design known as the Deuteronomistic Work of History.
4   A few examples of sequences: Jud.7:12-14, Gideon steals up on the camp of the Midianites and eavesdrops on the hostile soldiers; or Jud.7:15-18, he prepares the raid, mainly by giving orders; or vv.19-22, the final *denouement*; or Gen.1, where most days of creation are covered by a single sequence each.
5   A few examples of direct discourse: God instructs Gideon to go down to the enemy's camp, seven lines, Jud.7:9-11; Hannah expresses a vow, six lines, I Sam.1:11; or: Hannah addresses Eli, 1:26-28, seven lines.
6   I used to indicate the literary unit as 'scene', for want of a better term, and the unit at level 8 as a 'story part'. The scenes themselves (now in the sense of level 8) usually exhibit a strict pattern; for a discussion of Gen.27 (symmetry of 3 + 3 parts) and I Kings 1 (a concentric structure of nine parts) see NAG ch.III § 3 and NAPS I ch.XIII. An example from I Sam.1: this chapter contains three scenes (introduction and exposition: love and humiliation; Hannah's vow and birth of Samuel; after nursing Hannah keeps her vow) divided into seven sequences: vv.1-2/3-8/9-11/12-18/19-20/21-23/24-28. The crown on this series is sequence number 8: the embedded speech which constitutes the Song of Hannah. This poem has three stanzas and seven strophes.

levels: the parts are subordinate to the whole, and the whole is more than the sum of its parts.

This text model already works for a well-written newspaper article. It shows, however, only a very sketchy interest in the artistic side of stories and poems. This model mainly belongs to the field of linguistics and textual theory. It cannot pretend to do justice to the mode of existence of the literary work of art. We are still stuck with the question how to approach the language and text of the poet.

The poet and his language.
In the case of poetry, some rungs on the ladder have different labels. The poet uses language in the best sense of the word, he does not consume it or use it up in the way we do when we chat, give information, or write a newspaper article or a short note.[7] That sort of language is superficial and interchangeable, by definition it does not invite attention to itself and its unsuspected potential. Literary language is very different: by fair means or foul it draws attention to itself, so that the message for its own sake becomes interesting.[8]

The Hebrew poet ascends and descends along this ladder:

texture	*composition*
	(higher units)
6. verses	
5. cola	11. poem
4. phrases	10. sections
3. words	9. stanzas
2. syllables	8. substanzas
1. sounds	7. strophes

This seems to be a mixed model: it starts off with terms from linguistics, such as syllable and phrase, but switches to literary terms in order to refer to higher units: verses, strophes and so forth. The mixed aspect results from the poet's trade: the text he creates is an ingenious fusion of language and art. He takes the maximum

---

[7] The distinction between use and consumption (using up) of language comes from Martin Heidegger in *Sein und Zeit* (1926) and *Holzwege* (Frankfurt,1950), p.36. Contemporaries of his in St. Petersburg, the Russian Formalists, recognised the artificiality of art, so that we speak of foregrounding and alienating devices of language, necessary in order to attain a literary level. Cf. for this Victor Erlich, *Russian Formalism*, 1955 (3rd ed. Yale University Press, 1981).

[8] The message for its own sake: this is how Roman Jakobson described the poetic function, when he presented his communication model of six factors and six corresponding functions during a congress at Indiana University in 1958; this famous article is called Linguistics and Poetics and was originally published in *Style in Language*, ed. Thomas A. Sebeok, Cambridge, Mass. 1960; it has now also appeared in the collection published by his widow, *Language in Literature*, Harvard UP 1987, pp.62-94.

advantage of linguistic potential; in order to attain a high intensity of communication he aims for a high density. In principle the poet can employ practically any linguistic phenomenon, however humble, to create a new language.

I shall illustrate this with a series of examples, two from songs by David, two from Ps.132 and two from Deut.32.

The first example is about something as lowly as a preposition, and shows that we should not make the mistake of considering it unworthy of attention. I take the monosyllable *min*, and investigate how it is used in David's lament on Saul and Jonathan, II Sam.1:19-27. In a structural analysis of the poem I have shown that there are three stanzas, each consisting of two short strophes.[9] The middle unit (vv.22-23), a eulogy on the heroes and their victories in the more distant past, contrasts sharply with the stanzas preceding and following, which are elegiac as they commemorate the defeat on Mount Gilboa three days earlier. This radical difference in genre and in the period of time which is referred to is marked by a fourfold *min* which indicates head and tail of the stanza by occupying corner positions, on the edges of the six short (mostly containing 2 + 2 stresses) poetic lines.[10]

Whatever the poet picks up from the treasury of the language, he always uses it to some purpose. My second example comes from the great psalm of thanksgiving by the established King David, II Sam.22. Here, the poet employs such a simple device as the difference in length of various nouns. The beginning and end of the poem – and its variant, Psalm 18 - are full of substantives stating that God has proved himself to be a fortress for the speaker. There is an interaction between segholates, i.e. the shortest nouns possible for stems with three radicals, and substantives which are really long because they start with a *mem praeformans*.[11] In this way, a morphological element has become an element of style, and the poet provides extra structural weight by a strategic positioning.

This same transformation we find in the third example. Psalm 132, the poetic counterpart of what may be called the foundation charter of the Davidic

---

[9] The analysis and interpretation of David's lament can be found in ch. XV of *The Crossing Fates*, 1986 (= NAPS II). The 2 + 2 + 2 strophes which fill the three stanzas are preceded by one full poetic line, II Sam.1:19, consisting of a thematic sentence and a refrain sentence. This verse deserves to be called strophe 1, in which case the total of three stanzas contains seven strophes in all. This has only become clear to me since in chapter I, § 3 of *Vow and Desire*, 1993 (= NAPS IV) I have given a complete analysis of the Song of Hannah, a poem which also contains three stanzas and seven strophes; I have also shown there how closely the three poems I Sam.2, II Sam.1 and 22 are interrelated. The Song of Hannah is the culmination of the first prose unit of I Sam., *sc.* chapter 1, which consists of three parts and seven sequences.

[10] What happens to the preposition *min* in the first oracle of Bileam is comparable to and of equal structural weight as the strategic positioning of *min* in the lament. There, too, it occurs two times twice at the beginning of A and B-cola. Whilst the fourfold *min* in the lament is a form of inclusion and builds a sort of square around the central stanza, in the oracle of Num. 23:7-10 it marks the opening lines of two strophes and thus creates a parallelism at strophe level.

[11] For details and more analysis see *Throne and City*, 1990 (= NAPS III), in ch.VIII, § 1.

dynasty and the spiritual Jerusalem, II Sam.7, consists of strophes of two and three verses. The last strophe consists of 2 + 2 verses, which are kept together in a masterly way. The strophic unit is a series of promises by God to the Davidic king. He is continuously the first-person subject of Hiphil forms, (pattern *ʾaqtil*), which practically all have a segholate (singular, so originally a monosyllable) as their objects. The verb *lbš*, which in v.9a was already linked to a segholate (*ṣedeq*), returns in duplicate and polarised: the *ʾalbiš* of 16a has *yešaʿ* as a positive object, but its recurrence in v.18a has *bošet* as a negative object, to the detriment of the enemy.

The use of the Piel (fourth example) in Psalm 132 is also interesting. Verse 9 states, in the B-colon following the Qal of *lbš*, that "his faithful shout for joy"(*yᵉrannenu*). One of the most important decisions the poet took in favour of a tight structure is having most components of v.9 return in v.16. There we have God the speaker who in the A-colon is going to clothe the priests with salvation. In the B-colon the verb *rnn* appears again for the "loyal ones", but this time in a paronomasia: reinforced with the infinitive absolute. What does this mean? The answer comes in sight when we remember the verse preceding v.16:

צידה ברך אברך   /   אביוניה אשביע לחם
וכהניה אלביש ישע   /   וחסידיה רנן ירננו

In v.15a there is another such *figura etymologica*, so that we are now able to draw a diagonal line from blessing to jubilation (15a + 16b). This line is bisected by another diagonal connecting 15b + 16a. The first half of the long final strophe (vv.15-18) proves to have its own rigorous composition, a chiasm which determines the quartet of cola.

Examples five and six I derive from the long Song of Moses in Deut.32. Language often refers to language and communication; this is its metalingual function, as stated in the communication model which Roman Jakobson presented forty years ago.[12] The opening line of Moses' song - or rather the song which God put into the leader's mouth - has been dedicated to communication. Its arc of tension is determined by two poles, speaking and listening, and the surface chronology of this kind of linguistic contact suggests that one precedes the other. Before the first word has been uttered, however, the poet has decided to reverse this quasi-temporal arrangement. He puts the command 'Listen!' first in the verse, although this receptive act seems to follow that of speaking, and places the act of speaking at the end of the verse, "the words of my mouth".[13] Thus, the form *haʾᵃzinu* - which in the Jewish world has become the title of the

---

[12] See note 8 *supra*.
[13] This actually happens twice, as the verse is a bicolon and governed by parallelismus membrorum.

famous Song - has become the key which opens the lyrical space of Deut.32. How to explain the selection of this Hiphil imperative?

By placing the stem 'listening' next to the word 'heaven', the poet first rejects the obvious and attractive possibility of a double alliteration. He does not say *šimʿu šamayim*, a totally legitimate option which was actually used by another great poet, Isaiah. The very first and programmatic strophe of the collection bearing the name of the prophet starts with these two words.[14] And there is another thing which he rejects: we know that in classical poetry the nota objecti, the relative pronoun *ᵃšer* and the article are hardly used.[15] The article is in poetics not required to indicate the vocative either.[16] The poet of Deut.32, however, decided to use the article with the very first noun which he puts in and which he gives the function of vocative. His poem now starts with *haʾzinu haššamaym*, which in the original Hebrew has a balance of 3 + 3 syllables, and forms a twosome which does present a clear alliteration after all.

Yet this sound pattern does not manage to eclipse the repetition of consonants in *šimʿu šamayim*. So the question remains: Why did the poet opt for an opening with 'listen!' (stem *ʾzn*) instead of 'hear!'? He could have achieved the reversal of the order speak-listen just as well by using the verb *šmʿ*?

The answer is in the maker's plan, is inspired by the semantic isotopy of the vocal-auditory aspect, and serves the purpose of conclusion: having started by calling witnesses, in a gesture which encompasses the cosmos, the huge composition ends on another broad gesture, calling the peoples, who in v.43 are invited to praise the people of God. The coda, v.43 (two bicola, the last strophic unit), now issues the command *harninu*, another Hiphil imperative. This time, the form does not require a receptive action, but demands an act of expression, of spontaneous vocal activity.

In this way, an inclusio has been created which marks the beginning and end of the composition. The poem as a whole is a semiotic universe, in which this structural closure pattern has its own say. It suggests in a poetic way that the two actions, reception and expression, which encompass the entire vocal-auditory domain as a kind of merism, are linked in a natural and compelling complementarity. Those who listen closely to Moses' instruction (*tora*) are automatically led to a hymn of praise of the chosen people and their God. Thus, an ele-

---

[14] See Adele Berlin, *The Dynamics of Biblical Parallelism*, Bloomington IN 1985, pp.94 and 127-129 for a series of variants of hear + prayer.
[15] See the work of D. N. Freedman, who investigated in how far these instances of absence contribute to the definition of what constitutes poetry, see Another Look at Biblical Hebrew Poetry, in E.R. Follis, ed., *Directions in Biblical Hebrew Poetry*, JSOTS 40, Sheffield 1987 pp.11-28, and statistics for these so-called 'prose particles' in the *Festschrift* for Freedman, *The Word of the Lord Shall go Forth* (ed. C.L. Meyers and M. O'Connor), Winona Lake IN 1983, in the article Prose Particle Counts of the Hebrew Bible, by F.I. Andersen & A. Dean Forbes, pp.165-183.
[16] The place I just mentioned, Is.1:2, proves this.

gant gesture hands the last word to the surrounding peoples; it will probably be a word of total agreement.

This short exercise, which anticipates the extensive analysis of Deut.32 in chapters Three and Four, shows how minute details are linked with or subservient to wider outlines which have to provide the tension necessary to structure an extensive composition. The double *ha-* is not only a phenomenon at the textural levels 1 and 2 (sounds and syllables), but also at levels 3-5, by welding subject and predicate into a tightly-knit pair and appointing this to be the first sentence core. Then, the parallelismus membrorum procedure starts on the words "Give ear, O heavens!", doubles them in the B-colon and by thus filling out the verse (level 6) assigns them their final place in the poetic line. Finally, the *ha'zinu- harninu* inclusio shows that the alliteration with *ha-* and the selection of the Hiphil imperative together constitute an operation at level 11, for the purpose of closure.

B. *The poem under the rule of prosody; a finger exercise on Psalm 113.*
The poet is under tremendous coercion of more than one kind; he must obey different sets of rules or conventions regarding language, style, and structure. I limit myself here to the prosodic dimension:

1. He has to curb his expression through cola. A colon can contain 2-4 stresses and 6-9 syllables; sometimes it can have 5, or 10-11 syllables, rarely 4 or 12; syntactically speaking, in more than 50% of cases the colon is also a syntactic unit, usually a clause, sometimes even - on a small scale - a compound sentence.[17]
2. He has to construe a neat verse: this will almost always be either a bicolon or a tricolon. This aim implies a new set of rules, about the relations between the two or three cola which together form the verse.
3. The prevailing artistic conventions in the Syro-Palestinian territory for the creation of poetry, the evolution of which had started about a thousand years before the poet, prescribe in Ancient Israel that verses be arranged in strophes of limited length, usually two or three verses.[18] As the whole is more than the sum of its parts, the strophic textual unit cannot be absolute. This is a relative unit, occurring as one among equals. One level up the strophe is related to other strophes and grouped into stanzas. One stanza usually contains two to four strophes.[19] Both layers of the poem, levels 7 and 8 (stro-

---

[17] These figures are based on a count of pre-Masoretic syllables in about a hundred Psalms and about 30 chapters of the book Job.

[18] Although Van der Lugt's processing of a lot of material, as presented in his thesis on the Psalms and recently in his book on Job, could be improved on many points, it is a reliable indication that the poems in the book of Psalms and in Job largely consist of strophes containing two or three verses. See a) P. van der Lugt, Strofische structuren in de Bijbels-Hebreeuwse poëzie, Kampen 1981, and b) idem, Rhetorical Criticism & the Poetry of the Book of Job, Leiden 1995, = OTS xxxii.

[19] See once more the two books by Van der Lugt which I mentioned in the previous note.

phes and stanzas), carry the same message as the lower levels: their units are links in chains.

How does the strophe manifest and distinguish itself? How can we recognise a strophe? Which rules should we follow in order to delineate it correctly? For this part of the prosodic investigation there is no simple recipe, and I'm not going to look for it. The reality here is that the poet is able to employ every characteristic, every contrast, and every configuration hidden in the treasuries of his native language towards the organisation of verse and strophe. Sometimes he will use anaphora in order to have the same openings for his two or three poetic lines, and thus reveal the extent of his strophe,[20] another time he will use a quotation formula.[21] He may arrange two bicola by forcing the four half verses into a chiastic order.[22] Or he can have the strophe boundary coincide with a change in characters, speaker, genre or tone. And because poetry fully restores the sensory quality to the language, we as readers should be aware of the contribution made by sounds, syllables and stresses. Alliteration, assonance and rhyme occur frequently and often co-operate with other stylistic phenomena towards the characterisation of a verse or strophe; and the humble craft of counting syllables should also become one of our techniques.

So far I have not mentioned content, but a noticeable shift in subject matter, theme or content is equally important. The Greek word 'strophe' seems made for just such a turn. The poet may also exploit such differences as sing/plur, nominal/verbal, masc/fem, past/present or one grammatical person vs. another in order to mark off a strophe. The number of possibilities is so large that any attempt at categorisation seems futile. As stated before, there is no recipe, but it is possible to formulate a guideline, which a good reader will never lose sight of: to develop and use a great sensitivity to all phenomena of similarity and difference which we can observe in the poet's language.

This is a good moment to test the complexity of Hebrew poetry on an apparently simple example. For this I have selected a complete literary unit: a four-strophe poem which at the same time demonstrates the necessity of counting pre-Masoretic syllables. *Psalm 113* has nine verses, all but one of which contain the same number of 14 syllables. Many translations and commentaries have not been able to resist the temptation of perfect symmetry and claim that the poem is organised as three units of three verses.[23] There are, however, four strophes. In a bicolic arrangement and divided into strophes the text looks as follows:

---

[20] See for instance Psalm 121:7a//8a or Job 9:5-6 and 11-12.

[21] Thus in the Song of Songs 2:10a, followed by a poetic line from the lover, 10bc, which is repeated verbatim in v.13cd. These two elements prove that the poem 2:8-17, spoken by the girl, in the middle contains two strophes which belong to the young man and have been embedded in two strophes for her voice: vv.8-9 and vv.16-17.

[22] Thus for instance the Song of Songs 2:14cd and ef, or Ps.132:15-16, or Job 7:7-8.

[23] The model of 3 x 3 verses is found in Ley, Duhm, Mowinckel, Delitzsch, Buber-Rosenzweig

1	הללו עבדי יהוה	הללו את שם יהוה
2	יהי שם יהוה מברך	מעתה ועד עולם
3	ממזרח שמש עד מבואו	מהלל שם יהוה
4	רם על כל גוים יהוה	על השמים כבודו
5	מי כיהוה אלהינו	המגביהי לשבת
6	המשפילי לראות	בשמים ובארץ
7	מקימי מעפר דל	מאשפת ירים אביון
8	להושיבי עם נדיבים	עם נדיבי עמו
9	מושיבי עקרת הבית	אם הבנים שמחה

The first noticeable element is the chain of Hiphil forms, praising God's commitment to his creation. This decision is also a spectacular example of the poet's promoting a morphological category to a stylistic category; in this case, we even have a tool of structural impact.

The chain - this is my second observation - is introduced by a conspicuous question, to which there is only one answer: "Who is like the LORD?" The chain itself even represents an extensive answer. Containing two appositions (5b + 6a) and four predicative units (in vv.7-9) it proves the doctrine of God's matchlessness. Because of its length, it can serve at the same time as the basis for the lyrical argument that the deity is without parallel, and hence as the basis for praising God. Finally, all this praise is present in two ways: the poem exhorts the reader to it, and suits the action to the word by itself being a hymn.

The hymnic exclamation, in the form of a rhetorical question, is found in the middle verse of the poem. Verse 5 thus becomes the pivot of the whole. For the determination of the exact middle we have to descend to cola level. I draw a line between v.5a and v.5b, so that the poem is now articulated as 9 + 9 cola. This division immediately yields some features which are characteristic for the two halves but have strangely enough not been noted in commentaries. The cru-

---

(who print a blank line after v.3), BJ, Kissane, Beaucamp, NBE, D.N. Freedman (PPP 243-261), and recently also in Van der Lugt in his study of the Psalms: pp.385-387. In his inventory of repetitions, strophe markers etc. the last author notes as contraindications: $m^ɛth$ $w^ɛd$ $ɛwlm$ (v.2b), my (v.5a). The structural analysis I propose to carry out will put these features in their proper places within the networks of style and structure, so that these devices will require a better lay-out. The following translations and commentaries do not distinguish any strophes at all and print the verses without blank lines to separate the strophes (not a satisfactory option either): KJ, SV, LV, GNB, NEB, KBS, NBG, and Dahood (AB). The correct arrangement of four strophes is given by Briggs (ICC, 1907) and De Liagre Böhl & Gemser (Nijkerk 1968); Gunkel (Die Psalmen, Göttingen 1926, fourth edition) does distinguish vv.1-2/3-4/5-6/7-9 but states: "keine Strophenbildung". Kraus (BKAT) recognises the halves: vv.1-4 / 5-9.

cial colon 5a mentions God's proper name for the last time in the poem, and the poet has hurriedly put in an apposition assuring us that this YHWH is "our God". At exactly this point, the second half starts on its chain of Hiphils. Now, before the line dividing the nine verses into nine plus nine cola, the tetragrammaton occurs six times, without a single Hiphil form occurring; after, there is no proper name anymore and we get six Hiphil forms. The distribution of the Name is striking as well; this is a descending series 3-2-1, spread over strophes 1, 2 and (the opening colon of strophe) 3.

The opposition presence-absence and the balance six-six are supported by the changing position of God; in turn, they support this shift. In the first half, God is either grammatically or rhetorically the object of attention and praise.[24] In the second half, he is exclusively the subject, and an active subject at that, of verb forms which thanks to the Hiphil are pre-eminently active and transitive.

All these aspects become clearly visible when the poem is presented in the format of a single colon per line. This variant visualisation is here used for a purely heuristic purpose, as a typographic arrangement which might draw our attention to more and other things than the bicolic version does. In my experience it is efficient and helpful to the interpreter with more than one poem to have the text also available as a series of cola:

הללו עבדי יהוה	1
הללו את שם יהוה	
יהי שם יהוה מברך	2
מעתה ועד עולם	
ממזרח שמש עד מבואו	3
מהלל שם יהוה	
רם על כל גוים יהוה	4
על השמים כבודו	
מי כיהוה אלהינו	5
המגביהי לשבת	
המשפילי לראות	6
בשמים ובארץ	
מקימי מעפר דל	7
מאשפת ירים אביון	
להושיבי עם נדיבים	8
עם נדיבי עמו	
מושיבי עקרת הבית	9
אם הבנים שמחה	

The division of the poem in halves which do justice to the prosodic dimensions of verses, strophes and stanzas is more important than dividing it into 9 + 9 cola. The hymnic question "who?" is a strong structural signal, at the moment when God changes from object to subject. The question makes the pivotal line into the opening of the second stanza. This consists of a short and a long strophe. The short unit, strophe three, is distinguished from the fourth and last strophe in various ways, but the two main reasons to separate vv.5-6 from vv.7-9 by a strophe boundary are that the quartet of cola in vv.5-6, because of its chiastic organisation, has become complete and finished, and that its strophe is utterly nominal, with appositions for the Hiphil, whilst the causative forms in vv.7-9 function as verbs; all four of them are predicative.

The first part of the poem, vv.1-4, is a stanza as well, this time consisting of two short strophes of two poetic lines each. In this arrangement I depart from the 3-3-3 pattern which should be rejected. The difference is that v.3 does not belong to the first strophe any longer. Again, it is the syntax which guides us by means of two powerful signals: the first pair of verses has a jussive character, the second pair is in the indicative mode. What is commanded in strophe 1 is no more than a fact in strophe 2, and moreover known far and wide.

The second signal from the syntax is the creative order which the poet has bestowed on it. The first quartet of cola consists of three jussive and verbal cola, plus the broad gesture of a temporal merism in the last colon. The second quartet, i.e. strophe 2, consists of the broad gesture of a spatial merism (the first colon, v.3a) plus three predicative cola which are nominal and indicative. This results in a mirror-image organisation of the two strophes, which only comes into its own when we recognise the strophe boundary between v.2 and v.3 in the shape of a blank line. Corroborating details here are the facts that the merisms are contiguous, richly alliterate with the mem and are both based on the pattern *min .. w^{e}ʿad.*[25]

The strophe boundary is both put into perspective and articulated by a chiasm which connects the two pairs of cola in vv.2-3. The diagonal between v.2b and v.3a has already been discussed. On the other one, "the name of the LORD" is repeated as subject, and we find a synonymy which both times employs the Pual register and leans against the caesura: *m^{e}borak* and *m^{e}hullal.* And as soon

---

[24] God is the grammatical object only in the first two cola (v.1). The transformation from Piel to Pual exhibited by the participles of 2a + 3b prepares the way for the transition to God as grammatical subject. Nevertheless he is, either lyrically or rhetorically, always the object of attention and praise after v.1 and before v. 5.

[25] The expression "from .. to" usually has the conjunction w^e before the second preposition, but not always. The regular pattern here occurs in v.2b, but not in v.3a. Are we to insert the conjunction, as the BHS apparatus recommends? It is not strictly necessary, and moreover I suspect that the conjunction was left out for the sake of the extreme regularity of the syllable count: just like 7 other verses, this one has 14 syllables.

as we consider the sentence core of 2a + 3b closely, we discover a chiasm within the chiasm at this level of half verses: "the name of the LORD be blessed" is shifted almost imperceptibly to the indicative mode, but is clearly reversed to "praised ... the name of the LORD".

The chiasm between the cola of vv.2-3 puts the strophe boundary into perspective because it actually functions at stanza level. Its conjunctive force is no match for the separative power of the binary aspects jussive/indicative, verbal/nominal, and time vs. space. This last aspect introduces a new difference separating the first strophe from all other three. The dimensions of space are a major characteristic in the entire song, which comes into play from the second strophe onwards, and there immediately results in a new chiasm. In the inside positions, we find the tetragrammaton combined with a predicative participle (3b + 4a). In the outside positions we first get the horizontal dimension, which we may render freely but correctly as "from East to West" and then the vertical dimension, "his glory is above the heavens". The poet reinforces this diagonal with alliterations (*šemeš - šamayim*) and in particular with the successful assonances (including rhyme) of $m^e bo'o$ and $k^e bodo$ which both close their cola.

The crosswise organisation of the second strophe is intensively copied in the third strophe, a textual unit of the same length. Because this, too, consists of a quartet of cola it is eminently suited to a chiastic connection. The two participles of 3b + 4a are succeeded by the two of 5b + 6a and the final fourth colon (4b and 6b) contains "the heavens" in both strophes.

In v.6b there is again a spatial merism, the same one we remember from the first verse of the Bible: heaven and earth. When we look back to the second strophe we discover the hidden workings of this same complementarity. The earth is implicitly present in v.3, thanks to the merism of 3a and its horizontal dimension.

I also consider the B-cola of the second strophe. The elements "the name of *yhwh*" and "the heavens" both refer forward to their counterparts two verses away. The first element refers back, to v.1b, the second points forward to v.6b. Within the model of 2-2-2-3 verses these repetitions are responsions, keeping the three short strophes together by means of communication lines from their centre.[26] Another binding agent in these three strophes is an expressive chain of alliterations: *šem* (3x) - *šemeš* (1x) - *šamayim* (2x), running from v.1b through to v.6b.

The chiasm governing the quartet of half verses in the third strophe is essential for a better understanding of the message. Thanks to the crosswise organi-

---

[26] In the rejected 3 x 3 model they function adequately as instances of inclusion, but they are less striking, among other things because with this division - see the representation in Van der Lugt, p.385 - the diagonal lines of the chiasms have not been done justice, and the signalling function of the syntax has been greatly underrated.

sation we realise that the words "in the heavens and the earth" are not in the first place a complement to v.6a ("who looks far down"), and maybe are not dependent on this stich at all. It is clear that the other diagonal, 5b + 6a, is determined by the merism high/low. The remarkable point is that these two cola are the best, if not the only, pair here to realise a parallelismus membrorum. What is so exceptional about these two cola is the fact that they have been separated diagonally, placed in the positions of B and A-colon respectively. Once we have got all this straight, within the strophe the half verses 5a + 6b are left as a pair. This strongly suggests that the terms of space first of all, if not exclusively, have been intended to illustrate the extent of God's unicity. In this way, a correct interpretation of this strophe is justified in rearranging the parts of the sentence. The seamless connection shows how much 6b is subordinate to 5a: "The LORD, our God, is peerless, both in heaven and on the earth."

Finally, there is a linear connection between the 'cosmos' merism and the pair high/low in the appositions. The first term (heaven) fits in well with "seated on high" and the second (the earth) links up with "looking far down". It is no surprise that this last phrase is followed immediately by the great final strophe, exclusively concerned with God's commitment to people who need him.

If the reader will allow me to call the predicative participles within strophe 2 parts of nominal sentences, the difference between nominal and verbal enables us to arrange the four strophes of the poem according to the pattern AB-BA. The outside strophes are governed by three plus four verbal predicates, the inside strophes by three plus one nominal predicates. Indeed, not one finite form is to be found in strophes 2-3.

If we want to mark off strophes from each other we should not underestimate humble and unsightly contrasts. At first, the spacing we put in between vv.5-6 and vv.7-9 seems a rather hazardous blank. Can the formidable chain of Hiphil forms be interrupted? If we look closely we notice that the first two of these, the participles of 5b + 6a, are accompanied by the article, the dearth of which in classical poetry is thus belied. The two articles are supported again by another two, in the final colon 6b. In verses 7-8, however, there is no article at all, especially not near the new Hiphil participle which opens the final strophe. Moreover, this *m^{e}qimi* forms a word pair with the finite form *yarim* of the B-colon. In this way, our attention is drawn to the fact that Hiphil forms in the fourth strophe are predicates, and the verses of this unit are independent sentences.[27] The Hiphil forms in strophe 3 on the other hand are 'only' appositions, so that strophe 3 contains only one sentence core.

---

[27] In the two participial clauses in v.7a and 9ab ellipsis of the subject occurs: "he" is not verbalised, a phenomenon which can occur both in prose and poetry; see the grammar by Joüon-Muraoka, § 154c, and Waltke & O'Connor, Introduction to Biblical Hebrew Syntax, § 4.8g. The infinitive which opens v.8 is of course no final link, but a variant, parallel and continuation of the finite form

The short strophes all concluded their quartet of half verses by filling the last colon with a purely nominal complement.[28] The fourth strophe has an extra verse and consequently applies this principle twice: v.8b and v.9b are purely nominal, so that those verses have only one sentence core and the caesura is relativised by enjambment, after the example of vv. 2b//4b//6b.

There are more instances of repetition in the last strophe. The verb *yšb*, which illustrated the first Hiphil by means of a modal infinitive, is repeated twice: its causative provides the last two verses with their predicate. These forms are followed by a double preposition (*ʿim*) and a double "princes". Verse 7 is in fact the first and only verse in the poem to exhibit the maximum amount of parallelism, as it is completely filled by word pairs: a form of three-fold doubling. The duplication of the last object, a despondent woman, is festive and liberating because v.9b is a second object, this time predicative: "the joyous mother of children".[29] The words for 'house' and 'sons' alliterate and both are accompanied - rather conspicuously - by the article. The consonants of *bayit* and *banim* are no isolated occurrences; throughout the strophe there is a chain of alliterations on mem, bet and nun, starting in a minor key (*ʾebyon*), with the treble link of the stem *ʿmm* and the double *nᵉdibim* as the centre, and ending on the joyous note of the mother (*ʾem*). The poem as a whole frequently employs the mem: the sound occurs no fewer than 33 times (5 + 10 and 5 + 13 times in the four strophes). This is twice as many as the lamed (15 times) and the bet (16 times).

The liberating intervention of God takes place along a vertical axis. The cola of v.7 indicate a double movement upwards, away from misery (concretised as dust and ash heap) with the poor and needy at the receiving end and God as mighty subject. Next, 8a and 9a follow with a double movement downwards which creates tranquillity and dignity. V.8 is still concerned with the poor, v.9 moves on to the barren woman. The man/woman polarity is well-balanced; apart from that, it is also half of another polarity, so that the second stanza also balances the first as regards human characters. In stanza I there are two collectives which complement each other: the small group - probably the Israelites - which is called "the servants of the LORD" and is commanded to praise, plus the large group representing the rest of mankind and which is going to listen to that praise, "all nations". In II there are two individuals, or singular forms at least, who receive God's help: a man and a woman.

yarim; this, too, is no new phenomenon, Joüon-Muraoka § 124p and Waltke & O'Connor, § 36.3.2. The fact that three Versiones have "makes *him* sit", proves that the translators have understood the verse correctly, but not that their *Vorlage* had a suffix -*w* attached to the Hiphil infinitive of *yšb*. I do not change the last -i of *hošibi*, so that the chain of archaising long i-vowels remains intact.

[28] With 'purely' I here mean to exclude participles.

[29] There is a word play behind this: A house (*byt*) may be built (*bnh*) through having sons (*bnym*), as Sarah already knew - the pun is employed as early as Gen.16 and occasionally occurs elsewhere, too.

The final strophe is characterised by exact quantities. Its three verses each contain 3 + 3 words. The unit is framed by an associative connection. Having children is used in opposition to dust, a word which almost always is an emblem of insignificance, mortality and death. The association suggests that the poor can only be rescued from the dust of death when the barren woman becomes fertile.

Thus everything comes together. The poet manages to clinch this impression by means of the prosodic quantity of his verses. I give the figures for the pre-Masoretic syllables below; mine differ from those found by David Noel Freedman[30] by one point only and in this way achieves true regularity and a total of 124 syllables, which makes this Psalm the exact equivalent of its successor Ps.114. Like Freedman, I consider the words *hallᵉlu yah* at the beginning and end to be a liturgical envelope whose words do not belong to the poem. It is a kind of anacrusis, added by the singing community or by tradition.

verse			
1	3.2.2 / 3.1.1.2	7 + 7 = 14	
2	1.1.2.3 / 3.2.2	7 + 7 = 14	strophe 1 = 28
3	3.1.1.3 / 3.1.2	8 + 6 = 14	
4	1.1.1.2.2 / 1.3.3	7 + 7 = 14	strophe 2 = 28
5	1.3.4 / 4.2	8 + 6 = 14	
6	4.2 / 3.3	6 + 6 = 12	strophe 3 = 26
7	3.3.1 / 3.2.2	7 + 7 = 14	
8	4.1.3 / 1.3.2	8 + 6 = 14	strophe 4 = 42
9	3.2.2 / 1.3.3	7 + 7 = 14	

The total comes to 28 + 28 + 26 + 42 = 124 syllables. The greatest regularity is found at verse level: eight out of nine verses contain 14 syllables. Of these, five are symmetrical, 7 + 7; three have an extra point in the A-colon and one less in the B-colon, i.e. 8 + 6, with the same total. The only verse to contain 2 + 2 words is the only exception, counting 12 syllables. This is the dip before the poet presents his climax, the only strophe consisting of three verses.

My final verdict on Psalm 113: this poem did seem rather simple at first, but

---

[30] Freedman's count is given in an article dating from 1975, entitled: Psalm 113 and the Song of Hannah; it is now included in PPP pp.243-261. The only difference between him and me (except that Freedman advocates the 3-3-3 model) is that I count *yᵉhi* as a monosyllable, analogous to words such as *kᵉli* and *ṣᵉbi*. My counts of Job 3 constitute a strong argument in favour of this. I do, however, consider it possible that this apocope form should be counted as two syllables in some poetry.

appearances are deceptive. The impression of clarity largely results from a masterly command of the various techniques of syntax, repetition combined with variation, parallelism and prosodic control over verse, strophe and stanza structure. In actual fact this short hymn is complex enough.[31]

The 114th Psalm is no less sophisticated. Its 124 syllables are distributed over eight rather than nine verses. The poem has a transparent structure of four strophes representing the ABB'A' pattern. These four units each consist of two verses and four cola. In the outside strophes God and his people appear; in the inside strophes, which are almost identical as regards vocabulary but radically different as regards the direction of speaking, figures from Nature appear in twosomes. They have been made to witness the miracle of the Exodus; they are frightened in vv.3-4 and are made even more anthropomorphic by the poet when he addresses them in the mirror-image vv.5-6. By means of this address the poet turns the miracle into an event in his own present, as well as the present of his hearers.

There are five verses of 15 and two of 16 syllables, in an intriguing balance:

verse			
1	2.3.3 / 1.2.2.2	8 + 7 = 15	
2	3.3.3 / 3.4	9 + 7 = 16	strophe 1 = 31
3	2.2.3 / 3.2.3	7 + 8 = 15	
4	3.3.3 / 3.2.1	9 + 6 = 15	strophe 2 = 30
5	1.2.2.1.2 / 3.2.3	8 + 8 = 16	
6	3.3.3. / 3.2.1	9 + 6 = 15	strophe 3 = 31
7	3.2.2.1 / 3.2.2	8 + 7 = 15	
8	4.2.2.1 / 3.4.1	9 + 8 = 17	strophe 4 = 32

The total amounts to 31 + 30 + 31 + 32 = 124 syllables. Clearly, the norm per strophe is 31, which has twice been exactly realised, and twice has been varied by means of the smallest possible deviations upwards and downwards. The number of words is symmetrical, too: 12 + 12 and 14 + 14. The regularity at strophe level is perfect in the first and third units, which mirror each other: 15 + 16 = 16 + 15. The figures for the cola, arranged per strophe in ascending order, reflect the components of the ascending series 30-31-32 in strophes 2-3-4: 6-7-

---

[31] The *constraints* of prosody at colon, verse and strophe level, and their interaction with syntax hardly figure in P. Auffret, Hymne à l'incomparable: étude structurelle du Psaume 113, Studi Epigrafici e Linguistici 9 (1992) pp.35-52.

8-9 (strophe 2) in the third strophe becomes 6-8-8-9 and finally 7-8-8-9. Each strophe contains one colon of nine syllables.

The division of the second quartet draws attention to connections between v.5 and v.8 (water) and between v.6 and v.7 (mountains, earth). In the verses, three times the symmetry 8 + 8 is found, and as regards the four verses containing 15 in all, this total is based twice on 8 + 7 and twice on 9 + 6.

There is also a strict regularity in the words and stresses of Ps.114:

words	stresses	words	stresses
strophe 1		*strophe 2*	
3 + 4	3 + 3	3 + 3	3 + 3
3 + 2	3 + 2	3 + 3	3 + 2
strophe 3		*strophe 4*	
5 + 3	3 + 3	4 + 3	3 + 3
3 + 3	3 + 2	4 + 3	3 + 2

The odd one out in this respect, v.5a with five words, is of no consequence as it employs some monosyllables; this A-colon contains after all no more than 8 syllables, just like the B-colon.

Note on pre-Masoretic syllables.
Those who want to know the syllables as the poets wrote them will have to get acquainted with the ancient Hebrew, which does not differ much from the Masoretic Hebrew except in a few details. If you want to count pre-Masoretic syllables, you should find them first. To this end it is not really necessary to make a full reconstruction of the ancient Hebrew. How exactly this sounded is a problem which goes far beyond the question of the original syllables and their numbers. The state of the original Hebrew of ancient Israel is to us asymptotic: at best we can approach it, never fully attain it. But fortunately that is not necessary to get the finer measures of its poetry.

Counting the pre-Masoretic syllables is for over 90% neither difficult nor hazardous. Most pre-Common Era Hebrew words had the same structure as they have in the Masora. Hundreds of verses do not differ at all from the original. I give two examples in transcription:

Deut.32:6   *z^{e}kor y^{e}mot ʿolam / binu š^{e}not dor wador*
Job 9:25   *w^{e}yamay qallu minni raṣ / bar^{e}ḥu lo raʾu ṭoba*

The first verse I score as 2.2.2 / 2.2.1.2 and the second as 3.2.2.1 / 3.1.2.2.

There is no difference with their pre-Masoretic form, and this holds for many verses. What we do not know exactly is when the original a-vowels of such words as *bar^{e}ḥu*, *y^{e}mot* and *š^{e}not*, in the position where now we have the vocal shwa, lost their sound and have become the dull and ultra-short vowel.[32] That transition, however, has not affected the number of syllables or even their structure (open or closed).

The few remaining percent have to do with some awkward details. The problems arising from this I hope to deal with systematically in the course of this series, and partially solve. Among other things, it is about such puzzles as: should we treat forms such as *k^{e}li* and *y^{e}hi* in the same way, and following the usual treatment of segholate forms count them as monosyllables (considering their origins, **kily* and **yihy*, the verb form resulting from apocope)? I am inclined to say we should, irrespective of how these forms were pronounced some thousand-odd years before the Masoretes.[33] Then, there are various Piel forms which have undergone a so-called secondary dedoubling (virtual gemination) in the Hebrew tradition.[34] Does this reflect a historical, earlier state of affairs? Should we follow the Masoretes here when we count syllables? Maybe we often should, but not always. This, too, deserves closer scrutiny. I consider it perfectly possible that the solution of this problem may be reached by finding patterns in the figures for syllables per verse, strophe and stanza. For instance, I often come across strophes which are either completely symmetrical (e.g., three verses of 16 syllables each) or which form an ascending or descending series (15-16-17 or the reverse). The levels underneath this (cola) and above (stanzas) may also yield figures which conform to a pattern.

---

[32] At a very early stage the verb was of course **baraḥu*, and the singular of the nouns was **yawm* and **šanat*.

[33] *y^{e}hi* occurs both in Ps.113 and in Job 3. Freedman (PPP p.244) allocated it two syllables in the Psalm; I grant it only one, an allocation which I think is amply supported by a) the exceptional regularity of the figures per verse, which we have just noted, and b) the fact that Ps.114 has exactly the same number of syllables. (Cf. the fact that two more neighbours, Psalms 111 and 112, have an identical number of syllables, viz. 169 - see Freedman PPP pp.48 and 71.) My syllable count in Job 3 results in striking patterns which for that poem, too, argue in favour of one point as the value of the apocopated form. I take into account, however, the possibility that the value of *y^{e}hi* fluctuates, and should count as one with some poets, as two with others. Decisions here will only be possible on the basis of painstaking analyses, both on the score of dividing cola, verses, strophes and stanzas, and of scrutinising the syllables.

[34] The plural imperative *hall^{e}lu* is always spelled without dagesh forte by the Masoretes; I still think it should be written as three syllables, as confirmed by the pattern of Ps.113. The pattern *hamm^{e}dabb^{e}rim*, a cumbersome quintet of syllables, is usually reduced to *hamdabrim* by the Masoretes. Should we go along with this half way, all the way, or not at all? In Job 3:21a I count the first word, which forms half an anaphora with the first word (consisting of four syllables) of v. 22a and runs המחכים, as four syllables; see the total for its strophe as part of the network of strophe totals.

These pressure points merit a lot of thorough investigation, but have little effect on the analysis of the poems discussed here. With respect to the large majority of forms I follow the usual reduction procedure. In order to arrive at the pre-Masoretic syllables I eliminate those ḥatef-vowels which contrary to those in for instance ʾᵒhalim, ʾᵃni, and ʾᵉmet, cannot be traced back to an earlier vowel (as is in the case in moʿᵒmad, yaʿᵃqob, šaʾᵃnanu, including the furtive pataḥ as in ruᵃḥ). The auxiliary vowel which has crept into the singular segholate nouns is also eliminated (the last vowel in forms such as *melek, naʿar, bayit*).

What is the status of these syllable counts? In my investigation, counting syllables does not serve as a metrical theory, or as a replacement of it. It is descriptive rather than prescriptive, and is a welcome corrective for a different, much more speculative type of counting, that of stresses.[35] Syllable counts I consider a fine - in the sense of detailed - measure of quantity in cola, verses, strophes and stanzas. Words and their numbers are less suitable as a measure at the levels of cola and verses, because of their varying lengths. A colon can be fairly long because it contains ten syllables, and yet have only two words; so for instance Deut.32 in v.10c: *yesobᵉbenhu yebonᵉnehu*, a colon which exploits the Polel and brings it into a musical balance. Conversely, a colon can consist of many words and yet be short: Job 9:24c has five words, but no more than six syllables.

C. *The relations between syntax and the higher prosodic units.*
In Hebrew poetry the interaction between syntax and prosody, here especially the creation of cola, verses and strophes, is fascinating. It is also one of the biggest challenges for the poet as a craftsman. The construction of syntactic units does not exceed the boundaries of the strophe, with a few significant and occasionally spectacular exceptions.

Below, I give the results of a modest investigation for which I selected four chapters from Job (chapters 6-7 and 9-10: the first two speeches in which Job prepares the discussion with his friends) and the Songs *lammaʿalot* (Pss.120-134) as a pilot project. The figures in the columns below should be seen as approximations, as they depend on the definitions adopted for e.g. clause and compound sentence, and on the demarcation of cola, which in Job is almost always unambiguous but not in the group of Psalms.[36] On the two or three points I will discuss here, however, they are reliable. The capital P here means 'predicate':

---

[35] On this point I am in complete agreement with Freedman, whose syllable counting work deserves more attention than it has received, and with Raabe (in his book *Psalm Structures*, A Study of Psalms with Refrains, JSOTS 104, Sheffield 1990).
As regards metrics: for an account of the accentuating metre I advocate, see the introduction to my detailed analysis of the Song of Hannah in *Vow and Desire*, especially pp.79-80.
[36] Speaking of definitions: consider the disjunctive question, marked by hᵃ .. and ʾim ... Is this a compound sentence or not? Both parts have their own predicates and complete syntax, so that they may easily be accommodated in the halves of a bicolon, as for instance in Job 6:5-6, 30 and 8:3.

	Job 6-7, 9-10	*Pss. 120-134*
	4 poems	15 poems
	109 verses	121 verses
	222 cola	249 cola
one verb is P in one colon:	c. 130	c. 125
one noun is P in one colon:	18	28
two P in one colon:	57 !	9
colon without P	4	70 !
compound sentence covers an entire verse or more:	14 (c. 37 cola)	10 (c. 30 cola)
compound sentence in one colon:	15	2

These two control groups compare well as regards the most frequent phenomenon. At least half of their cola are governed by one verbal predicate; these half verses are clauses, short and independent syntactic units. Obviously, the syntactic weight or attraction of the colon is great. The small corpus from Job differs from the Psalms in two noticeable characteristics. There are many cola, more than 25%, with two predicates in one colon. In all probability this is a much larger percentage than that in the Psalter. Furthermore, the book has very few cola without predicate. This means in the first place that the poet, having completed an A-colon containing a sentence core, does not then wind down by adding no more than a complement, but takes off again and places a new predicative unit in the B-colon. This contrasts sharply with the group of Psalms, where out of 249 cola no less than 70 cola have no predicate. These are almost always B-cola consisting of a complement or apposition, and sometimes even a

---

For the purpose of poetical analysis it is perfectly possible to describe the half verses as independent, predicative units. And what about the relative clause? This, too, fits its own colon and has its own predicative structure. To put it differently: a purely linguistic approach may not always be productive or sufficient for a structural analysis of verse and strophe construction.

nominal word group indicating the subject. I would estimate that this use of B-cola occurs frequently in the rest of the Book of Psalms as well.

I will now consider both groups together. Their 230 verses number more than 65 cola which, in combinations of two or more, contain compound sentences. This amounts to more than 14% of the total number of cola, a considerable group. Both in the lyrics by and for the pilgrims, and in the critical wisdom of the Book of Job, it is not at all unusual for complete verses and even larger textual units to be filled up with one long and complex syntactic unit. This circumstance alone means that we should not consider the colon as the basic building-block of Hebrew poetry. If we add to this the phenomenon of parallelismus membrorum - since Collins' work not such a decisive element in poetry as many used to think and still do - which, although not required for the construction of the verse, still occurs frequently enough, it leaves us with the full poetic line as the number one candidate for the title of 'building-block'. Finally, there is the third aspect that in the one place in the Psalter where the colon really should be the number one building brick (the two poems which are alphabetic acrostics per colon, Pss. 111 and 112), it is not: instead, the large majority of the cola is there dutifully linked as twosomes, bicolic verses.

D. *Hermeneutics interacting with structural analysis.*

The complexity of the Hebrew literary genius cannot be adequately explored and described through a mere enumeration of repetition, strophe markers, separators and so forth. Verses and strophes do not only exist by virtue of elements defining their parameters. They often lead a highly individual life, and in co-operation or contrast with their equals often show fluctuating moods, contents, and motifs. Consequently, a full-fledged poetics is not the same as an inventory of poetic tools, or a *summum bonum* of the poet's tricks.

Our relation with poetics is a form of discursive interaction. We are dealing with two types of discourse here: the poet has delivered a creative discourse through his lyrics, and it now falls to us to present a re-creative discourse which in a way emulates the artist. The poet's lyricism is a discourse in the sense that, just like the narrative prose of the Bible, it is rhetorical in the classical meaning of the word: it practises the art of persuasion. This is not affected in any way by differences of degree. Moses standing on the shore of the Reed Sea (Ex.15), or Deborah and Barak looking back on the unexpected defeat of the seemingly invincible Canaanite chariots (Jud.5), express themselves mainly in songs, in rapidly changing, colourful images. In the proverbs of wisdom literature the rhetoric is much more argumentative, as it is in the nature of much *chokma* to teach and admonish. The verses of Deut.32 and Job 3 are no less artistic than those of the two songs of victory mentioned above, but their rhetoric is more long-winded and is of a more argumentative character. These poems want to set up an extensive line of reasoning and exercise a more compelling influence on the congenial listener than does Ex.15.

The argumentative quality of Deut.32 and Job 3 should be emulated by the interpreter. His own discipline, poetics, is still young; that is why it is not enough to use enumerations of characteristics, markers and repetitions as main supports.[37] The argument of the interpreter should, I think, avoid a partial approach and offer a full discussion of the interaction between syntax and prosody, and between form and content, in order to present a clear view of structure and organisation, and should not stop adducing arguments when the final stage of the actual interpretation has been reached. This work is the practical form of hermeneutics.

Hermeneutics is the art of explaining. Hebrew poetry is so complex - read: rich in meanings and sense - that it can only come into its own when it is reflected through hermeneutic awareness. This implies that the interpreter should be open to, and exhort himself all the time to remain open to, the impressive array of artistically and thematically relevant signals given off by language, style and structure. This book is an exercise in that state of openness - an exercise, because this state is no permanent achievement, but has to be won every day against one's own blind spots, prejudices and instances of foreclosure - and discusses three long poems, all equally famous representatives of the literary genius of ancient Israel.

---

[37] As an example of this I may mention the two representatives of the so-called Kampen School whom I will be confronting later, when I analyse Job 3 and Deut.32. Pieter van der Lugt and Paul Sanders have written important works on the book of Job (in 1995) and the Song of Moses (in 1996) respectively - see the bibliography. Their extensive material is largely presented in the form of rather indigestible lists, so that the reader can hardly determine how much weight their observations carry as regards a correct division into strophes and stanzas. A complicating factor here is the fact that in recent work the Kampen School has been interpreting ever more language and style elements as so-called strophe markers, which has the paradoxical result of reducing their effect and value as evidence. If almost everything can serve as a strophe marker, enumerating them correspondingly becomes less persuasive. And exactly because poets do have a lot of devices at their disposal for the demarcation of textual units, the interpreter should provide us with a sincere discourse which both describes and argues, so that this can have its own persuasive effect.

Chapter Two

A full description of Exodus 15

0. The text of Moses' Song at the Reed Sea, which is the subject of the present chapter, reads in English as follows. I print here the translation of the Jewish Publication Society of America, but I anticipate the results of my investigation by offering the text of Exodus 15:1-18 in sixteen strophes and in a slightly changed colometrical order.

Then Moses and the Israelites sang this song to the LORD. They said:

	strophe
¹I will sing to the LORD, for He has triumphed gloriously; Horse and driver He has hurled into the sea.	1
²The LORD is my strength and might; He is become my deliverance. This is my God and I will enshrine Him; the God of my father, and I will exalt Him. ³The LORD, the Warrior – LORD is His name!	2
⁴Pharaoh's chariots and his army He has cast into the sea; And the pick of his officers are drowned in the Sea of Reeds. ⁵The deeps covered them; they went down into the depths like a stone.	3
⁶Your right hand, O LORD, glorious in power, Your right hand, O LORD, shatters the foe!	4

⁷In Your great triumph
    You break Your opponents;
You send forth Your fury,
    it consumes them like straw.

⁸At the blast of Your nostrils
    the waters piled up,
The floods stood straight like a wall;
    the deeps froze in the heart of the sea.

⁹The foe said,
    "I will pursue, I will overtake.
I will divide the spoil,
    my desire shall have its fill of them.
I will bare my sword—
    my hand shall subdue them."

¹⁰You made Your wind blow,
    the sea covered them;
They sank like lead
    in the majestic waters.

¹¹Who is like You, O LORD,
    among the celestials;
Who is like You,
    majestic in holiness,
Awesome in splendor,
    working wonders!

¹²You put out Your right hand,
    the earth swallowed them.
¹³In Your love You lead
    the people You redeemed;
In Your strength You guide them
    to Your holy abode.

¹⁴The peoples hear,
    they tremble;
Agony grips
    the dwellers in Philistia.

> ¹⁵Now are dismayed
>> the clans of Edom;
> the tribes of Moab–
>> trembling grips them.   12
>
> ¹⁶Terror and dread
>> descend upon them;
> Through the might of your arm
>> they are still as stone–   13
>
> Till Your people
>> cross over, O Lord,   14
> Till Your people
>> cross whom You have ransomed.
>
> ¹⁷You wil bring them and plant them
>> in Your own mountain,   15
> the place you made
>> to dwell in, O Lord,
> the sanctuary, O Lord,
>> which Your hands established.
>
> ¹⁸The Lord will reign   16
>> for ever and ever!

§ 1. *The key to the poem: textural units*

In this chapter I am defending the view that Ex.15 is a well-integrated poem consisting of 4 stanzas, 16 strophes, 39 full poetic lines of bicolic structure resulting in 78 cola, containing 169 words.[1] There are about 158 stresses and 408 pre-Masoretic syllables.

I start looking for the correct way into the poem and allow myself to be led by a question which is always productive when dealing with a work of art: is there anything that strikes me? I notice three characteristic cases of staircase parallelism. This forceful pattern shapes vv.6 and 11, and the second half of v.16.

---

[1] I refer to the Masoretic verse (i.e. the *pasuq*) by using v. and vv., almost exclusively in combination with the number, instead of the word 'verse'. This last word I will use only in a literary sense to indicate the full poetic line, usually a bicolon, sometimes a tricolon; here in Ex.15 it is always a bicolon. Sporadically, I will use the term 'half verse' as a variation of 'colon'. Verses (in the literary sense) are numbered separately, to facilitate exact reference. In this way, v.6 (more precisely, v.6abcd) equals ll.9 and 10, and the [full poetic] lines 34-35 equal (Mas.) v.16efgh.

A close scrutiny of the text immediately yields a number of fundamental clues as to heartbeat, tone and structure of the poem. The English translation is as follows:[2]

v.6	Your right hand, O LORD,	/ glorious in power,
	Your right hand, O LORD,	/ shatters the foe!
v.11	Who is like You, O LORD,	/ among the celestials;
	Who is like You,	/ majestic in holiness,
	Awesome in splendor,	/ working wonders!
v.16ef	Till your people cross	/ over, O LORD,
gh	Till your people cross	/ whom You have ransomed.

It is the repetition of the A-colon which constitutes the force of the pattern; actually, we have here a considerably expanded anaphora. In v.16 the repetition even moves beyond the caesura, so that the B-cola start in the same way with ʿam.

Vv. 6 and 16e-h show a practically identical pattern.[3] This structure may be schematically represented in a few letters:

a b / c d
a b / e f

In these cases there are two verses; v.11, however, contains three. These three verses are situated roughly in the arithmetical middle of the poem, and a reasonably trained reader will quickly discover them to be in all respects the centre of the poem, so much so that I would like to designate them as the thematic power supply of the work of art.

Partly because of the addition of a third verse, the ordering of the staircase parallelism in v.11 is very different from that of vv.6 and 16. There is a different syntax: in vv.6 and 16(efgh) each verse is a predicative sentence which can only be realised as a syntactical unit thanks to enjambment.[4] In the long v.11 the relation between the A and B-cola is far less direct. Twice, the A-colon contains a nominal sentence core, 'Who is like you?' – an independent type of pred-

---

[2] This is the JPS translation; I have inserted a slash to indicate the caesura. The Hebrew text of v.16efgh has the verb in the A-colon and the people opening the B-colon. In English this word order is unpleasant, so that the slash is placed a little awkwardly in the translation.
[3] See also Wilfred G.E. Watson, *Classical Hebrew Poetry, A Guide to its Techniques*, JSOTS 26, Sheffield 1984, pp.150-156. Watson also gives a diagram for this figure, to show the staircase.
[4] In v.6 subject plus vocative occupy the A-colon, and the predicative core does not appear until the B-colon. In v.16 the order is reversed: the verbal predicate comes first and the B-colon opens with the subject.

icate which does not need any syntactical extension. Once (v.11b) this hymnal מִי כָמֹכָה is accompanied by a complement ('among the celestials, O Lord'), the other time (v.11d) it is continued through an apposition: 11d reads נֶאְדָּר בַּקֹּדֶשׁ. This, however, is not all. The poet decided to reinforce this Niphal participle, which forms part of a $s^e mikut$ construction, by two more instances of $s^e mikut$. Each of these occupies a colon in v.11ef, and this verse again starts out with a Niphal participle. The n, r and o-sounds contribute to the over-all coherence, together with an evident two-beat-rhythm:

Ne'daR baqqOdeš // NORa' t^{e}hillOt / 'Ośe pele'

These observations now enable us to describe the structure of the hymnal strophe. Three times two is two times three. By drawing a diagonal line, bisecting the strophe, the three bicola may be divided into two halves: two trios.[5] The first half of the six cola is predicative and consists of a repeated rhetorical question, whilst the second half forms an imposing chain of appositions, all construct state combinations; together, the three of them express the almost inexpressible: they formulate exactly why God is as peerless as the head sentence 'Who is like You' states, and they formulate it through descriptive terms singing his praise.

The time has come to appraise the three verses containing staircase parallelism in their mutual relations, and adopt an interpretative approach. All address God with his proper name YHWH in the vocative. They constitute a subsystem not only through their striking form, but through their content as well:
- the first verse pair (ll.9-10 = v.6) sings of the people of Israel being delivered from the enemy Egypt by the mighty right hand of their God.
- The central verses (v.11 = ll.21-23), being a trio, form a longer strophe. They address God personally and sing his praises; impressive attributes such as holiness and wonders serve to illustrate the fact that God is incomparable. All references to a concrete situation are lacking.
- The last verse pair, with the extended anaphoras (ll.34-35 = v.16efgh), refers to the journey of the chosen people to the promised land.

In this way, these three strophes tie in well with the underlying chronology. In the first half of the Song leave is taken of the superpower Egypt, and on the other side of the hymnal centre the people are on their way to a new territory while their future neighbours watch with trembling knees. The three verses in v.11 rise above the masses of water and the clouds of dust being kicked up before and after, and exclusively refer to the greatness of the true God, who has just redeemed Israel and in doing so gave it its identity.

It need not now surprise us that the strophes containing extended anaphora

---

[5] In the next chapter, dealing with Deut.32, we shall encounter three more cases of a three-line strophe whose three bicola may be re-arranged as two threesomes.

constitute the main supports of the structure.⁶ They occupy strategic positions within the poem, to the extent of indicating the over-all division of the poem into stanzas. I will illustrate their normative influence on prosody, and their function as cornerstones within the structure, by a few observations. These three passages, standing out so clearly from the surrounding verses as to become strophic units, I will henceforth call refrain strophes.

The three units are also marked by a stylistic decision on the part of the poet which expresses his evocative power. Three times a simile is used which has been placed just before the refrain strophe, whose content is at the expense of the enemy, and which literally or metonymically⁷ evokes death:

v.5b   They went down into the depths *like a stone*
v.10c   They sank *like lead* in the majestic waters
v.16cd Through the might of Your arm they are still *as stone*

In this way, the silence of terror and death three times concludes an entire stanza.

In between the refrain strophes, in vv.7-10 and 12-16d, there are two blocks of exactly the same size: both contain four strophes = ten verses = twenty cola. The refrain strophes themselves have a centripetal aspect. In the first place, strophes R_1 and R_3 (ll.9-10 and 34-35) revolve as parts of their own subsystem around the three-line strophe R_2. Secondly, strophe R_1 refers forward by addressing God in the second person. This unit has been placed in a delicate spot; before, the poet was speaking *about* God, but from now on, i.e. starting at the first refrain strophe, he will only be speaking *to* God and refer to him in the second person.⁸ A vertical parallelism ("the foe .. your opponents") links v.6 to v.7.

Thirdly, the centripetal tendency of the refrain strophes may be deduced from the syntax of R_3. Although this unit is a strophe, it is strangely enough a dependent temporal clause. Therefore, it should be linked either to the preceding or to the following verses. Where do these two ʿad-lines belong? Does the conjunction here mean "until, before" or "while"? If we choose to link v.16efgh

---

⁶ The strategic position of the three passages containing staircase parallelism has been clearly established by James Muilenburg, "A Liturgy on the Triumphs of Yahweh", in: *Studia Biblica et Semitica*, 1996 (the *Festschrift* for Th. Vriezen), Wageningen 1966, pp.233-251, and underlined by D.N. Freedman, "The Song of the Sea", in the *Festschrift* for Muilenburg, 1967, now in PPP pp.179-186.
For my study of Ex.15 Freedman's "Strophe and Meter in Exodus 15", 1974, now in PPP p.187-227, is even more important because of his patience, love of detail and literary sensitivity.

⁷ The stone and the lead of vv.5b and 10c depict the death of the chasing Egyptians, but the stone of 16d in the first place indicates being paralysed and dumb with terror.

⁸ This applies to all verses in which God appears. In vv.9 and 14-15 the poet focuses on the enemies. To refer to God, the second person is used up to and including v.17. The final line, v.18, returns to the third person.

to what precedes it - that is, following the Masoretes - there is not much difference between *while* and *until,* so that we can keep the JPS translation "till" as cited above.

Equally remarkable is the fact that from a purely grammatical and semantic point of view a link between v.16efgh and the following verse cannot be ruled out.[9] What should we choose? A clue is offered by a form of repetition which has structural impact. The colon containing "the people whom you have purchased" is the counterpart of the colon in v.13b, "the people whom you have redeemed". The Qal perfects explain and support each other. This connection indicates an inclusio. It is considerably reinforced by the fact that the movement of the people, עם + עבר in ll.34-35, has already started in the same strophe (vv.12-13) and there has an obvious counterpart in God's guidance. Between these strophes, occupied by God and his people, there are verses exclusively populated by those terrified observers, the neighbouring tribes (vv.14-16d). We may conclude that the third refrain strophe is through inclusio so closely connected to vv.12-13 that it should be linked to the preceding text. We will therefore retain the translation quoted above.

One lesson to be learnt from the refrain strophes remains: the lesson about the heartbeat of the poem. The staircase parallelism makes it easy to scan the verses of these strophic units. Here we obviously have a metre of 2 + 2 stresses; the number of stresses is even identical to the number of words in the seven verses of the refrain strophes.[10]

It seems that the prosodic lesson is going to be that the metrical 2 + 2 pattern is also the metrical theme of the poem. Are the refrain strophes a standardising signal in this respect? I am inclined to think so. A few observations confirm the two-plus-two proposition. Let us start at the beginning, for that is where the poet immediately shows his metrical hand. The first verse contains two clauses, each consisting of a colon. Because of this we need have no hesitation in making the second syntactic unit a bicolon as well, this time with an enjambment. Both verses have 2 + 2 stresses, a scanning which is fairly straightforward:

ʾašira lᵉyahweh / *ki gaʾo gaʾa*
o ó o   o o ó   o o ó o ó

sus wᵉrokᵉbo / *rama bayyam*
ó   o o o ó   o ó   o ó

---

[9] This leads to the following rendering: "While your people pass by (..), you will bring them in and plant them on the mountain which is your inheritance". This temporal combination of the movement and the planting is not very elegant.

[10] Note that all cola in the refrain strophes consist of two words, except for v.16h. This colon contains one extra monosyllable which, however, does not detract from the iron regularity of the two-beat.

This extremely compact rhythm is all the more significant because in the next two strophes (making up the rest of stanza I) the poet likes to create the impression that verses with three stresses per colon matter a lot to him. From v.6 onwards he will systematically dispel that impression.

A second observation in favour of the 2 + 2 structure is the following. The only strophe which contains embedded speech and ironically enough offers the Egyptian enemy room to voice their illusions is v.9 (= ll.16-18), and is a convincing example of cola which all consist of two words in combination with two stresses. The two-beat-rhythm in "I divide the spoil, my desire has its fill of them, I bare my sword, my hand dispossesses them" is evident in the original language. The first two words, with their alliterating alephs, also occupy an entire colon since they constitute the quotation formula, and the two remaining words, אריק אשיג, indeed continue the alliteration, but again form a separate colon as the beginning of the embedded speech, as an asyndetic pair, and as verbs without objects.

It is now possible to expand this observation into a third, far broader generalisation: the poem is full of word couples.[11] There are scores of examples; in this respect, the poem resembles David's lament.[12] To mention a few sets: there is a long series of word couples which each constitute a complete predicative sentence and fill an entire colon: vv.1a, 3b, 5a, 7c, 7d; all six cola of v.9; then 10a, 10b, 11a, 11c, 12a, 12b, 14a,[13] 18 cases in all. Another series of no fewer than 15 cola contains instances of *s^{e}mikut*.[14]

Further proof is not necessary. We have pinpointed the poem's heartbeat: *the metrical cell of 2 + 2 stresses*. This pattern is so powerful that it governs about 30 out of the 39 verses. Now that we have established the pattern, it is extremely helpful in finding the correct division into cola for the poem. Moreover, the structure supports me when occasionally I decide to divide off an exceptionally short colon. The usual length is six to nine syllables,[15] but here we have cola con-

---

[11] I use 'couples' or 'twosomes' rather than 'word pairs', in order to save the latter as a technical term for those pairs which, spread over adjacent cola, constitute parallelism.

[12] As early as 1922, W.F. Albright already noted that the *qinah* in II Sam.1 is dominated by a two-beat rhythm. A detailed elaboration and structural application of this perception I have given in NAPS II. The typographical arrangement in twosomes (*op. cit.* p.657) turns out to be more productive for description and interpretation of the lament than its prosodic (metrical) face, which I've given as well (NAPS II p.676).

[13] If we don't attach too much importance to word counts, vv.1b, 3a, 7d and others also belong in this series.

[14] The *s^{e}mikut* is also used frequently in the *qinah*. Here in Ex.15 it occurs in v.4c, 7a, 8a, 8f, 11d, 11e, 11f, 13d, 14d, 15b, 15c, 15f, 16c, 17b, 17c. Compare this to the situation (relative clause) in v.13b // 16h, and the couple in v.10d.

[15] A count of pre-Masoretic syllables in about a hundred Psalms and a number of chapters in Proverbs and Job yielded this average. (Such a count presupposes a correct demarcation of cola, which is not always easy. Space does not permit a more detailed argumentation here.) The figures

sisting of four or even three syllables. This is exactly the aspect where again we get support from the staircase parallelism. I am giving R_3 below as an illustration:

עמך יהוה / עד יעבר		l.34	v.16ef
עם זו קנית / עד יעבר		l.35	gh

The anaphoric repetition of the A-colon and the precedents in vv.6 and 11 help us to mark out the cola in the way they are given here. Whilst the B-cola each contain five syllables, the A-cola are much shorter still. After eliminating the ḥaṭef-vowel only three syllables remain. A tentative scanning might fit the binary pattern: ó oó. The same holds for the stresses in l. 28a ($ḥil$ $'aḥaz$): two stresses for three syllables. Allocating two stresses, however, to the three pre-Masoretic syllables in lines 23b ($'o\acute{s}eh$ pal') 14b (noz^elim), 15b (b^eleb yam) and 27b ($yirgazun$) is not possible: these cola all have only one stress, I would guess.

How can we be sure we are justified in marking out cola containing only three or four syllables? There is another verse which unexpectedly contributes to our argument. In ll.29-30 (= v.15ab + cd) we read:

אלופי אדום	/	אז נבהלו
יאחזמו רעד	/	אילי מואב

The correct division into cola is in fact already determined by the neat chiasm which places two well-known neighbours on one diagonal and their fears on the other. The crossover-structure does us another service by closing off the two verses so that we immediately know we are dealing with a complete strophe.

There is, however, a more subtle phenomenon in the second verse (= l.30) which alerts our attention. This line opens with the "rams of Moab", and because of its close succession to l. 29 we assume them to be the subject of the new sentence. But no, we have been misled; in l. 30b, $ra'ad$ is the subject, with the suffix -mo referring to the leaders of Moab. Suddenly, they prove to be 'only' the object! As a result, they are allotted their syntactical place as *casus pendens* in l. 30a. The verse has acquired a bump, situated at the position of the caesura. The bump serves both as signal and as proof that the sudden transformation of subject into object (here: victim) presupposes a bicolic articulation.

The chiasm which so inescapably gives us four times two words has another function which exceeds the levels of cola, verses and strophe. The two

---

for Deut.32 also conform to this pattern. Above the 6-9 syllables average, every now and then 10 and 11 syllables occur; this length is still acceptable. At the lower end of the scale we sometimes find 5 syllables, which is not problematic; four, however, is exceptional.

verses dealing with fear in Moab and Edom are framed by a ring of adjacent verses:

r.27	The peoples hear,	/	they shudder;
r.28	Agony *grips*	/	*the dwellers in Philistia.*
r.29	Now are dismayed	/	the chieftains of Edom;
r.30	The rams of Moab	/	trembling *grips* them.
r.31	Aghast are all	/	*the dwellers in Canaan.*
r.32	Upon them descend	/	terror and dread.

This ring refers to the inhabitants of Philistia and Canaan, as shown by my italics, and is supported by the verb אחז which twice occupies first position. We observe that the chiastic opposition of people and fear continues to be effective in de adjacent strophes ll.27-28 = v.14 and ll.31-33 (= vv.15ef + 16abcd); this gives us the courage to break up lines 27-28 and 31-32 into bicola. These are all syntactical units with one predicate, presupposing enjambment.

Thus, the heart of stanza III (vv.12-16) is occupied by three strophes full of fear. This fear affects peoples (plural). Around all this a positive ring appears, devoted to the people (singular), and this ring is supported by the repetition we have already noted, that of "the people whom you have redeemed/purchased" with its poetical demonstrative *zu*. In this way, stanza III annexes the third refrain strophe and is a concentric composition of five strophes: ABXB'A'. We shall see later that strophe R_3 does a form of double duty: on prosodic and quantitative grounds it should be distinguished from strophes 10-13 (= vv.12-16cd) which form a quartet. One of those grounds is that the refrain strophe remains a part of the centripetal subsystem which articulates the body of the poem into two large stanzas.

I will close this 'entrance' paragraph by printing the poem in the desired colometric and strophic arrangement. The Roman numerals on the left indicate stanzas, the Arabic numerals next to these the 16 strophes. On the right-hand side, each full poetic line is accorded its own number, and on the far right the numbers of the Masoretic verses are given. The letters a, b, c etc. indicate the cola within the verses.

On the page following that an overview of the poem's proportions is presented, with figures for five levels. Strophes containing two lines are indicated by the letter S (short), and those containing three lines by the letter L (long).

stanza	strophe			line	verse
	9 = R	באלים יהוה	מי כמכה	21	11ab
		נאדר בקדש	מי כמכה	22	cd
		עשה פלא	נורא תהלת	23	ef
III	10	תבלעמו ארץ	נטית ימינך	24	12ab
		עם זו גאלת	נחית בחסדך	25	13ab
		אל נוה קדשך	נהלת בעזך	26	cd
	11	ירגזון	שמעו עמים	27	14ab
		ישבי פלשת	חיל אחז	28	cd
	12	אלופי אדום	אז נבהלו	29	15ab
		יאחזמו רעד	אילי מואב	30	cd
	13	ישבי כנען	נמגו כל	31	15ef
		אימתה ופחד	תפל עליהם	32	16ab
		ידמו כאבן	בגדל זרועך	33	cd
	14 = R	עמך יהוה	עד יעבר	34	16ef
		עם זו קנית	עד יעבר	35	gh
IV	15	בהר נחלתך	תבאמו ותטעמו	36	17ab
		פעלת יהוה	מכון לשבתך	37	cd
		כוננו ידיך	מקדש אדני	38	ef
	16	לעלם ועד	יהוה ימלך	39	18ab

Exodus 15 — The Song of Moses at the Reed Sea

stanza	strophe			line	verse
I	1	כי גאה גאה	אשירה ליהוה	1	1ab
		רמה בים	סוס ורכבו	2	cd
	2	ויהי לי לישועה	עזי וזמרת יה	3	2ab
		אבי וארממנהו	זה אלי ואנוהו אלהי	4	cd
		יהוה שמו	יהוה איש מלחמה	5	3ab
	3	ירה בים	מרכבת פרעה וחילו	6	4ab
		טבעו בים סוף	ומבחר שלשיו	7	cd
		ירדו במצולת כמו אבן	תהמת יכסימו	8	5ab
	4 = R	נאדרי בכח	ימינך יהוה	9	6ab
		תרעץ אויב	ימינך יהוה	10	cd
II	5	תהרס קמיך	וברב גאונך	11	7ab
		יאכלמו כקש	תשלח חרנך	12	cd
	6	נערמו מים	וברוח אפיך	13	8ab
		נזלים	נצבו כמו נד	14	cd
		בלב ים	קפאו תהמת	15	ef
	7	ארדף אשיג	אמר אויב	16	9ab
		תמלאמו נפשי	אחלק שלל	17	cd
		תורישמו ידי	אריק חרבי	18	ef
	8	כסמו ים	נשפת ברוחך	19	10ab
		במים אדירים	צללו כעופרת	20	cd

Survey of Exodus 15: the figures for five levels

strophe #	1	2	3		4	5	6	7	8		9	10	11	12	13		14	15	16
S/L	S	L	L		S	S	L	L	S		L	L	S	S	L		S	L	S
verses	2	3	3		2	2	3	3	2		3	3	2	2	3		2	3	1
cola	4	6	6		4	4	6	6	4		6	6	4	4	6		4	6	2
words	9	17	16		8	8	12	12	8		12	14	7	8	12		9	12	4
stresses	8	16	14		8	8	10	12	8		11	12	7	8	12		8	12	4
syllables	20	40	40		19	23	28	29	22		25	36	16	18	30		16	37	9
	stanza I			R_1		stanza II				R_2		stanza III				R_3	stanza IV		

§ 2. Structures and contours: a description of strophes and stanzas

Stanza I.
The first strophe contains a compound sentence whose halves each occupy a colon, and a clause which thanks to an enjambment fills the cola of l.2. The poet immediately shows his enthusiasm by a cohortative and the expression of his urgent desire to sing, which he straight away motivates by a *ki*-clause. The function of this sentence, however, is rather wider than just to explain why the poet is so eager to sing. As a hymnal half verse it reflects in a nutshell the message of the poem as a whole: God is exalted. The open vowels of *ga'o ga'a* form a beautiful example of the stylistic use of the infinitive absolute.

The very first colon presents us with a puzzle. What does the preposition *l^e* mean here? The usual translations interpret this as Moses wanting to sing *to* God. In that case, we should expect him to address the deity in the second person — which for the next eight verses he does not do. Recent research has increased the probability that the correct translation is "I will sing of God".[16] My own explorations into the use of שׁיר ל lead me to agree with this rendering.[17]

The reading that Moses wants to sing of/about God is strongly supported by the special function of the strophe which contains his intention, and by the structure of the first stanza. The opening strophe has a programmatic significance and impact, to such an extent that its structure is reflected on a larger scale by the stanza.

The structure of the first strophe is simply one verse pro God, and one verse anti enemy. This dichotomy is supported by aspects of language and genre. The first verse is hymnal, the second refers to an action in the strong sense of the

---

[16] P.A.H. de Boer, "Cantate Domino: An Erroneous Dative?", OTS xxi (1981), pp.55-67. He ends his exploration of a wide range of passages including LXX and Vulgate with the words: "The translation of the *lamedh* as a *lamedh* of reference, designating an accusative of theme, brings grammar into entire agreement with the contents of the songs, sing of the Lord, celebrate God, *cantate dominum*." He is supported by Waltke & O'Connor in their *Introduction to Biblical Hebrew Syntax*, Winona Lake IN, 1990, p.210 = §11.2.10g. HAL still refuses to concur when faced with a series of passages, see p.1372a point 2, *sub voce* שׁיר. It prefers "zu Ehren von Jahwe singen".

[17] I would particularly prefer "sing of/about God" for two reasons: a) in the passages Ps.33:1-3, 96:2-3, 98:1, 4-6 and 105:1-3 various synonyms of *šyr l* appear in veritable clusters where God is not being addressed but is praised and celebrated, and thus really is (in De Boer's words) "accusative of theme". b) De Boer rightly points to the content of the texts, art. cit. p.62: "The songs are not simply in honour of the deity but they tell how God has shown himself, in nature and to his people as life-giving and as saviour."
Very similar to the opening of the Song of Moses at the Reed Sea is the first strophe of the Song of Deborah, Jud.5. There, too, *šyr l* is used, and for that too I have advocated the translation "to sing of" in "The Song of Deborah and Barak: Its Prosodic Levels and Structure," pp.595-628 of *Pomegranates and Golden Bells*, Studies in Biblical, Jewish, and Near Eastern Ritual, Law, and Literature in Honor of Jacob Milgrom (edited by David P. Wright, David Noel Freedman, and Avi Hurvitz), Winona Lake, Indiana, 1995.

word. The verb which precedes everything denotes an action which is vocal and refers to the subsequent poem as an oral event. The meaning of the verb here *is* indubitably "to sing the praises of". The climax follows in the splendid paronomasia of the B-colon, where the long vowels *i* and *a* assonate well with the *'ašira* in front. The second verse follows rather abruptly; not only by the asyndetic connection, but also because it presents in its A-colon a rather unexpected character, "horse and rider". The B-colon offers the solution: this enemy turns out to be the object of the powerful action, in the strong sense of the word. The sentence refers to deliverance, and in retrospect the reader sees that verse 2 documents and justifies the elevated mood and enthusiasm of verse 1. Putting the enemy in first position is an insult.

The hymn/action dichotomy which determines the two sentences about God now characterises fully the two subsequent strophes which complete stanza I. Consequently, strophe 2 is essentially[18] nominal, whilst on the other hand strophe 3 consists entirely of verbal sentences. Strophe 2 celebrates God's qualities, strophe 3 reports on the decisive event.[19]

The scale-up of the first strophe in/by the first stanza is also reflected by the cornerstones of strophes 2 and 3. The very first colon ended on God's proper name, and we find the same in the first colon of the hymnal-nominal strophe 2. The final verse of that unit, sc. v.3 (= l.5) makes even more of the name. The tetragrammaton is the anaphora of both cola, apart from the word *šem* itself. When next we consider the relation between the initial and the third strophe, we see that the first unit finished on the two iambs of *rama bayyam*, immediately after *rkb*. The third strophe opens with *mrkbt* and in its first B-colon contains the same iambs, *yara bayyam*. This statement is developed thoroughly in the two B-cola immediately following, in an ominous crescendo (ll.7b//8b).

Strophe 2 = ll.3-5 = vv.2-3. This unit opens with a verse describing God through three abstract concepts. With their one-two-three syllables, these form an ascending series. The word *zimrat*, being surrounded by "strength" and "salvation", probably means "my protection".[20] The two consonants of the mascu-

---

[18] The verb *wyhy* in l.3b could denote a process, but *hyh*, an oddity in the grammar anyway, leads to the nominal predicate "salvation". The two verbs in the central verse do refer to actions on the speaker's part, but this action is oral (synonymous with "I will sing") and itself refers to lauding God.

[19] Note that only in the first sentence, l.6 = v.4ab, God is present as agent with a transitive verb, whereas the two subsequent verses, ll.7-8, focus on the enemy, first with a passive and then with an intransitive verb.

[20] I derive it from זמר III, as does HAL p.263, a stem which is sufficiently attested (cf. the name Zimri) and which has cognates in three Semitic languages. The taw added to זמרה here occurs in exactly the same way in the well-known parallels/quotations Is.12:2 and Ps.118:14, so that corruption of the text or haplography of the yodh seems improbable. The form זמרת may be viewed as an archaic form of the feminine - cf. *'emata* in v.16b -, or one may assume double duty of the suffix (from עזי).

line עַז recur in the two feminine forms which follow. The four long *i*-vowels, the *sin* and the rhyme on *-a* in l.3 find their echoes in l.5a. If we connect the feminine *yᵉšuʿa* to the feminine *milḥama*, which is of equal length and belongs to the same semantic field, and also draw a diagonal from *yah* to *yhwh* in v.5b, we have a chiastic arrangement which links the first and last verses of the strophe and thus marks and closes off the unit. This pattern seems the more apt because it sets off the central verse, l.4.

The middle line has its own syntax and so conspicuously forms the axis of the strophe. Each colon now contains two predicates, nominal alternating with verbal. The deictic opening ("this is") does double duty and its predicate *ʾeli* is considerably expanded[21] into five syllables in the B-colon, "the God of my father". The subsequent single-word verbal clauses rhyme, make God into a celebrated object and are also expanded: from *ʾanwehu* to *ʾᵃromᵉmenhu*. The concept of "exalted" (*רוֹם) is the successor to *גָּאֹה.

In the opening strophe, the first person singular has been acknowledged through the verb which started it all. Here, in the second strophe, we have the morpheme "my" two plus two times in ll.3-4, a good balance, and the aleph which denotes the first person imperfect appears twice in l.4. After this, the I-morpheme does not occur again.[22] To make up for this, God is soon promoted to second person in the text, so that the very personal tone of the poem is maintained.

The fact that five out of six cola contain three words clearly sets off this strophe against the rest of the poem, with its norm of two words and two stresses per colon. Scanning this strophe is not easy – and this, too, deviates from the norm in Ex. 15.[23]

Strophe 3 is the last unit to accept three words per colon every now and then.[24] Lines 6 and 7 each have one twosome and one threesome; the final verse

---

[21] This expansion follows the recipe formulated by Kugel as "A is so, and what's more, B." J. Kugel, *The Idea of Biblical Poetry*, Parallelism and Its History, New Haven 1981, pp.10-58. Robert Alter speaks of intensification (in various forms: heightening, strengthening, specification, focusing, etc.) in Chapter 1 (The Dynamics of Parallelism) of *The Art of Biblical Poetry*, New York 1985.
[22] The "I" remains presupposed from v.6, as from that point the poem constantly addresses 'you' (= God).
[23] To my mind, the deictic זֶה and the proper name יָהּ (however short) should be allocated a stress. The monosyllable אִישׁ should possibly have a stress as well, being a title and because of emphasis. This would result in the following pattern:
l.3 o ó   o o ó   ó   /   o o ó   o o ó
l.4 ó   o ó   o o ó o /   o o ó   o ó   o o o ó o
l.5 o ó   ó   o o ó   /   o ó   o ó
If this is correct, collision of accents occurs in l.3a (end) and l.5a.
[24] After strophe 3 the powerful rule holds that no colon contains more than two words. Very occasionally there is an extra word, but then only a monosyllable (thus ll.12a, 25b//35b). In ll.14b and 27b there is even a word less.

reaches a total of four words (with, incidentally, only nine syllables in all) in the B-colon. 'Reach' is the correct word here, as the three B-cola form an impressive series of 2-3-4 words which all refer to death by drowning:

l.6b	.... /	yara bayyam
l.7b	.... /	ṭubbeʿu beyam suf
l.8b	.... /	yaredu bimṣolot kemo ʾaben

The indications for 'water' (always preceded by b^e) become longer and longer, they become more and more specific and grow from a monosyllable in the singular to the plural "depths" in 8b, whilst there the enemy acquires the opposite quality of "stone" so that their fate is sealed. The simile is striking: *in cauda venenum*.

For just a moment longer God remains in the picture as an agent in this sequence, then his role is taken over by the Egyptians. Admittedly, they get the subject position in ll.7b//8b, but this is in ironical inverse relation to their fate. Moreover, they first get a passive form – isn't it their suffering, *passio*, which is highlighted – and next an intransitive form, as if the going-down movement is an automatic process. Their humiliation is stressed even more in l.8a when "the waters" themselves are the subject and make the Egyptians into the object (read: the victims). The other collective, the people of Israel, have not been allowed a single morpheme of space in the text at this stage. Ironically enough they will not appear until the seventh strophe, as a suffix to the enemy's bragging.

While the waters are rising in the B-cola, an opposite movement takes place in the A-cola. The enemy shrinks and shrinks, from three to two words and then to one syllable:

l.6a	Pharaoh's chariots and his host /	....
l.7a	and the pick of his officers /	....
l.8a	the floods covered them /	....

It is only too clear who is winning, and we can also hear this in the rhyme of the awesome t^ehomot (a word with mythical connotations) and $m^eṣolot$. Finally, I note that k^emo in l.8b echoes both *-mot* and kaph + *-mu* in 8a, and that the labials mem and beth occur frequently throughout the strophe (7 and 8 times respectively, for instance in the alliterations *mark^ebot - mibḥar*). In the A-cola I hear a series *mar-*, *par-* and *-ḥar*, apart from the correspondence between *yara* and *yaredu*. The u-sounds in *suf*, *ṭubbeʿu*, *yekasyumu* and *yaredu* sound threateningly dark for the enemy.

Thus the first stanza ends on a glut of terms for 'water' and 'enemy'. This fascinates the poet so much that he decides to continue this pattern in the next stanza. In stanza II another three out of four strophes are completely filled with it. Here, however, one element is added: that of heat. The heat of God's nose (ll.12a-13a; his רוח in l.19a) is of course his wrath. First, however, we pass his right hand, which is so powerful as to be awarded a refrain strophe – as stated before, a pillar of the composition.

I leave the first stanza with a few remarkable figures about its proportions. The extent to which strophe 1 as a programmatic unit is enlarged by strophes 2 and 3 is perfectly mirrored in their lengths.[25] Strophe 1 contains 20 syllables, strophe 2 exactly twice that number, and strophe 3 also contains 40 syllables. Their total number of syllables, which is also that of stanza I, is 100. The four strophes occupying stanza II are almost the same length, 102 syllables, and again, the four strophes in stanza III have exactly the round number of 100.

Strophe 4 is the first strophe showing the iron regularity of twice 2 + 2 words and exactly the same number of stresses. The anaphoric start of the verses expands to include the entire A-colon, which results in a staircase parallelism; this is the first characteristic of the unit. The second is discursive and rhetorical: the dramatic shift from third to second person for God, which is maintained right up to the last verse of the Song. The direction of the discourse changes: the I is no longer speaking about a 'he', but addresses a 'you' before him – a direct address with all the power and immediacy that entails. Because of this phenomenon I do not read strophe 4 as the ending of the first stanza, but, following the centripetal recipe include it with the body of the poem, just as R_3 (= strophe 14 = v.16e-h).

The second person appears in the shape of the double *-ka*, followed by the vocative *yhwh*. This poem does not contain any enjambments across verse boundaries, so I read l.9 as a predicative sentence: "Your right hand, O LORD, *is* glorious in power." The participle נאדר provides us with a keyword which fulfils roughly the same function with respect to the composition as the similes of lead and stone.[26] It also occurs in the central verse of the central refrain strophe,

---

[25] Counts: strophe 1 contains 3.3 / 1.2.2 plus 1.4 / 2.2 = 20 syllables; strophe 2 contains 2.3.1 / 2.1.3 plus 1.2.4 / 3.2.6 plus 2.1.3 / 2.2 = 40 syllables, and strophe 3 contains 3.2.3 / 2.2 plus 3.3 / 3.2.1 plus 3.4 / 3.3.2.1 = 40 syllables.
Freedman, on the other hand, counts 102 in PPP p. 223; see also his reconstruction and transcription of the pre-Masoretic Hebrew on pp.195-197. The difference between his result and mine is caused by his resolving *yksymw* (being a Piel) to five syllables (yakassiyumu) and allocating 3 syllables to *wyhy*. In strophes 5-8 = vv.7-10 Freedman counts 106 syllables, likewise 106 in vv.12-16d. Whatever the exact figures, the message from both of us is clear: there is an extensive quantitative balance before and after strophes R_1 and R_2.
[26] The form *neʾdari* is less strange on account of its final vowel (which I view as an archaic, atrophied case ending) than because of its gender: a masculine form after the feminine subject *ymyn*? I explain the incongruence as a *constructio ad sensum* chosen by the poet because he had the figure of YHWH (through the synecdoche "hand") in mind. In l.10b *ymyn* does get a feminine predicate again: תרעץ.

in l.22b, which is almost identical to l.9b. The adjective אדירים occupies a strategic position very close to it, as the very last word of stanza II.
Strophe 4 contains one verbal colon and three nominal cola. Its antipode, strophe 14 (R_3), has the exactly opposite structure of one nominal colon and three cola containing a verb. The central refrain strophe 9 is completely nominal in all three verses.[27] An excellent choice for the hymnal heart.

Stanza II = strophes 5-8 = vv.7-10.
This stanza consists of four strophes which collaborate in pairs. We can see this in the mirror effect of their lengths: S + L for strophes 5-6 and L + S for strophes 7-8. Thanks to the strict norm of two words per colon their symmetry is perfect at word level as well: 8 + 12 and 12 + 8 words. And even at syllable level the differences between the two S-units and those between the two L-units are minute: 23/22 syllables for strophes 5 and 8, 28/29 syllables for the long strophes 6 and 7. These figures might lead us to expect these strophes to exhibit a concentric ABBA relation. This, however, is not the case; rather, their meanings are parallel. The contents of the strophes may be summarised as follows:
- strophe 5: God's wrath destroys the enemy   2 verses
- strophe 6: the waters pile up into a dam   3 verses
- strophe 7: the illusions of the enemy, who is speaking   3 verses
- strophe 8: the enemy sinks in the mighty waters   2 verses.

This requires an alternating phrasing; in 5 and 7 God and the enemy are in turn victorious, in 6 and 8 the waters are, on behalf of Israel (in 6) and at the cost of Egypt (in 8). The systematic order is inescapable, closely interweaving a parallel arrangement (of content) with a concentric arrangement (of proportions).

Strophe 5 starts off with a complement (l.11a) and then has three cola with a verb as predicate. Consequently, there is a lot of action here, by God (three times *-ka* in rhyming position, two times the *t-* of the *tqtl* pattern) against the enemy ("those who rise against you .. them"). The A-cola are beautifully attuned to each other thanks to a nominal formation (stem + *-on*), so that "your majesty" is explained as, and fused with, "your [heat =] fury":
- three syllables + $g^{e\prime}onka$
- three syllables + $h^a ronka$.

The word "majesty" appeals to the sensitive reader, as this opening of stanza II echoes the *ga'o ga'a* which served as a signboard at the beginning of stanza I. We hear the long *o* again in *rob* and *tahros*, and two more times in *yok^{e}lemo*. The destruction itself takes place in the B-cola. By way of *ga'on* the poet has found

---

[27] Of course, the three participles there, just like the נאדר in strophe 4, do not function as verbs here but as adjectives. NB.: the sereh underneath the sin of עשה reveals that פלא is not governed verbally by עשה, but nominally: it is not the object, but part of a *s^{e}mikut*.

ḥaron, which now leads him to an image quite the opposite of the frequent drowning: the heat of God's fury "consumes them like stubble" – end of strophe.

Various forms of balance keep strophes 5 and 6 together as a pair. The simile "like stubble" receives a companion in "like a dam" in l.14a. The beginning of strophe 6 closely parallels the beginning of strophe 5 in syntax, alliterations and rhyme:

l.11a   *ub^{e}rob g$^{e\rangle}$onka*
l.13a   *ub^{e}ruḥ ʾappeka*

This results in the acknowledgement that strictly speaking "the blast of your nostrils" is the same as God's wrath, which in turn is identical to "your great triumph". The combination "the blast of your nostrils" is varied rather nicely in l.19a (= v.10a):

l.13a   *ub^{e}ruḥ*   *ʾappeka*
l.19a   *našafta*   *b^{e}ruḥ^{a}ka*

The smouldering nose (plus *-ka*) moves up along the diagonal and becomes the verb 'to blow' (plus *-ta*). Together with the other diagonal (רוח, twice) this results in a chiasm which itself functions as a support for the arrangement of the four strophes into parallel pairs: ll.13a // 19a are of course the opening lines of strophes 6 and 8, respectively.

Strophe 6 is the first (and not the last) unit which is going to make much of the alliteration with the *nun*. There are two perfect forms from the same register, that of the Niphal, followed by two nouns which usually are irreconcilable (dam vs. streams), but which now explain each other thanks to the miraculous coagulation of the waters:

ll.13b + 14ab   . . . .   / *Ne^{c}ermu mayim*
                Niṣṣ^{e}bu k^{e}mo Ned   / *Noz^{e}lim*

Marking out cola is not easy here in the middle of strophe 6, especially as regards allocating an entire colon to one three-syllabic word, but we are guided by the alliterations. What is more, we get support from a new chiasm which crosses the halves of l.14 with those of l.15, so that the *noz^{e}lim* (masc., three syllables) become the *t^{e}homot* (fem., three syllables), and the three syllables of the adjunct *k^{e}mo ned* balance the three of the adjunct *b^{e}leb yam*. This balance may also be phrased 'vertically': the 3+3 / 3 syllables of the one verse exactly reflect the 3+3 / 3 syllables of the other. The strophe as a whole is framed by two parts of the body, one of which is more metaphoric than the other: the blast of your nose ... in the heart of the sea. The characters they represent, however, collaborate very well against the enemy.

Strophe 7 forms a remarkable break by undermining the chronology. In strophes 3 and 6 the hostile host has been drowned already, and here the adversary is still talking of success! Hence, strophe 7 is noticeable as a separate unit for two reasons: this section is embedded speech, which strangely enough is given to the enemy, and also a flashback with respect to the developments, which largely respect the chronology of events.

Strophe 7 offers an ideal opportunity to present students with a puzzle. Does this unit consist of three bicola or two tricola? As I have given the bicolic arrangement above, I here present the strophe in tricolic lines:

v.9abc   אמר אויב / ארדף אשיג / אחלק שלל
v.9def   תמלאמו נפשי / אריק חרבי / תורישמו ידי

This arrangement, though not the best, is not bad. The sustained alliteration of the aleph, the consonant which here links the enemy and three of his verbs, is now contained in one verse. The same holds for the iambs *nafši - ḥarbi - yadi* and their rhymes. The C-cola are synonymous as regards meaning, as both refer to the spoils. Still, I prefer the bicolic arrangement, which looks as follows:

l.16   ארדף אשיג   אמר אויב   v.9ab
l.17   תמלאמו נפשי אחלק שלל   cd
l.18   תורישמו ידי   אריק חרבי   ef

Which arguments can we use to beat the tricolic proposition? In the bicolic arrangement, the aleph is still important, and now it also appears anaphorically at the beginning of all three verses. The asyndetic pair of verbs without object in v.9b now finds itself next to the similarly unique couple occupying v.9a which forms the quotation formula. The verse now contains twice 2 + 2 syllables. The half verses of ll.17-18 all have a verbal predicate, followed by nouns which all have two syllables; in the A-cola they are object (spoils, sword), in the B-cola they are subject and refer to parts of the body (my [eager] throat, my hand). In the half verses of l.18 a Hiphil is used both times.

These observations more or less balance the arguments in favour of two tricola. In the bicolic arrangement, however, two vertical and two diagonal lines are added. Vertically, we notice "I" as the subject of the A-cola of ll.17-18 and the rhyme on *-emo* in the B-cola, which all have a feminine subject in the third person (pattern *tqtl*). Moreover, there are crossing lines confronting us with the fascinating semantics of a chiasm. We have the opposition full/empty (מלא - ריק) in "my throat shall have its fill of them" versus "I will draw my sword", whereas 17a and 18b again refer to stealing and plundering. This results in what I will now call the quartet of greediness. Finally, there is an important prosodic argument which to me is decisive: this poem is totally bicolic, and strophe 7 will just have to fit in.

The enemy is portrayed as extremely energetic. This is the effect not only of a consistently sustained asyndeton, but also of the staccato rhythm of the verbs. The enemy is full of confidence and in a triumphant mood. An attractive counterpoint in a song of victory by ... his victims, who ended up not being victims at all. And how very sad that the enemy has no way of knowing that he has been honoured with a strophe in the Song of Moses!

Strophes 6 and 8, complementing each other through the element of water, represent opening and closing. The waters open up to allow the Israelites to pass through by rising to form a dam and freezing - strophe 6. The water closes over the enemy's cavalry and army - strophe 8. Its *ʾaddir* quality has been copied from and approved by God, who himself is of course *neʾdar* "by his power and by his holiness". The movements of the water cover the chronology of events. Between dam and floods the enemy is allowed his say; the retrospect lends an almost surreal quality to his discourse.

Strophe 8. Whereas the beginning of this unit closely links up to that of the previous water strophe, the main characteristic of the three cola which follow (l.19b and l.20ab) is that they, themselves forming the end of stanza II, have been inspired by the end of stanza I. The מצולת of l.8b here receive a clever echo in the verb צללו of l.20a.[28] The latter form is fully assonant with the ירדו of l.8b. Hence I propose to view *ṣalᵉlu* as a fusion, as regards sound and meaning, of the terms *yarᵉdu* and *mᵉṣolot*.

The relation between strophe 8 and strophe 3 also becomes clear from the following. The contents of l.8a (the floods covered them) is identical to that of l.19b (the sea covered them). Moreover, a chiasm of terms denoting water links up strophes 6 and 8:

strophe 6:	water (end of l.13)	....	sea (end of l.15)
strophe 8:	sea (end of l.19)	....	water (l.20b)

Between the components of this cross we then also find the similes "like a dam" and "like lead", which yet connect the comparisons in strophes 5-6 to the network of similes which helped to mark out the ends of the stanzas.

The connection between strophes 6 and 8 is reinforced by several contrasts. Strophe 6 does not mention any people at all, neither as agents nor as objects. In strophe 8, on the other hand, the enemy is noticeably present, but as a target: the ignominiously sinking victim of the angry sea. This is linked to another contrast: in strophe 6 the waters always are the grammatical subjects, but not the agents of the action. They occur mainly in passive forms (two Niphals, as we have seen). In strophe 8, however, the sea is extremely active and eliminates the Egyptian army through *kissamo*.

Strophe 9 (= v.11) is the central refrain strophe, R_2. It differs from R_1 and R_3 in that it consists of three verses. The *-mi- .. -ka* sounds of strophe 4 are here continued in the double *mi kamoka*, the famous rhetorical question which especially refers to God's matchlessness. Fittingly, the figure of God himself and his

---

[28] I refer to the phonetic link here, and do not imply that these words originate from the same root.

perfections are at the centre of attention, which also is the centre of the poem. Having been alerted to the *nun* of the Niphal in strophe 6 we notice that here, too, a Niphal has been used twice. The first form occurs in l.9b, so that the phrases "majestic in power" and in l.22b, "majestic in holiness", support each other and their second terms (כח and קדש) become synonymous. Immediately after that, i.e. asyndetically, a new phrase follows containing a Niphal participle, *nora' t^{e}hillot*, plus the combination *'oseh pele'*. As regards sound, this bicolon with its three o-sounds has been partly inspired by the o-sounds of the double *kamoka*. I translate the phrase occupying l.23a as "terrible in/through glorious deeds". The hymnal centre does not link any of the terms celebrating God to the concrete situation, as if to indicate that God cannot be contained and that his perfections utterly transcend the horizon of human knowing.

Stanza III plus refrain: strophes 10-14 (vv.12-16).

This section celebrates a new development. Egypt and its discomfiture at and in the Red Sea are behind us, according to cantor Moses. By subject matter alone strophes 10-14 clearly form a group. The business now is to move on: "your people" are on their way "to your holy abode", and under your guidance. The one people, the group "whom you have redeemed", is pitted against the many peoples mentioned in strophes 11-13 and indicated by name. To accommodate all this the poet has created a circular structure with the cowering neighbours in the middle (strophes 11-13, = vv.14-16d) and around these the ring of strophes 10 + 14 for God, the chosen people and their relationship.

On the basis of several prosodic aspects we seem justified in taking the series 10-13 as stanza III. The systematic articulation of stanza II, 102 syllables accommodated in a unit pattern S + L − L + S, is here turned inside out and yet mirrored exactly: the strophic units exhibit the pattern L + S − S + L and contain 100 syllables (exactly the same number as stanza I). The quantitative factors are supported by stylistic and structural elements. Strophes 10-13 are also marked out as a quartet through several cornerstones. The first which strikes the eye by its strategic position is the simile "as a stone" in l.33b; as the cornerstone of stanza III this is the successor to "as lead" (end of stanza II) and "like a stone" (end of stanza I). In v.16c (= l.33a) we have "the might of your arm" which may be linked to "your right hand" in v.12a (= l.24a), resulting in an inclusio. The element of ימינך is in itself a cornerstone because it occurs in the very first colon of stanza III, and because it echoes "your right hand, glorious in power" in the strophe which managed the transition from stanza I to II. The repetition makes sense: that same right hand which destroyed the hostile power (negative, stanza II) is now taking positive action to guide Israel past all sorts of neighbouring tribes which would probably want to be just as hostile, if they were not suppressed and shown their place by the numinous terror of this awful deity called *yhwh*.

Strophe 10 retains the inspiration from the *nun*. The three perfect forms which open the verses constitute an anaphora of sounds (*n...-ta*), and are supported by the three nouns which follow and which themselves rhyme on *-ka*. Moreover, the B-cola of v.13 also end in *-ta* and *-ka*. In this way, the strophe is credited fully to the deity. Through the inner rhyme *ga'alta - nehalta* and the recurrence of ayin, u and zayin from ʿ*am zu* (l.25b) in ʿ*uzz-* (l.26a) ll. 25b and 26a show a phonetic chiasm.[29]

This L-strophe has a strongly 'vertical' structure. The nouns of the A-cola may be pushed into each other like a telescope, and also explain each other: "your hand" is the manifestation of "your love" and both coincide in "your strength" . The B-cola are related dynamically. Around " the people whom you have redeemed" (the middle B-colon) there is spatial information covering the people's itinerary and expressed in polar opposites. In 24b the earth swallows the enemy of yesterday and today, in l.26 the other end of the route appears, "your holy abode" (another initial nun). The substantives קדש and עז which close off the strophe refer to the exact middle of the poem (where God is called "majestic in holiness") and the start of the nominal, hymnal strophe 2 (the very first noun which Moses applies to God in praise is "my strength"). Again, this link makes good sense: the holiness and strength which characterise God are more than just words. In strophe 10 they become operational, by means of redemption and guidance towards a joyful destiny.

Strophes 11-13. The enumeration of peoples also echoes the circular structure through increasing and decreasing precision. The chiasm which forms the core and defines strophe 12 contains two proper names of tribes from Transjordan. Around these we find the wider terms Philistia and Canaan, which refer to the Cisjordan and which in this context are both names of countries because of the word "inhabitants".[30] "Inhabitants" itself is a wider term than the "chiefs" who occupy the centre, flanking the sounds *-om* and *mo-* with their alliteration *'allufe - 'ele*. Around these four verses (ll.28-31) there are even vaguer indications: ʿ*ammim* who tremble, and ʿ*alehem* and "they/them" (in 32a + 33b) whom terror and dumbness befall.

In vv.14-16 two sound patterns for fear are conspicuous: *-gaz-* and *'ahaz* (strophe 11), *'az* and *-haz-* (strophe 12), coupled to the striking pair of segholates closing off ll.30 and 32: *raʿad* and *pahad*. Their strophes 12 and 13 both open on Niphal forms (same choice again!). There is not a single transitive verb

---

[29] Some more phonetic phenomena: the difference between *nahita* and *natita* is just one sound. Because of the inner rhyme of *ga'alta - nehalta* and the recurrence of ayin, u and zayin from ʿ*am zu* (l.25b) in ʿ*uzz-*(l.26a), 25b and 26a show a phonetic chiasm. The nouns in second position all start with a short syllable based on a hatef-vowel; the monosyllables *ḥasd and *ʿuzz are provided with a counterpart in *qudš.

[30] Note that it is not only the two proper names in strophe 12 which are symmetrical (in sound), but also the two surrounding names: the forms *p^elišt and *k^enaʿn have a comparable structure.

here which might give these neighbours the illusion they can act with dignity. All the time they are the objects of what seizes, surprises or terrifies them, or they are the subjects of passive verbs, which boils down to the same thing. Contrast that to Israel's position: admittedly, they are objects in strophe 10, but of God's care and favour, and they rise to subject status in strophe 14.

Strophe 14. The people which is being guided in strophe 10 now moves of its own accord in strophe 14. The repetition which results in staircase parallelism here goes on longer than in the other two refrain strophes and extends beyond the caesura. If we indicate each word by a letter, the pattern looks like this:

l.34   ab / cd
l.35   ab / cef

The letter c here denotes "people', or rather, "your people". This singular contrasts with the anonymous plural ʿ*ammim* in l.27a, and the entire colon 35b forms a ring together with l.25b.

The unit thus acquires an oscillating position: as a part of the five-fold ring structure and because of its syntactic dependence on the main clause in l.33 it requires a place in stanza III. If we take the cornerstones in the structure of strophes 10-13 into account, however, neither R_3 nor the unit as part of the subsystem of the three refrain strophes belong in stanza III. The same phenomenon, in a slightly less pronounced form, also occurs with R_1. In a way, R_1 is included within the body of the poem – mainly because of the centripetal force – yet preferably its place seems outside it, given the self-sufficient structure of stanza II. R_3 is attached more to the body of the poem, but tries to escape. We might call this to-and-fro a form of double duty at strophe level.

Stanza IV = strophes 15 and 16 = vv.17-18.

This unit, consisting of only 16 words, quickly finishes off the poem. In essence it consists of one L-strophe, following which a single verse (l.39), half an S-strophe long, constitutes the ending. This v.18 returns to the third person for God and forms a kind of coda, perhaps a liturgical exclamation or proclamation.

Strophe 15 shows an interesting balance as regards nominal vs. verbal elements. Two verbs with objects (the "them" suffix, *bis*) fill the first A-colon, following which a spatial term occupies the B-colon - actually no more than a complement. In the two verses which follow we again encounter two terms denoting concrete spatial objects, but this time they occupy first position in the A-cola and in both cases are the grammatical objects of one single verb which occupies the B-colon with its subject. Twice, God is addressed directly in the vocative. This structure is schematically presented in the following diagram, where P indicates predicate, N = noun and V = vocative:

$$\begin{array}{lll} P + P & / & N + N \\ N + N & / & P + N = V \\ N + N = V & / & P + N \end{array}$$

Three times God is the "you" of a verb form, three times he is represented by the rhyming *-ka*. The two verbs in front are the last involvement on God's part with his people in this text: "you will bring them in, and plant them on the mountain which is your inheritance". The two verses which follow show God only in relation to the holy place. Their A-cola are synonymous with l.36b, which results in a chain of three nominal pairs, each link of which explains and pervades the others: "the mountain of your inheritance" is identical with "the place ... to dwell in" is identical with "your sanctuary, O Lord". This chain provides an argument for making the nouns in 37a//38a dependent on the preposition b^e in l.36b, which does triple duty. As a result of this connection ll.37b//38b then become asyndetic relative clauses.[31] In these two verses there is a diagonal line from the noun *makon* to the action which formed the abode: your hands *kon^{e}nu*. It is bisected by the line connecting the vocatives *yhwh* and "my Lord".

The chronological aspect is interesting. God's taking care of the people (two verbs) comes after the completed crossing. Being planted by God is the completion of their journey, and of the constituent phase of the history of the covenant. The action which follows (another two verbs) is in the perfect tense and refers back in time. God had long acquired himself a throne and founded it with his own hands. This movement of the poem back in time is an apt finishing touch to the splendid lyricism which has largely respected the chronology of events.[32]

The retrospective gesture intimates how God has prepared himself for subsequent developments. Now, a new era starts: the people's 'dwelling' takes place - literally - in the land which God had chosen as a dwelling place for himself, and in this respect will coincide with His living. This is illustrated by the repetition of the root "holy" (*miqdaš*, in l.38a). The God who is "majestic in holi-

---

[31] Thus for instance the JPS, and see also C. Houtman, Exodus vol.II, (in the series COT = Commentaar op het Oude Testament, Kampen), 1989, p.263.
[32] However vivid, expressive and changeable the images and strophes of the lyricism in Jud.5, there, too, we may discern the retention of the underlying chronology. In Jud. 5 it is even more important than here, because in the song of victory the lyrical present of the singers Deborah and Barak alternates with the history and the yesterday of the battle. See my analysis in the *Festschrift* Milgrom, p.599 (see for the title note 17 *supra*).

ness" (hymnal: nominal, l.22b) has purposefully guided his people to his "holy abode" (l.26, action!), which coincides with "the sanctuary (=holy place) ".

A form of complementariness links up strophe 15 with the beginning of the poem. The terms of space and movement create an inclusio at strophe level. The lofty deity who in one dynamic gesture cast the seemingly powerful enemy into the waters of the sea is the same person who founded a secure throne in a high place, the mountain which he chose, and there, with a vertical movement and a positive gesture plants the people which elsewhere is called "his inheritance", just like the mountain.

The coda "keeps up with the times" by looking way past them. God will be King "for ever and ever". The hymn *cum* song of victory has amply proved - in the special mode and with the particular tools of lyricism - that this title belongs to him.

§ 3. *Proportions*

The Song of Moses contains strophes of two or three verses, which I indicate by the letters S (short) and L (long). Now that the text has been printed and discussed, we can easily observe some quantitative aspects without losing sight of their relation to the essential issue: meaning and quality.

The first point to be noted is purely arithmetical. The poem's sixteen strophes show a strict balance between S and L. There are eight short and eight long strophes, in the following order:

S L L S S L L S L L S S L S L S

This symmetry is maintained one level down, a level which closely resembles the level of the stanzas, but which is not the same when we divide the set of 16 into quartets:

S L L S / S L L S / L L S S / L S L S
    R   R   R

To this set I have added the letter R for the three units which are characterised by staircase parallelism.

Each quartet now has a binary division, insofar as it has two short and two long strophes. Their sequence varies. The first two sets of four show a concentric symmetry with 2 x 3 verses being surrounded by 2 x 2 verses. Each of the last two quartets represents yet another possibility.

The first half of the poem still largely keeps to the division of the stanzas, but after the middle the series given here is no more than a quantitative reality. That is not necessarily bad, since in matters of metrics and prosody a restrained and quantitative approach is called for. This sort of counting is permitted as long as we can avoid the pitfall of deducing statements about content, meaning or value directly from figures.

I will now consider the set of short strophes and leave the last, which only contains one verse and forms the coda, aside. The remaining set of seven then shows the following proportions, given in ascending order irrespective of the order in which they appear in the text: 16-16-18-19-20-22-23 syllables. This is a smooth series whose maximum links up very well with the minimum of the scale which applies to the eight L-strophes, and which, again sorted in ascending order, runs as follows: 25-28-29-30-36-37-40-40 syllables.

The two longest strophes are situated at the beginning: these are units 2 and 3 which develop the 'hymnal' line and the 'action' line of the opening, respectively. The units containing 36 and 37 syllables each open a stanza: the third and fourth respectively. This positioning makes good sense as well, because both deal with the dwelling place of the deity, and complementarily and chronologically belong together: God leads the people, the people arrive and are planted by him. The shortest L-strophe is the hymnal centre of gravity: strophe 10, about "who is like you?"

We creep closer to content and meaning when we write down the entire series following the structure of the poem and its articulation by the refrain strophes:

$$S+ L + L \quad / \quad S \quad S + L \quad L + S \quad L \quad L + S \quad S + L \quad S \ / \quad L + S$$
$$\qquad\qquad\qquad R_1 \qquad\qquad\qquad\qquad R_2 \qquad\qquad\qquad\qquad R_3$$

The slash here shows how the refrain strophes belong to the body of the poem, taking into account their interrelations and their centripetal tendency. Between these units, stanzas II and III, each containing four strophes, have been more clearly demarcated by inserting extra spaces.

If we write down the same series giving the figures for the number of words per strophe, the result is as follows:

$$9 + 17 + 16 \quad 8 \quad 8 + 12 + 12 + 8 \quad 12 \quad 14 + 7 + 8 + 12 \quad 9 \quad 12 + 4$$
$$\qquad\qquad\qquad R \qquad\qquad\qquad\qquad R \qquad\qquad\qquad\qquad R$$

Words vary so much in length that they are unreliable as a unit of measure, but in this case it is certainly striking that there are eight strophes containing eight words and four containing twelve words. The structural analysis in the previous paragraph has clearly shown that the body of the poem consists of 2 x 4 strophes and that each stanza has its own, forceful symmetry. Under those circumstances it is certainly no coincidence that stanza II contains the series 8-12-12-8. Stanza III deviates slightly with 14-7-8-12. Stanza IV has 12 + 4 = 16 words in all, which is the same number as that of the strophe which precedes the body of the poem.

The numbers 8 and 12 I would like to call key numbers at this relatively unimportant level of word counting. This is the case in at least seven strophes; there are three more strophes which, containing 7 or 9 words, differ by only one point from the norm of eight. At this level, the refrain strophes also exhibit their mutual involvement; their series of 8-12-9 words again reveals the axis of the poem. The figures for the stresses in these strophes run 8-11-8.

As we have seen, one of the main characteristics of this poem is the fact that almost all cola consist of two words. Because of this exceptional stability of the colon it is also useful to carry out a colon count which takes into account the alternation of stanzas and refrain strophes. The numbers of cola per strophe and stanza are given below; strophes are separated by a full stop:

per strophe:	4.6.6	R=4	4.6.6.4	R=6	6.4.4.6	R=4	6.2
per stanza:	16	[4]	20	[6]	20	[4]	8

The systematic alternation of S and L is here of course translated into the numbers 4 and 6. The series 4-6-4 for the refrain strophes again proves that they mark a middle and two boundaries. Their figures collaborate splendidly with those of stanzas II and III in showing the perfect regularity of the body of the poem. The figures per stanza reveal something new about head and tail: the short closing stanza contains exactly half the number of cola of stanza I.

I will close my argument by descending to the level of the smallest units of measure, the syllables. Here we see the following numbers:

strophe	1	2	3	4	5	6	7	8	9	10	11	12	13	14	15	16
				R					R				R			
	20	40	40	19	23	28	29	22	25	36	16	18	30	16	37	9

Per stanza this means (the figures for the three intervening R-strophes are given in brackets):

stanza I	R_1	stanza II	R_2	stanza III	R_3	stanza IV
100	[19]	102	[25]	100	[16]	46

I do not want to go too far in drawing conclusions from these figures; caution should be used when taking figures as a basis for profound interpretative statements, if only because what has been counted here are pre-Masoretic syllables and their totals are only tentative, with an approximation error of about 2 %.

Nevertheless, we are justified in taking these last series of numbers as a striking proof of the poem's careful construction. It would be a pity not to point out that these numbers prove that stanzas I-III are in principle equal in length, and that stanza IV is half-size.

More in detail I think the following details should be noted. Strophe 1 is exactly half the lengths of strophes 2 and 3. Strophes 2 and 3 have exactly the same length; this is not the result of, but it is linked to the fact that these are the only strophic units which for a fleeting moment suggest that the poet is interested in cola containing three stresses/words. Stanzas I-II-III form a series 100-102-100. In stanza II, the difference between the two S-strophes is minimal, as they contain 23 and 22 words; the same holds for the two L-strophes, containing 28 and 29 words. As a result, strophes 5-6 and 7-8 form two pairs of exactly the same length – and this harmonises perfectly with their contents, which make 5-6 the parallel pair to 7-8.

Chapter III

A comprehensive description of Deut. 32 as a work of art

Text

I begin this chapter by offering the full text of the poem Deuteronomy 32 as rendered by the JPS. I present this translation in my own colometry and with few slight alterations, on the grounds which are given in my subsequent analyses.

	strophe

¹Give ear, O heavens, let me speak;
    let the earth hear the words I utter!
²May my discourse come down as the rain,
    my speech distill as the dew,
Like showers on young growth,
    like droplets on the grass.
	1

³For the name of the LORD I proclaim;
    give glory to our God!
⁴The Rock!–His deeds are perfect,
    yea, all His ways are just;
A faithful God, never false,
    true and upright is He.
	2

⁵His non-children–that crooked, perverse generation–
    their baseness has played Him false.
⁶Do you thus requite the LORD,
    o dull and witless people?
Is not He the Father who created you,
    fashioned you and made you endure!
	3

⁷Remember the days of old,
    consider the years of ages past;
Ask your father, he will inform you,
    your elders, they will tell you:
	4

⁸When the Most High gave nations their homes
    and set the divisions of man,
He fixed the boundaries of peoples
    in relation to Israel's numbers.
⁹For the LORD's portion is His people,
    Jacob His own allotment.

¹⁰He found him in a desert region,
    in an empty howling waste.
He engirded him, watched over him,
    guarded him as the pupil of His eye.

¹¹Like an eagle who rouses his nestlings,
    gliding down to his young,
So did He spread His wings and take him,
    bear him along on His pinions;
¹²The LORD alone did guide him,
    no alien god at His side.

¹³He set him atop the highlands,
    to feast on the yield of the earth;
He fed him honey from the crag,
    and oil from the flinty rock,

¹⁴Curd of kine and milk of flocks;
    with the best of lambs,
And rams and he-goats,
    with the very finest wheat—
        and foaming grape-blood was your drink.

¹⁵So Jeshurun grew fat and caroused—
    you grew fat and gross and coarse—
He forsook the God who made him
    and spurned the Rock of his support.
¹⁶They incensed Him with alien things,
    vexed Him with abominations.

¹⁷They sacrificed to demons, no-gods,
    gods they had never known,
New ones, who came but lately,
    who stirred not your fathers' fears.
¹⁸You neglected the Rock that begot you,
    forgot the God who brought you forth.

¹⁹The Lord saw and was vexed
 and spurned His sons and His daughters.
²⁰He said: I will hide My countenance from them,
 and see how they fare in the end.
For they are a treacherous breed,
 children with no loyalty in them.

²¹They incensed Me with no-gods,
 vexed Me with their futilities;
I'll incense them with a no-folk,
 vex them with a nation of fools.

²²For a fire has flared in My wrath
 and burned to the bottom of Sheol,
Has consumed the earth and its increase,
 eaten down to the base of the hills.

²³I will sweep misfortunes on them,
 use up My arrows on them:
²⁴Wasting famine, ravaging plague,
 deadly pestilence, and fanged beasts
Will I let loose against them,
 with venomous creepers in dust.

²⁵The sword shall deal death without,
 as shall the terror within,
To youth and maiden alike,
 the suckling as well as the aged.

²⁶I might have reduced them to naught,
 made their memory cease among men,
²⁷But for fear of the taunts of the foe,
 their enemies who might misjudge
And say, "Our own hand has prevailed;
 none of this was wrought by the Lord!"

²⁸For they are a folk void of sense,
 lacking all discernment.
²⁹Were they wise, they would think upon this,
 gain insight into their future:

12
13
14
15
16
17
18

30"How could one have routed a thousand,
    or two put ten thousand to flight,
Unless their Rock had sold them,
    the LORD had given them up?"
31For their rock is not like our Rock,
    in our enemies' own estimation.

32Ah! Their vine is from Sodom,
    from the vineyards of Gomorrah;
Their grapes are poison,
    a bitter growth their clusters.
33Their wine is the venom of asps,
    the pitiless poison of vipers.

34Lo, I have put it all away,
    sealed up in My storehouses,
35To be My vengeance and recompense,
    at the time that their foot falters.
Yea, the day of disaster is near,
    and destiny rushes upon them.

36For the LORD will vindicate His people
    and take revenge for His servants,
When He sees that their might is gone,
    and neither ruler nor helper is left.

37He will say: Where are their gods,
    the rock in whom they sought refuge,
38Who ate the fat of their offerings
    and drank their libation wine?
Let them rise up to your help,
    and let them be a shield unto you!

39See, then, that I, I am He;
    there is no god beside Me.
I deal death and give life;
    I wounded and I will heal:
        none can deliver from My hand.

40Lo, I raise My hand to heaven
    and say: As I live forever,
41When I whet My flashing blade
    and My hand lays hold on judgment,

19

20

21

22

23

24

25

Vengeance will I wreak on My foes,
>   will I deal to those who reject Me. 26
> ⁴²I will make My arrows drunk with blood–
>   as My sword devours flesh–
> Blood of the slain and the captive
>   from the long-haired enemy chiefs.

⁴³O nations, acclaim His people!
>   for He'll avenge the blood of His servants, 27
> Wreak vengeance on His foes,
>   and cleanse the land of his people.

Introduction

The long poem in Deut.32, which Moses recites by God's order, is an extremely complex edifice. Its 461 words have been accommodated in 140 cola. These have been grouped 67 times as bicola and twice as tricola, resulting in 69 verses in the sense of full poetic lines. The verses have been arranged into 27 strophes which in turn combine into 11 stanzas. Because of the length of the poem we have to consider one more level above the stanzas before we can say that the text is a well-integrated whole: that of the sections. There are four sections in all; their main function is the articulation of the Song as an unfolding discourse, an argumentative structure.

As spoken language the poem is complex as well, containing speeches on at least four discursive levels. Delineating these levels, which result from embedding, is essential for a correct understanding of the poem. The correct demarcation of this particular articulation is a preliminary task, which is why I start with it straight away. It seems sensible, however, to first say something about the number of four levels by means of a comparison.

The Samuel books (including I Kings 1-2) form an extensive composition. This piece of narrative art is the core of the so-called Deuteronomistic History. The proportions of narrator's text and direct discourse are about equal.(a) There are 693 speeches in all, varying in length from one syllable to 43 lines - leaving aside for the moment the long Song of Thanksgiving in II Sam.22 with its 110 cola. The main portion of these 693 speeches, 545, contain one to four lines. There are 103 cases in which embedding occurs as a result of quotation: this means second-degree direct discourse. There are only seven cases of third-degree speech, five of which are extremely short; there is only one case of a long speech,

---

a   The data and figures which follow I derive from the tables in the Appendix to my *Vow and Desire*, = NAPS IV, Assen 1993, pp.587-593.

namely II Sam.7:8c-16b, the actual oracle of salvation to David containing God's promise of a lasting dynasty: 23 lines. And however complex the material in the Samuel books, there is only one text which is embedded even further as fourth-degree direct discourse; this is also found in II Sam.7. "It is a unit consisting of only one line which is a paradox by containing words of God which he quotes himself and has, nevertheless, never uttered: a reproach in the form of a rhetorical question, in a certain sense taking part in the counterfactual mode, in view of the status of v.7b." ([b]) The line in question is II Sam.7:7c.

Against this background it is certainly spectacular how the Song in Deut.32 traverses one level after another. Moses is speaking for a long time and produces eleven strophes in first-degree direct discourse. After v.19 (= l.30) it is God's turn, introduced by the shortest and most familiar form of the quotation formula, 'and he said', at the beginning of v.20. He speaks five strophes (vv.20-25) which of course are second-degree discourse, but what happens next? In v.26a we again have a quotation formula, but this time God is quoting himself! From that point we hear a soliloquy in the third degree. In the following I will argue that this speech occupies most of the text through to v.35. This, however, does not complete the tiered structure of the Song. It is not long before God quotes (in v.27cd) a second party in his soliloquy: Israel's enemies. They receive seven words filling most of the bicolon l.44 (= v.27cd). This makes a fourth-degree discourse, with a very special status: it describes an illusion on the part of the enemy which God is eager to dispel.

Next, God himself speaks vv.28-29, which returns us to the third-degree level. Immediately, however, two very curious complications follow. In the four cola of v.30 (= ll.47-48) God again allows the enemy to have the floor, so that we once again 'descend' to the fourth degree, and again the status is intriguing: this is an imaginary speech (counterfactual) which thus has never actually been spoken. Verse 31 is immediately linked to the previous one and seems to be some sort of aside, serving as an explanation. It is a dry, unpoetic line consisting of two cola functioning as an interjection or a gloss, and definitely not spoken by God.([c])

As from verse 36 we find words speaking *about* God. This suddenly takes us right back to the first level, that of the leader reciting a didactic poem. Moses himself speaks short strophes here and at the end, in vv. 36 and 43. In between these, in vv.37-42, God speaks for the last time, and this time, too, his contribution contains various levels. In v.37a Moses introduces him by 'he will say', so that the following speech by God is a second-degree discourse, lasting through to v.40a and occupying two strophes. In the middle of this verse, however, God quotes himself in the same way as in v.26a, using the perfect tense of

---

b   NAPS IV, p.593.
c   In the following I will allocate this line to the author and hence call it a zero-degree discourse.

אמר, after which nine cola in the third degree follow. These are vv.40b-42d, again filling two strophes.

If we now size up the two main speakers and count their words, cola, and verses, a remarkable balance appears at the three levels of textual units:
- Moses speaks vv.1-19 (plus ויאמר of v.20a),
  and resumes in vv.36 (plus ואמר of 37a) and 43.
- God speaks vv.20-30, 32-35 and 37-42; when he quotes himself and the enemy, those words are still spoken by him, so that these embedded speeches still come under the heading 'God speaks' and should be included in the count.

The figures, then, are 227 words for Moses and 228 for God. This minimal difference dissolves when we consider the verses and cola, which perfectly balance each other: both speak 34 verses and 69 cola. The number 69 is remarkable for two reasons. In the first place, it is the total number of verses. If these were all bicola, we could link the first 69 without problem to the second 69. However, there are two tricola, and it is these which bring the total number of cola in the poem to 140 – a number we should probably interpret as twice the beautiful number 70.

Secondly, the number of 69 cola per speaker is remarkable in that this doubling does not yield the total number of cola in the poem. We might add the two cola of v.31, but these are not spoken by either Moses or God. The odd numbers are explained by two more surplus cola elsewhere in the poem; these are the C-cola of v.14 and v.39. The former is spoken by Moses, the latter by God.(d)

On the one hand, two cola which do not belong to either Moses or God are subtracted from the 140, and on the other both speakers get an extra colon each, so that their 34 verses per person eventually do contain the odd number of 69 cola which, one level below that of the poetic lines, reflects the number of verses. I propose that we view the bipartite verse in brackets - the interruption by v.31 - in relation to the two C-cola and consider this relation a hermeneutic circle. The almost perfect match of the numbers of words, cola, and verses divided between Moses and God presupposes separating v.31, but also confirms it. And vice versa, putting that aside between brackets is necessary in order to find the balance between the main speakers, but at the same time confirms this balance.

The articulation of the various speeches into degrees one through four, according to the level of embedding, has been mainly marked by the verb 'to say' used as a quotation formula. Close inspection shows us that this root occurs eight times,

---

d There is another application of the number 69. If we include the simple form *w'mr* in v.37a, which has God as its subject, in the count for the strophe in question which is spoken entirely by God (sc. vv.37-38 = ll.58-60 = strophe 23), God's last speech contains 69 words. This regards the four strophes 23-26 which form the climax, as God here finally fixes his relation to Israel and to the enemy.

always in pairs, and that in two strategic positions it is used in a collocation with a double ראה. The first pair is nominal, appears in the introduction (in the B-cola, in rhyming position) and does not contribute yet to the discursive articulation. Its placement is nevertheless a modest signal of the importance of this root.

The second pair is already verbal and constitutes an opposition which is helpful in marking out large textual units. Both are imperfect masculine singular forms and are governed by the two large collectives, Israel versus the enemy. The יאמרו of v.7d (= l.11b) is the 'telling' by the elders which according to Moses is urgently needed to instruct and rebuke his audience, threatened by corruption. It occurs in the strophe which is not only the linear or arithmetic beginning of the large narrative section II (= vv.7-18), but also the discursive start by constituting the opening, i.e. an introduction which is not yet part of the narrative mode. The יאמרו of v.27c (= l.44a) is the adversaries' 'saying' which frustrates and infuriates God. It occurs in the strophe which opens section IIIB (= vv.26-35) as a variant of the quotation formula and takes us straight into the local hornets' nest of embeddings. Both these future tenses of 'to say' relate to each other as the sensible speech of the Israelites, desired by Moses, relates to the enemies' deluded speech which God rejects.

Four occurrences of 'to say' remain to be discussed. From a purely temporal point of view they divide into a pair for the past tense, v.20a + v.26a, and a pair for the very near future, v.37a and v.40b. The entire quartet goes to God as the subject of the verb forms. Other and more exciting subdivisions, however, are possible. Two of these are perfect forms ending in -*ti* pronounced by God himself, the other two are quotation formulas spoken by Moses in order to hand over the floor to God from his first-degree level of first speaker. Moreover, the forms in vv.20a and 37a (= ll.31a and 58a) each have an ally in that both of them are flanked by a double 'seeing'.

The systematic pattern of this second quartet of forms (all of them verbal, with God as subject) now looks as follows:

	Moses introduces God		*God quotes himself*
v.19a	וירא יהוה		
+ 20ab	ויאמר ... אראה		
		v.26a	אמרתי
v.36c	כי ראה		
+ 37a	ואמר		
+ 39a	ראו עתה כי ..	v.40b	ואמרתי

We shall see that the three occurrences from vv.36-39 given here are well distributed over three closely related strophes which together form the penultimate stanza.

Anticipating the results of §§ 1-4 which contain a strophe by strophe and stanza by stanza description of the poem, I would like to mention at this point that at four levels the composition is based on the prosodic principle, and on the measures of 'two or three'.

The overwhelming majority of the 140 cola contains two or three stresses. There are only 8 cola with four stresses, while there are 21 cola containing two stresses and no less than 111 cola containing three. This last group covers more than 79 % of all cases; the 132 cola containing two or three stresses constitute more than 94 % of the total number.

At the next level up the full poetic line appears, the verse in a literary sense. 67 times the verse is a bicolon, and two times a tricolon. The only striking thing about these figures is that the bicolon has an overwhelming majority, much more so than the average percentage in representative classical poetry.

The 'two or three' -principle is powerfully and significantly active at the next level up, that of the strophes. There are 12 strophes containing two verses and 15 containing three verses. Denoting these as 'short' and 'long', respectively, I will call the first group S-strophes, the second L-strophes. The long strophes contain 45 of the 69 verses, the remaining 24 verses are placed in short strophes.

I will go up one last time, to the level of the stanzas. The eleven stanzas which I am going to distinguish below and whose demarcation will be accounted for contain either two or three strophes. There are six slim stanzas which each contain no more than two strophes, and five stouter stanzas of three strophes each.

The main structure of the poem is as follows:

section	quantities			verse numbers
	stanzas	strophes	verses	
I	1	3	9	1-6
II	4	4 + 4	20	7-18
III	4	5 + 5	26	19-35
IV	2	6	14	36-43

The text itself is extremely sound, there is not a single word to be deleted or inserted. The consonant text is nearly impeccable; I myself see only three instances where minor surgery might be necessary, no more than revocalising a syllable.(ᵉ)

ᵉ I read תשׁי in v.18a as תשׁה = *tiššeh*; in v.23a I read an imperfect (cohortative) of *אסף, and in v.35a, by means of repunctuation, I read the noun *šillum*. If the form ʾfʾyhm in v.26a has not been derived from *pʾy, but from pʾh (that is, with a consonant *he*, not the *mater lectionis*), one should read ʾafʾihem (with long ḥireq and ṣereh). Finally, we have v.5a: probably slightly corrupt, but the paradox here is that the constituent parts and the statement they support are totally clear.

§ 1. *The first section: one stanza, three strophes*

The first strophe consists of three verses (ll.1-3 = vv.1-2).[x] The main structural characteristic here is the maximum use made of word pairs. Although Lowth has taught us that parallelismus membrorum is already defined by the distribution over two cola of only one word pair, actually every position within this strophe is occupied by a word which has its counterpart in the adjacent colon. This type of tight packing to achieve completeness with all word pairs is linked to the fact that in the strophe the words have essentially only been grouped into threesomes.[1]

The second characteristic of the strophe is vertical parallelism, which is applied so powerfully that it immediately guarantees the unity of the strophe.[2] The first verse contains the all-embracing merism of heaven and earth which so many readers know from the opening of the book of Genesis, and as the pair which is also invoked in the very first verse of the book of Isaiah. Through a kind of metonymy this word pair is succeeded in l.2, and made fertile and friendly as it were, by rain and dew; the former originates in heaven, the latter covers the earth. These are flanked by the words 'my teaching' and 'my speech', which make the cola in l.2 rhyme on the same long vowel as l.1 ended on. Their main contribution, however, to the strophe structure is that each closes off its colon and that thus their meanings coincide with the phrases 'let me speak' and 'the words from my mouth' which also close off their respective cola.

In this way, there are two strong hooks of symmetry keeping l.1 and l.2 together. These are extended through another set of hooks which by means of telescopic extension appears out of the central line and grips the third verse, thanks to a concerted effort on the part of syntax and the use of simile. The third line, consisting 'only' of complements, provides the strophe with a tranquil ending. Two images of mild nature slow down the speed of one verbal predicate per colon which governed ll.1-2. Their cola are determined by the telescopic repetition of the preposition 'as'. The singular forms *maṭar* and *ṭal* are

---

[x]) The term 'verse' only indicates the traditional text unit when abbreviated to 'v.', or immediately followed by a number; in all other instances it refers to the full poetic line.

[1] Essentially, but in one respect not literally or purely arithmetically, as the word פי at the end of l.1b is the only instance of a fourth word jutting out. It is, however, a monosyllable and moreover only a part of the construct state combination and stress unit אמרי פי, which itself is the counterpart of the single אדברה in l.1a and the single אמרתי in l.2b which it rhymes with.

[2] This makes it so puzzling why Sanders would give the two Masoretic verses a strophe each, op.cit. p.267 and p.289. This division immediately raises doubts about whether the 'Kampen method' is scientific. After this one, Sanders will mark off single-line strophes eight more times: in the case of vv.3, 5, 18, 26, 31, 38b, 40 and 43a. In at least five of these cases this division and isolation ignores connections which are immediately sensed in a natural communication with poetry, if not already evident: v.3, 5, 26, 38b and 40. (Verse 43a is an 'improvement' based on the LXX and a Qumran fragment).

here intensified and refined to the plural forms *śeʿirim // rebibim*, with their maximum and pleasant assonance. These words, a relatively exclusive selection from the lexicon, expand and illustrate the regular words for 'rain' and 'dew'. Next, these extended complements each get a complement in turn, i.e. 'upon the grass' and 'upon the herb', in order to fill out the half lines 3a//3b. In this way, long words rhyming on *-im* are varied by two short singular forms based on monosyllables (the origin of the segholates).[3]

In order to view the contours of a strophe clearly it can sometimes be productive to print the text colon by colon, as given below:

האזינו השמים ואדברה	1.1	(MT v.1)
ותשמע הארץ אמרי פי		
יערף כמטר לקחי	1.2	(MT v.2)
תזל כטל אמרתי		
כשעירים עלי דשא	1.3	
וכרביבים עלי עשב		

Each separate verse shows the strict word order abc//a'b'c'. Moreover, the second verse copies this pattern from the first, as the verbal predicate is again in first position. There are, however, subtle shifts which protect the strophe from monotony. The objects[4] from the opening verse are promoted to grammatical subjects in the second, which is accompanied by a shift in meaning in the verbs. In spite of this, the poet even manages to intensify the vertical parallelism slightly by assonance in the B-cola: *tišmaʿ* and *tizzal* balance each other, and both are followed by 2 + 3 syllables ranging from alliteration (*k-* ... *k-* ...) to rhyme.

The only completely new element in the second verse is the preposition of comparison. That one syllable, however, is exactly the morpheme which is copied in the third verse, and has even been promoted to anaphora there. It has thus become clear in various ways that the central verse of the three-line unit lives up to its position by fulfilling a mediating function both formally and as regards content. This delineates the strophic unit once more.[5] The quartet of terms for 'my speech' meets the quartet of terms for 'water' in the middle, and

---

[3] I remind the reader that my syllable count is based on the pre-Masoretic shapes and lengths of the words.
In my study of II Sam.22 I have shown how the poet manages to transform nominal formations into stylistic categories. In that long poem, segholates occupy strategic positions as contrasts to nouns which have been formed by means of a *mem praeformans*. See *Throne and City* (= NAPS III), pp.337, 354.
[4] The word 'in order for me to speak' of v.1a from a purely grammatical point of view is not an object, but (syntactically speaking) a final clause of its own; nevertheless, materially (i.e. in the deep structure of the colon as a whole) it is the object of the command 'Give ear, ye heavens!'
[5] Observing this mediation yields a new argument against isolating v.1 as a single-line strophe.

the way they intersect in the central line is a form of powerful integration.⁶

The various correspondences in the exordium may be schematically represented in various ways, but I hope that the following letter sequences best express the organisation of the strophe as an aesthetic object. I am giving a slightly simplified⁷ notation:

$$
\begin{array}{l}
a \quad b \quad c \ / \ a \quad b \quad c \\
a' \ b' \ c \ / \ a' \ b' \ c \\
b'' \ d \quad e \ / \ b'' \ d \quad e
\end{array}
$$

The tight cohesion of the strophe goes even deeper, and may also be seen – or rather heard – at the level which should be considered the most elementary as it concerns the sensory perception of language signs: the level of sounds. Out of several phonetic devices I here mention three patterns whose contributions to the over-all cohesion I find the most striking.⁸ The labials and the rolling consonant r in *rᵉbibim* aptly echo *dabber* plus *'imre-pi* from v.1. In v.2 the liquidae m, l and r become prominent, as onomatopoeic representations of water. The combination of ayin and pe in l.2a is continued in l.3a and l.3b, and is supported there by the repetition of *ᶜᵃle* and two sibilants; the latter take us back to v.1 where the combination shin + mem occurs twice.⁹

What is the poetic origin of this interwoven structure? A sound answer to this question should contain at least two components, relating to core and genre. The core of the strophe is at the same time its source of energy: linking the four terms for 'my speech' and the four for 'water' is more than a matter of verse technique. The fourfold preposition 'as', responsible for the interweaving,

---

⁶ If we indicate the four terms for 'speaking' by an x, and the four terms for 'water' by a y, their entwining becomes visible in the following linear notation: x x / y x y x / y y (the slash separates the verses). In the diagram of the strophe and its cola this looks as follows (this time the slash functions as caesura within the verse):

$$
\begin{array}{cccc}
 & x & / & x \\
y & x & / & y \quad x \\
y & & / & y
\end{array}
$$

⁷ A more sophisticated notation, which however is hardly more productive, would look as follows:

$$
\begin{array}{l}
a \quad b \quad c \ / \ a' \quad b' \quad c' \\
a' \ b' \ c' \ / \ a'' \ b'' \ c''' \\
b'' \ d \quad e \ / \ b''' \ d \quad e'
\end{array}
$$

⁸ Other phonetic links: the ṭet in the central images *ṭal* and *maṭar*; their -a- and -l- sounds underneath, in the middle of ll.3a and 3b, in the double ᶜᵃle.

⁹ The poet Isaiah exploits the alliteration of shin and mem differently, by juxtaposing 'heaven' and 'hearing' in the very first colon of his book of poems: שמעו שמים. In his second colon this also results in alliteration of the aleph, האזיני ארץ. In *The Dynamics of Biblical Parallelism*, Bloomington IN 1985, Adele Berlin discusses several variations of the exhortation to listen, pp.127-129; see also pp.54, 60, 94.

65

in itself means comparison. It brings about a fusion, so that the one foursome does indeed cover the other. Elements which in everyday life do not share the same semantic field, such as 'word' and 'dew', are being accommodated within one isotopy by the poet's creativity. This unexpected coupling is the result of using metaphors – and good metaphors redescribe reality.

How the speaker's reality takes on a new form and a new meaning may also be expressed in terms of genre and subject matter. The first verse separates the cosmos into two components, heaven and earth. These halves of the universe are given a new orientation, as they are turned into witnesses of an authoritative lesson by means of an order which not only creates a centre but also gravitates towards it in a centripetal movement. This *Zweizeugenruf* shows the poet's high stakes: a more pretentious opening can hardly be imagined. These high stakes also force the poet to exploit his powers of design to the utmost – hence the high density of devices and lines of organisation.

The images in the centre form the intersection of two strategies. They are created not only by the preposition whose natural task it is to denote a simile, but are also the products of a metonymical operation: the vertical coupling of heaven-rain and earth-dew. Still, a semantic or logical gap remains which presents a considerable interpretational challenge. There is no easy transition from a listening earth to dripping speech, or from heavens giving ear to teaching which 'drops' like the rain. The actions denoted in l.2a and 2b do not follow from the preceding appeal. From v. 1 to v. 2 the poet makes a jump which is masked by the metonymy. Only when we understand the jump and are able to express its meaning can we hope to pinpoint his inspiration. The surprise signalled by the jump consists of the qualities of two lyrical characters, who had been told 'only' to act as receivers, being taken over by the speaker and transferred to his song. We, the readers, who at first are in analogous positions to heaven and earth, – being the receivers of the song – now realise that this song might possibly have some characteristics in common with heaven and earth. Is the lesson going to be a merism all through? Will the song be as natural, pleasant and fertile [for the listeners] as rain and dew are for nature? Could the grass or herb longing for life-giving water be an image for the audience? Another poet now starts to smile; it is Deutero-Isaiah, who compared his fellow exiles to grass and in his overture (Is.40:1-11) had to come to terms with two irreconcilable interpretations of this simile. His depressed audience only heard futility in the comparison, but the author of the Book of Consolation made a completely different connection: the people are grass, all right, but 'the word [sc. the promises] of our God will stand for ever'.

Some characteristics of the opening strophe remain which have not yet been discussed, as for instance the opposition nominal/verbal. These will be dealt with at stanza level where they will prove to be productive. I conclude here by mentioning some other aspects. Characteristic for this unit is the fact that the lyrical 'I' appears here. The four morphemes referring to him are right next to the four terms of cosmos and water in ll.1-2, and suddenly we notice that each component of this quartet is accompanied by the article.[10] In the remainder of the poem the article is extremely rare, even according to the standards of classical poetry. It is being saved for the metaphor allocated to God in this song, namely at the moment when he is introduced as *the* Rock, l.5a (= v.4a).[11] In the first strophe it is the job of the definite article to postulate assertively the halves of the cosmos and their life-giving water. Its first appearance, in *haššamayim*, alliterates with the very first word, the imperative *haʾªzinu*. Together with the five syllables of *waʾªdabbera* they immediately present a massive colon (11 syllables in pre-Masoretic Hebrew). Starting off at maximum power and ending in a lower gear (l.3 contains 6 + 7 syllables) sums up the prosodic contours of this unit.

The 'I' appears only one more time, at the beginning of the very next strophe, and then soon merges with the party labelled 'us' in l.4b (= v.3b, of which the 'us' in v.31 = l.49 is a stray echo). Who is this 'I' anyway? There are no fewer than four candidates. It could be the lyrical 'I', i.e. a character with primarily literary and semiotic status from the world evoked by this poetry. He could also be Moses, a character created by the narrator of the book of Deuteronomy – I mean the narrator responsible for the frame text of the introductory chapters 1-2 and the prose text at the end, mainly Chs. 31 and 34. The third candidate is another character of the same narrator, i.e. the God of Israel. He has excellent credentials in the eyes of readers who, like me, are not automatically willing to carry out an atomistic reading of Deut.32 by studying the poem entirely out of context. Stated positively: if we respect the context of Deut.32 we learn in Chapter 31 that this is God's own text. He not only instructs Moses to recite the poem to the collected people, but even dictates it to him, so that it is recorded in writing for future generations – 'then this poem shall confront them as a witness, since it will never be lost from the mouth of their offspring' (31:21).[12] Finally, the fourth candidate is an almost invisible figure: the person who actually wrote the poem himself. He, the author, is a historically untraceable indi-

---

[10] This is not without significance if one takes into account that classical poetry hardly uses the article, nota objecti and relative pronoun, as has been investigated and measured in the work of, among others, D. N. Freedman.

[11] The article does not appear until later, and only in l.27a (= v.17a), to indicate the competition ('the demons').

[12] In a diachronic orientation, the various terms which 31:16-29 has in common with Ch.32 will have been derived from the poem itself, and so will be of little value other than a form of later and even intra-biblical re-interpretation. In a synchronic and linear reading of the book as a whole, however, the text of Ch.31 is of great value to prepare the reader for the Song. Especially with respect to questions of ideology and authority Ch.31 (including the rest of the prose context) is of great significance.

vidual hiding behind his mask, the narrator - who in turn is already a disembodied voice, nameless and faceless.[13]

God's candidature is not altogether straightforward. In verse 3 it says: 'For the name of the LORD I proclaim', which diminishes the Lord's chances, as the 'I' here simply has got to be Moses - especially if, primed by the imperative in the B-colon, we hear a volitive note in this אקרא. Moses here means no more than the person who in first instance speaks until v.20 and no further, in the varying tones of hymn, reproach, exhortation, and especially (vv.8-19) of retrospection and narration. Moses means: the second candidate, the character depicted by (the narrator and) the author of the book of Deuteronomy. For the moment it also seems feasible to have him coincide with the first candidate, the lyrical 'I' who is part of the world drawn by the poetry itself. God's nomination becomes less realistic and at the same time more so in the light of Ch.31, when as from v.20 he is introduced obliquely by quotation. On the one hand, his words are 'only' embedded, which means included in the wider text written by somebody else. They cover the larger part of vv.20-35 and all of vv.37-42. On the other hand, they are and will be nothing less than the words of God, and it is not for nothing that the embedding speaker allocates them so much room in the text which appears to be 'his' song.[14]

I will postpone a decision on the identity of 'I' for the moment, but at this stage I will only point out that it is closely linked to two crucial aspects: authority, both real and claimed, and levels of argument. The authority of the song cannot be dissociated from the authority of the book or from the claim to authority made by the author. The texture of voices making up Deuteronomy is so complex that the reader is regularly thrown off balance. He is probably meant to be. The writer has withdrawn even further behind his characters than an author of mainly narrative texts would do. He delights in letting us flounder on the question where Moses' words end and God's words start. His aim in doing this is to blur the border lines between the authority of the great leader and 'prophet' and that of his deity.[15] A mature reading of the Song should be aware of this ideological trap.

The texture of voices in the Song is highly complex. We will have to distin-

---

[13] These terms from Meir Sternberg, *The Poetics of Biblical Narrative*, Bloomington IN 1985, Ch.2 and especially p.71.

[14] At this point, some critical reflection might be in order on the fact that the poem, in commentaries and other learned discourses, is indiscriminately called 'The Song of Moses'.

[15] This 'blurring' strategy has been introduced by Robert Polzin, first in *Moses and the Deuteronomist*, New York 1981, and later, among other publications, in his contribution on Deuteronomy in R. Alter & F. Kermode (eds.), *The Literary Guide to the Bible*, Harvard Univ. Press 1987. A similar case I tried to establish in a chapter which is treacherous to naive readers, and challenging to ideology criticism: I Sam.12, see Ch.VIII in my *Vow and Desire* (= NAPS IV), Assen 1993.

guish no fewer than five levels if we are to determine the status of the spoken word. This stratification is of essential importance for an accurate representation of the work of art and its structure, and equally indispensable for the question of the authority of 'my teaching'.

Strophe 2.

כי שם יהוה אקרא	4	(MT v.3)
הבו גדל לאלהינו		
הצור תמים פעלו	5	(MT v.4)
כי כל דרכיו משפט		
אל אמונה ואין עול	6	
צדיק וישר הוא		

The second strophe is immediately recognisable and set off by its affirmative tone. It is a short hymn, the actual contents of which are in ll.5-6 (= v.4). The first line (l.4 = v.3) forms an introduction. In the A-colon the 'I' announces his intention to praise, in the B-colon he adds an appeal. The cola are perfectly joined in three ways: the 3 + 3 words of the verse (after *ki*) link up as word pairs, resulting once more in a maximum parallelismus membrorum. The characters are presented through a precise addition, where 'I' plus 'you' are brought together in 'our', whose morpheme *-nu* nicely finishes off the verse. Finally, the poet has subtly attuned appeal and intention to each other by means of a syntactic chiasm governing both half verses: after the affirmative *ki* we have O + P / P + O.[16] This collaboration of cola leads me to interpret the first predicate, 'proclaim', as a volitive, so that it has the same modality as the second. Suddenly we see that this אקרא is in exactly the same position as the אדברה of the first strophe: at the end of the first colon. This verb, being a cohortative, also indicated an intention. In this way, the words explain each other thanks to the parallelism at strophe level (responsion).[17] Moses' 'speaking' is the proclamation of the name (read: fame) of YHWH. Reading along the linear axis we are now thinking that Moses' 'teaching' is the praising of the Lord. A beautiful theory, of which strophe 3 will swiftly cure us ...

---

[16] O = grammatical object, P = predicate. In l.4a the object is a construct state combination, 'the name of the Lord', in l.4b the situation is slightly different: גדל is the direct object, while 'our God' is the beneficiary after 'give', and hence an indirect object.

[17] This correspondence at strophe level motivates why the poet rejected the most obvious option of inserting an object as for instance *d^ebari* or *dibrati* into l.1a. I further notice that שם occupies the same position in the initial A-colon as שמים in v.1; again, this cannot be coincidence. And the line containing this שם is at the same time the first to present the tetragrammaton itself.

The 'I' addresses the collective called 'you', but does not dissociate himself from them or raises himself above them, as proven by 'our' at the end of the verse. Together, 'we' (= you and I) will 'avow the greatness of our God' (acknowledge, lit. 'to give'). The synonymous clauses in v.3 are still verbal, but the actual praise of God, in v.4 (four cola, ll.5-6), is completely nominal. The content is static, which here in a positive sense means: exceeding the limitations of time. God's perfections are timeless. After a strophe about water agreeably flowing from above and below, the second strophe immediately and bluntly confronts us with a rock. The poet turns the introduction of the rock into a surprise by adding the article, almost for the last time, and underlines this forceful positioning of the rock by a syntactic measure: הצור is a *casus pendens*. At the same time it is the first explicit metaphor, and no insignificant one, either.

The rock contrasted to all this water - what exactly is the opposition? Not that of life and death, but that of peaceful flowing contrasted to unshakeable fixity, which here does not have the threatening connotation of grimness, but should rather be seen as expressing admiration and pride: God is steady and completely faithful. The reciter employed by the author, Moses, can certainly agree with that: earlier in his life, as a leader in the desert, he struck water from a rock following God's instructions. That action has thoroughly undermined the equation water : rock = life : death.

The poet takes a lot of trouble over the message of God's faithfulness, devoting two complete verses to it in which he employs a lot of variation. The two sentences in l.5 he again arranges chiastically, this time following the pattern P + S / S + P. In this verse the substantives are prominent; besides the *casus pendens*, stubbornly preceding, both subjects and one predicate are also substantive.

In the verse which follows, the A-colon again sings of the deity by using substantives. They have been arranged as plus and minus; what characterises God is 'faithfulness' and not 'inequity'. The negation of the negative is a case of litotes and intensifies the positive.[18] A shift follows, so that the B-colon by contrast prefers adjectives, 'true and upright'. If we connect the monosyllables which constitute the head and tail of the verse with each other, because the referents are identical, l. 6 (= v.4cd) also shows a chiastic construction with God's qualities in the centre. Meanwhile, the pace has been doubled: each colon now contains two nominal predicates indicating praise. This is accompanied by a greater directness. In l.5 the poet was still speaking of 'his work' and 'his ways', in l.6 he regards 'God' and praises his person through four characteristics. In the

---

[18] There is a diagonal line connecting כל and אין as an opposition. For the Scripture writers, the opposition אין - יש is less productive than that between אין and כל; relevant details I have included in a contribution to a Festschrift: Iterative Forms of the Classical Hebrew Verb: Exploring the Triangle of Style, Syntax, and Text Grammar, in: *Studies in Hebrew & Aramaic Syntax* presented to Prof. J. Hoftijzer, edited by K. Jongeling, H.L. Murre-van den Berg & L. van Rompay, Leiden 1991, pp.38-55.

verse which calls God 'straightforward' (יָשָׁר) the poet's own speech has become very straightforward.

The long vowel -u- in *ᵉmuna* is a station on the way from *ṣur* to *hu*, the words which demarcate the panegyric proper and refer to the same person.[19] These two monosyllables are accompanied by three predicative adjectives, in ll.5a + 6b; in-between there are five substantives, in ll.5b + 6a. The creation of parallelismus membrorum requires doubling techniques.[20] In the first strophe doubling was only used to balance the half verses. In line 6, however, the technique is explicitly used within the colon. From now on the poet will make regular use of it - immediately and intensively in the next strophe.[21]

Strophe 3.

שחת לו לא בניו מומם	7	(MT v.5)
דור עקש ופתלתל		
הליהוה תגמלו זאת	8	(MT v.6)
עם נבל ולא חכם		
הלוא הוא אביך קנך	9	
הוא עשך ויכננך		

After all this praise Moses' audience must feel hit by a sledge-hammer in the third strophe. The first word is already right on target: corruption! Again, the strophic unity of three verses is quickly found on the basis of genre. This fragment is about reproach and accusation. Moses addresses his audience directly; four of the six cola address a second person who in l.8 is plural, in l.9 is singular. Tone and contents make this strophe as different from the previous one as black from white.

---

[19] Adele Berlin, op. cit., writes on p.79: "It is not word pairs that create parallelism. It is parallelism that activates word pairs."

[20] In the introduction they had been preceded, in l.4b, by *habu ... lelohenu*, which means an inner rhyme.

[21] The technique of doubling occurs about 30 times in Deut.32. Intracolon parallelism occurs, besides ll.7b//8b//9b, in ll.22a, 23a, 24a, 24b, 30b, 38a, 41a, 41b, 54a, 57b, 62a, 62b, 67a. Two verbal predicates in one colon: ll.11a, 11b, 16a, 18a, 24a, 24b (*ter*!), 30a, 31a, 42a, 44a, 46a, 57a, 60a, 62a, 62b.
Another form of duplicating, i.e. immediate repetition of words, is found in 10b, 16a (Polel forms), the suffixes in ll.9 and 11, 30b (**bn*), 49a, 50a, 51a, 61a, and 68b-69a (**nqm*).
This strong application of doubling - instant repetition of words - can be found fifty-fold in the Song of Deborah, Jud.5. See my contribution on this subject, The Song of Deborah and Barak: Its Prosodic Levels and Structure, pp.595-628 of *Pomegranates and Golden Bells*, Studies in Biblical, Jewish, and Near Eastern Ritual, Law, and Literature in Honor of Jacob Milgrom (edited by David P. Wright, David Noel Freedman, and Avi Hurvitz), Winona Lake, Indiana, 1995.

Although the first sentence of v.5 has probably been subject to some corruption, the separate elements can be placed easily enough, so that I will not change the words and translate them as: 'They have spoilt everything for him, his non-children, because of their blemish.' In case *lo* indicates the indirect object, the first words mean 'they have treated him corruptly'.[22] The colon which starts with a shin and ends in three mems interrupts the positive line of *šamayim* and *šem*.

The speaker goes on in the same breath, because the B-colon follows in an enjambment and is entirely taken up by an apposition, 'that crooked and perverse generation'. Out of its three words two are pejorative, balancing the two negative words which open and close the A-colon. The doubling technique is here active within the colon, and expands. The next B-colon, in l.8, also consists of two disqualifications, 'foolish and imprudent', again in the form of an apposition, this time with the force of the vocative.

The assertive and forceful colon 7a is the first to use the past tense. Colon 8a returns to the present by using the address form. It poses a question, but it is a rhetorical one as the speaker already knows what he is supposed to think of this 'requiting'. A rhythm emerges: verbal clause in first position, nominal condemnations in appositions. The syntactic unit twice coincides with a verse, for the first time in this poem.

The rhetorical question, being a vehicle for great indignation, goes on and occupies the third line as well, so that the interrogative particle *ha* becomes anaphoric.[23] This pattern is semantically confirmed by the fact that the third morphemes in lines 8 and 9 have the same referent: 'he' is identical to YHWH.[24] The pronoun itself is almost anaphoric within l.9 as it also opens the B-colon. And, noticing that it is also the last word in the preceding strophe, we realise that after four cola of rot and misery the poet is returning to God's qualities. Since, however, these qualities – father and creator – are in themselves relational and also come equipped with a fourfold *-ka* they are still functioning within a discourse of retribution. How sad that you should desert your own Father in this way: is this how you return his kindness? The element of 'your father' is the

---

[22] The combination 'not-his-sons[-anymore]' becomes acceptable when we come across this special use of the negation in v.17a, v.21a and v.21c. The word *mumam* I interpret as a causal or modal adjunct; such an adjunct can be used in poetry without preposition. The verb in front position does not have to agree with the subject in number.

[23] A subtle detail here is the fact that the lamed, which was a preposition in l. 8a, returns in l.9a, but this time as the consonant of the negation; this reinforces the anaphora.

[24] Sometimes this pronoun 3 masc. sing. has a special connection with God's proper name, or his identity; and in this poem we find an instance of this at a very sensitive moment, that of the self-revelation, with the unusual turn of l.61a (= v.39a). Cf. the parallels in Deutero-Isaiah, e.g. 43:10 and 13, 52:6.

opposite pole of '(not-)his sons'.²⁵ Meanwhile, the doubling technique has expanded to cover the entire final verse.²⁶ The use of the negation has also increased: twice it is used to attack the integrity of the addressees (not his sons anymore, imprudent), once it recalls God's commitment, through the detour and force of a rhetorical question.²⁷

Stanza I = Section I (Overview)

We get a slightly different view when the strophes are presented in their regular division of three times three verses. I am giving the text again, this time placing each verse on its own line and only using the numbers of the poetic lines.

ותשמע הארץ אמרי פי	האזינו השמים ואדברה	1.1
תזל כטל אמרתי	יערף כמטר לקחי	1.2
וכרביבים עלי עשב	כשעירים עלי דשא	1.3
הבו גדל לאלהינו	כי שם יהוה אקרא	1.4
כי כל דרכיו משפט	הצור תמים פעלו	1.5
צדיק וישר הוא	אל אמונה ואין עול	1.6
דור עקש ופתלתל	שחת לו לא בניו מומם	1.7
עם נבל ולא חכם	הליהוה תגמלו זאת	1.8
הוא עשך ויכננך	הלוא הוא אביך קנך	1.9

These are all L-strophes belonging to one stanza. Further down there are a few more stanzas containing three strophes, but this is the only one which exclusively contains three-line units. A special characteristic of this trio of L-strophes is the fact that at the same time it forms a section of the poem.

The obvious function of the first stanza is introductory and preparatory. Its first member, strophe 1, is not only an exordium, but at the argumentative level also provides a 'definition' of what is to come by means of a term familiar from

---

²⁵ This relation ll.7a - 9a is supported by manipulations with the sounds in ll.7b - 9b. The reduplications of *ptltl* and its o-vowel are echoed in the Polel form *konen*, while generous alliteration marks the polarity between *'qš* and *'šk*. And the second words of ll.7a and 9a, *lo* and *hu* respectively, have the same referent. The *knnk* are of course also counterparts of *qnk*, and serve the parallelism within l.9. The long u occurs twice in words which charge the people (*mum* and *tigmᵉlu*), versus two times in *hu*, in a verse which tries to save God's honour.

²⁶ The two predicates with the object 'you' in l.9b clearly have their opposite numbers in l.9a which also contains a double 'you'. The syntax is not symmetrical, by the way; l.9b contains two verbal predicates which each form a clause, in l.9a 'your father' is the only and nominal predicate, while the קנך following that is an asyndetic relative clause.

²⁷ Its vowel, the long o, now occurs eight times, against one o-vowel in strophe 1 and five in strophe 2.

wisdom literature: *leqach*, 'instruction, lesson, insight', and by means of the image of the grass stalks indicates the target group: you, the people of Israel, my audience. Within the stanza this strophe serves as an introduction in relation to the next pair, but its function goes beyond this stanza; it is also an introduction to the poem as a whole.

The second and third strophes inextricably belong together, exactly because they contain such a harsh antithesis. They form a pair on the basis of antonymy. Their main function regards the entire song: they constitute the exposition of the theme. God is dependable, you are corrupt - this simple antithesis is the source of a sweeping dynamics pervading the whole poem, including the heart of the final strophe. There is a fight to the bitter end between good and evil, in which Israel and its enemies will change position rather unexpectedly. Israel passes through both positions, as does the enemy.

Are we justified in using the term 'exposition'? Does this not primarily belong to the tools of narratology? True, but we are in fact allowed to call the first stanza the exposition since the Song itself continues with a long narrative section: Moses acts as narrator in vv.7-18 (and a bit further on). In the form of a story he confronts the people with their origin and election, for which he receives no fewer than twenty verses and eight strophes. This is a remarkable decision on the part of the poet, if we take into account the fact that storytelling in the classical period on principle employs prose. Biblical poetry fans out in a multitude of lyrical forms, and every now and then there is a hint of storytelling or a shred of narrativity, but epic poetry in the sense of a-story-in-verse never occurs.[28]

Moses' account contains hardly any plot, but appears as a real story by stating a lacuna at the beginning (strophe 4) and then working towards an outcome, albeit a negative one (apostasy, strophe 11).[29] The route from strophe 5 to strophe 11 emulates a story by taking the form of a long string of imperfect forms which nevertheless strictly remains within the boundaries and limits of verse and strophe structure.[30] If we take a closer look, however, the defect proves

---

[28] The exceptions only serve to confirm this rule. They receive a chapter of their own in Robert Alter, *The Art of Biblical Poetry*, New York 1985; this is Ch.2, From Line to Story.

[29] A 'story' in this context I take to be a prose text which usually starts with the formulation of a problem or defect, then follows a hero (the actantial subject) who is looking for an object of value and/or the solution of the problem, and to this end has to overcome obstacles or weather a conflict, after which the end brings the satisfaction of the defect or the solution of the problem. Sometimes, the very lack of a solution makes the story escalate; the stakes become much higher and a new quest starts. Example: Jud.19. The hero (the Levite) collects the object of value, but her death after a gang rape on the way back makes him appeal to the national assembly. They decide to start a civil war in order to exterminate Benjamin - a new value object of a new quest (which will not succeed either!), a new hero, etc. In this way, the Outrage of Gibeah is the spark in the powder keg of Jud.20-21 (the sequel at a higher level).

[30] As the chain forms part of a poetic text, the major form of the narration is not the *wyqtl* type as in narrative prose, but *yqtl*. There are 16 of these in vv.8-18 (v.11a does not count: two *yqtl* forms

not to be the cause of a plot, as it takes place at a different discursive level. The lack of understanding presupposed in strophe 4 should lead to self-examination, Moses says. However, that is his problem, not that of the hero of vv.8-14 (= strophes 5-9), YHWH. What the deity aims at is the settlement of the chosen people in a land of plenty, hoping that they will prove to be good partners in the covenant and will repay his care with awe and never-ending faith. What is related in strophes 5-11 precedes in time the reproaches of strophe 3 and the exhortation to gain insight which constitutes strophe 4. The long string of *yqtl* forms characterising the second section is in fact embedded in an argument by Moses. This argument is very well structured, both poetically and thematically, but it is not narrative. Moses' argumentation is set in the lyrical present, while the account of vv.8-19 regards the past with a far from neutral eye.[31]

The first stanza is at the same time the first section. The main internal reason is the typical character and function of these three strophes as exordium and exposition. The main external reason is the fact that the subsequent four stanzas (vv.7-18 = ll.10-29 = strophes 4-11) are a completely new entity, with their own devices (especially the narrative *yqtl*), a new tone and a different task.

Moreover, the poet deploys all sorts of formal devices in order to clarify the difference between sections I and II. The sections are sharply contrasted on their common boundary. Strophes 3 and 4 rub against each other because of the dialectics of similarity and difference. A basic similarity between verses 6 and 7 is the fact that Moses directly turns towards his audience: he addresses them. At the same time, there is the difference between asking (v.6) and commanding (v.7), which is the contrast between condemning and reproaching on the one hand, and urging and encouraging on the other. At the heart of this contrast sits the view of their origin. This similarity becomes visible in the word for 'your father' in l.9a which returns in l.11a. This one word itself, however, already embodies the dialectics of similarity and difference! At the end of the exposition it refers to God, at the beginning of the narrative section it refers to the human being - the biological father whose judgement you (according to Moses) should profit from.

Similarity serving contrast – this may simply be gleaned from the use of *-ka*, the suffix in the second person masculine singular. The poet puts four instances of it at the end of section I, and four at the beginning of section II. The one quartet is in l.9, the other in l.11; these are the final verses of strophes 3 and 4.

---

which constitute cores of relative clauses and parts of a simile). Yet, besides these there are seven cases of *wyqtl*, in v.13bc, 15a (bis), 15cd, 18b (plus three narrative forms at the threshold of section III, in v.19a and 20a). Finally, there is the perfect: only in v.15b (but there as many as three times, and in a remarkable second pers. sing.). Strophe 11 has three more perfect forms, but they do not belong on the narrative line; they occur in asyndetic relative sentences.

[31] Further below we shall see that this past is partly illusory; the events, and especially the people's attitude, are presented by Moses as past for the purpose of his rhetorical and ideological goals.

In both cases, these suffixes have been distributed in pairs over A-colon and B-colon. Later we shall see how strategically this form of the second person has been used.

Now that the first section has been delineated, I zoom in on its structure and prosodic contours. This stanza is the only one to consist of three long strophes. The regularity of three times three verses is considerable. The number three is metrically prominent as well: out of 18 cola there are no less than 15 containing three stresses. The ringing out of the exordium through the images (no more than complements, syntactically speaking) of l.3 remains balanced but is shorter: 2 + 2; l.7a probably contains four stresses.[32]

There are two parallelisms at strophe level which help to support the structure of the stanza; observing them provides us with new arguments for the delineation of the strophes and their stanza. One parallelism has to do with the opening verses of strophes 1 and 2, the other with the final verses of strophes 2 and 3. Lines 1 and 4 (v.1 // v.3) differ from the verses which follow them in their strophes by their jussive and introductory character, and by the oral-auditory aspect. Semantically, 'the word of my mouth' in the opening line even largely coincides with recognizing 'the greatness of our Lord'. These opening lines are followed by the contents of the 'words' (the unit of praise) in 4 + 4 cola, containing the contrast of water and rock.

The second parallelism is caused by lines 6 and 9 both speaking about God, and in both cases by the form of doubling which sometimes is called intracolon parallelism. The pace with which predicates are used rises so sharply that in these two final verses we find four plus four qualifications to the greater glory of God.

At stanza level, the three strophes follow a 1 + 2 pattern. The single strophe which forms the exordium introduces the pair which contains the exposition. This same pattern is applied one level down, i.e. at strophe level. These units each contain three verses which can also be read and articulated according to the 1 + 2 pattern:
- strophe 1: two jussive clauses/cola, followed by four cola governed by four times 'as' plus a quartet of words for water;
- strophe 2: two cola with verbal predicates for a intention or command, followed by four strictly nominal and hymnic cola;
- and strophe 3: two stern cola of condemnation in the third person, followed by four cola of reproaches = rhetorical questions in the second person.

At the same time, however, there is an opposite effect in the third strophe, so

---

[32] My highly tentative scan of l.7a looks as follows: o ó - o   ó - o ó   o ó.
This means that I attach the first *lo* to the verb via enclisis, among other reasons in order to prevent collision with the next *lo*; this syllable, that is, the negation, is so important that I would not dare not to allocate a stress to it. The result is very regular: four iambs even.

that there we also see the 2 + 1 pattern at work: two verses which treat the Israelites in extremely unfavourable terms, plus one verse which speaks very favourably of God and thus becomes the counterpart of strophe 2. The moral of this observation: a sensitive reader of this poetry cannot easily be fooled.

The difference nominal/verbal results in a balance between strophes 1 and 2 which at stanza level reverses the 1 + 2 pattern. The first strophe contains four verbal cola which each are a predicative unit and an independent sentence, plus two nominal cola. The second strophe reverses this: there are two verbal clauses/cola, and then four completely nominal cola. The third strophe contains a new mixture. Two verbal A-cola are followed by two nominal cola (appositions), while l.9 is first nominal, then verbal.[33] Thus, within this strophe there is a balance of 3 verbal versus 3 nominal cola. The symmetry between strophes 1 and 2, and that within the single strophe 3, realise the 2 + 1 model at stanza level.

At the semantic level there is a balance between the units filling the exposition. In strophe 2, there are six predicates in favour of God which all are nominal. In strophe 3, there are six negative terms (four as appositions) for the people. A subtle connection between the first and the second series is the fact that each has a single instance of litotes. In l.8b, 'not wise' means that the people are extremely foolish, in l.6a 'there is no iniquity [in him]' means that God is totally just and impartial.

I give the proportions of the first section here on the basis of two different counts. The metrical figures are only tentative, but provide an idea of the prosody and its relative regularity. The syllable count is primarily meant to be a gauge of quantity. As I try to count the original, pre-Masoretic syllables there is an approximation error which I estimate at around 2 %. There are figures for cola, verses and strophes.

First the stresses in the three strophes:

```
 L  +  L  +  L

3+3    3+3    4+3
3+3    3+3    3+3
2+2    3+3    3+3
```

The number of three metrical accents (ictuses, stresses) seems to me non-controversial in four verses, ll.1-2, 4-5. I allocate a stress to the monosyllables *hu* (end of l.6) and *zo't* (end of 8a) because of their deictic force. In a number of cases I combine a monosyllable with the preceding or following word for the

---

[33] Note: the *qnk* of l.9a is only an asyndetic relative clause, so that this colon contains one nominal predicate; in l.9b 'he' is the subject of two verbs.

purpose of stress unity.³⁴ I estimate l.7 to be an iambic quartet. Maybe 8b should run: o-oó oó oó. In l.3 the preposition plus segholate results in only one ictus per colon.

The figures for the syllables are the following:

strophe 1	*strophe 2*	*strophe 3*
11+8=19	6+7=13	8+ 7=15
7+7=14	6+7=13	8+ 7=15
6+7=13	7+6=13	9+10=19
__+	__+	__+
46	39	49

Striking here is the compactness of the middle strophe: it is much shorter than the adjoining two which are of about equal length. This fits in very well with the image of the Rock, with solidity and loyalty. Head and tail of the stanza have been weighted (containing 11 and 10 syllables). In between there is a reasonable regularity, as 13-15 syllables per verse is clearly the norm here. The final verse of the first strophe already contains the combination 6+7 which governs the entire second strophe, and thus prepares this quantitative aspect of the centre. The fact that the totals for the central trio remain equal at 13 is remarkable. In the third strophe, the balance of 8/8 for the A-cola of ll.7-8 and 7/7 for their B-cola, found on the vertical axis, perfectly fits the parallel syntax: a verbal and predicative A-colon plus a nominal B-colon consisting of appositions.

§ 2. *The second section: four stanzas, eight strophes (vv.7-18)*

The second section as a whole: contours and preview
Moses is the only speaker in the first half of the poem; in the second half he will say no more than the short strophes 22 and 27. Out of the total of 34 verses spoken by him, nine come in the first section and twenty in the second. It is this narrative section which gives him the most space.

Section II is a long part. How is it delineated? The poet decided to employ the device of inclusio, and realised that a framework based on only one form of correspondence between head and tail would be too flimsy and too tenuous. Consequently, he created a frame which can and should be clearly discerned, and is built on at least five elements.

---

[34] I take $h^alo\ hu$ of l.9 as a unit of stress, and also $w^{e\jmath}en\ {}^cawel$ (l.6a), *ki kol* (l.5b) and *ki šem* (l.4a), after the example of the non-controversial *ʾimre-pi* of the first verse. This decision avoids in all cases an unwanted collision.

The narrative section begins and ends with the language of the direct address. In strophe 4 its tone is didactic and insistent, in strophe 11 the cat is let out of the bag when Moses reproaches and condemns. This first aspect can only exist thanks to morphemes of the second person. These have been distributed so carefully, that their use may safely be called aspect two. In l.11 of strophe 4 (the first verse of the section, = v.7) the suffix 2 masc. sing. occurs four times; in the very last line of the section (v.18 = l.29, the final verse of strophe 11) there are also four morphemes for the second person.[35]

The second person deserves closer scrutiny. Before the verse (l.9) containing the quartet on *-ka*, Moses had used the form 'you', (plural, that is), just once in each strophe of section I, and only in the form of the verbal ending *-u*.[36] In section II, this 'you' only appears at the boundaries and in this way itself contributes to the inclusion.[37] Now, what of the distribution of the forms for 'you, your' (sing.)? Besides the 4 + 4 morphemes for this singular in the outside strophes we find another four you forms inside the section. They are remarkable in more than one respect: they, too, form a series and fulfil a delineating function, namely on the boundary between stanzas IV and V - not coincidentally the border where the scourge is unleashed. Moreover, the first morpheme of this quartet sticks out by being inside the apparently lost C-colon l.23c (= v.14e), while the next three conjugate an asyndetic series of perfect forms and occupy an entire colon. This is an unexpectedly direct and vehement outburst on Moses' part: the awesome staccato of v.15b (= l.24b).[38] Looking back on section II, I now count twelve (!) cases of the second person sing. Since this morpheme does not occur anywhere else in the poem, except for the adjacent line 9, we may conclude that the singular 'you' forms especially serve this section and its delineation.

Elements three, four and five of the frame which delineate the section together form a metonymic chain: father and birth, old and new, remembering and forgetting.

The days of yore receive a lot of attention in the first verse (l.10 = v.7ab). Studying history by asking questions of one's elders leads to wisdom, Moses says in strophe 4. In strophe 11 he points to the idols with mounting anger; he calls them 'the new ones' which is not exactly a recommendation. They are still wet

---

[35] In v.18 = l.29 this concerns the suffix *-ka (bis)* around the two imperfect forms in the centre. In l.11 the division over the bicolon is also two-two.

[36] These verb forms on *-u* are in ll.1a, 4b and 8a. After the second section 'you' (plural) only occurs in v. 43a (in *harninu*, the beautiful counterpart of the opening with *haʾᵃzinu*), and twice as the suffix *-kem* in v.38cd = l.60.

[37] The imperative of v.7b (= l.10b) ends in *-u*, and v.17d (= l.28b) has the suffix *-kem* once.

[38] This asyndetic trio is at the same time the maximum number of predicates possible per colon. As such, it was discussed by Michael O'Connor, in the perceptive studies of syntax versus verse structure contained in his *Hebrew Verse Structure*, Winona Lake IN 1980; see p.75. Deut.32 is one of the crown witnesses in this book, but is unfortunately presented in a completely arbitrary division.

behind the ears, these upstarts: *miqqarob* = recently. This opposition old-new is not only linked to the opposition God/gods, but also to that of remembering and forgetting: *zkr* is the very first word of the section, *škh* is the predicate of the very last colon. They form an antithetical word pair.[39] This gives rise to another opposition, that of wise/foolish, which we already know from v.6.

Moses wants his audience to become aware of its past, and exactly through section II he is going to argue that that is where their true identity lies. The facts, however, which he successively will have to pass in his account of strophes 5-10 (vv.8-16) bring him to a negative conclusion: the powerful agent who chose you (stanza II), protected you (stanza III) and raised you to a prosperous, even pampered existence (stanza IV), you have forgotten and abandoned (stanza V). The exhortation to remember the past (strophe 4) is no match for the harsh and scandalous reality of your desertion (strophe 11).

In strophe 4 we meet the pair 'your father' // 'your elders'. In strophe 11 they are called 'your fathers' with two plural morphemes (l.28, slot), but after that the poet leaves these people and in his final line returns to the singular and the deity. He honours him again through the metaphor צור, and calls him 'the Rock that begot you // who brought you forth', ילדך // מחללך. This is a daring choice of words, as it relativizes and almost transgresses the biological man/woman boundary.[40] The aim of these original terms is to underline God's status as a parent. Moreover, his fatherhood explicitly takes on an aspect of origin via the terms *yld* and *ḥolel*, and this origin is something which Moses has touched on in l.9 and then went on to elaborate in detail in strophes 5-6 (= vv.8-10).

Thus, section II is clearly marked off by means of elements which appear in pairs, form oppositions and are mutually connected by metonymy. A considerable number of the phenomena I discussed, however, serve on the next level up by contributing to a parallelism at section level. Sections I and II correspond with each other through their endings. I shall compare their opening strophes first, and then the concluding units.

Strophe 1 opens section I, strophe 4 opens section II. They have a lot in common. First, these strophic units open with addresses in the form of commands. They represent a sort of dialogue by means of their terms for oral/auditory aspects: listening, asking, being informed. This in turn has to do with the

---

[39] In I Sam.1:11 Hannah prays to God, in her vow: 'remember me (זכרתני) and do not forget (לא תשכח) your maidservant'. See also Deut.9:27 and Job 24:20. Consider also that זכר is a key word for the whole of Deuteronomy.

[40] Note that *yld* in the Qal usually means 'to give birth', and is exclusively reserved for the woman, who thus becomes a mother; and that the Polel of *ḥyl* refers to contractions and hence also to giving birth: thus the subject Sarah in Is.51:2, mountain goats in Job 39:1. The verse about God who 'brought forth the earth and the world' in Ps.90:2 is just as daring as our verse, theologically speaking, and Gen.2:4, where 'the *toledoth* of heaven and earth' is an *objective* genitive. Actually, heaven and earth do not originate from an act of procreation. (Ps.29:9, being a causative, is a separate case.)

important underlying concept of instruction and wisdom. The teaching, persuasion and insight which Moses announces with his first strophe - all of them aspects of the word לקח which we mainly know from Proverbs - largely coincides with the lesson the Israelites should receive from their fathers and which he recommends to them in the admonitory vocabulary of the *chokma*, strophe 4. The correspondence between these opening strophes is accordingly expressed by the use of the verb אמר, which in strophe 1 cannot be missed. We might overlook the 'telling' of l.11b, were it not for the fact that this verb occupies the same strategic position at the beginning of a section in v.20a, serving section IIIA, in v.26a serving section IIIB, and in v.37a serving section IV.[41] The exact form of the imperfect 3 masc. plural moreover receives a counterpart which is allocated to the opposing collective in v.27c (= l.44a - still at the beginning of section IIIB).

The parallelism of the first and second sections is also supported by similarities between their final strophes. Strophe 11 (three verses, 47 syllables) is as thoroughly devoted to the people's corruption as was strophe 3 (three verses also containing 47 syllables). Both units end on the series of four 2nd person singular morphemes already discussed. The combination 'not his sons' which already became acceptable because of the nearby litotes 'not wise', turns out to anticipate the couple 'not-god' in v.17a (l.27a) which Moses immediately after mentioning 'the demons' wants to use to reveal their true character. The sting of that couple is in the לא, and it is no coincidence that this negation is used twice more in strophe 11. Finally, the designations of God as father in ll.9 and 29 contribute to the parallel connection of sections I and II. This even goes as far as the poet's in both cases aptly granting the last word to a Polel form plus suffix: מחללך and יכננך.

Strophe 4.

זכר ימות עולם	10	(MT v.7)
בינו שנות דור ודור		
שאל אביך ויגדך	11	
זקניך ויאמרו לך		

Like the first, this strophe essentially consists of threesomes.[42] Because everything has been organised into word pairs, there is a maximum amount of paral-

---

[41] The verb 'to say' in v.37 introduces the four strophes spoken by God himself and, as opposed to the framework provided by Moses (i.e., strophes 22 and 27), form the substance of section IV. I remind the reader that the אמר of vv.20 and 37 is part of a collocation as in both cases it co-operates with a double ראה.

[42] Note that the doubling of דור provides the only instance of four words in a colon; the couple דור ודור, however, is a stylistic and metrical unit and obviously the counterpart of עולם.

lelismus membrorum. The 'command' mode is consistently maintained, so that it governs each colon.[43] The A-cola contain mainly singular forms, the B-cola mainly plural forms. The first verse has 3 + 3 o-vowels. This balance could only be achieved through the choice of the exclusive plural y^emot which tallies perfectly with $š^enot$. Apparently, the poet wanted forms with an -o- and rejected the common forms *yamim* and *šanim*.

Strophe 5.

בהנחל עליון גוים	12	(MT v.8)
בהפרידו בני אדם		
יצב גבלת עמים	13	
למספר בני ישראל		
כי חלק יהוה עמו	14	(MT v.9)
יעקב חבל נחלתו		

The previous strophe abounded in verbal predicates; this one has only one, the sentence core in l.13a. Following it, there are two nominal clauses which each get a colon (v.9 = l.14); preceding it, there is a generous use of enjambment, not only crossing the caesura between l.12a and 12b, but also crossing the verse boundary. This more or less mirrors the relation between ll.2-3.

The unity of the three-line strophe is guaranteed by an inclusio which employs the root *nḥl*; at the same time there is the variation between verbal and nominal, from בהנחל to נחלתו. This difference even determines the strophe as a whole: there are three cola with Hiphil verb forms plus three cola which are completely nominal. This division into halves leads to the discovery of remarkable twosomes. To this end I print the text again, this time in verses:

בהפרידו בני אדם	בהנחל עליון גוים	l.12
למספר בני ישראל	יצב גבלת עמים	l.13
יעקב חבל נחלתו	כי חלק יהוה עמו	l.14

We carry out some 'vertical' observations. The construct state combination 'the sons of man' is directly above 'the sons of Israel'. The vertical line at the end of all A-cola goes even further: underneath the plural 'nations' there is that of the 'peoples', but right underneath that there is the same stem in the singular, 'his people', almost capitalised. The structure of the strophe becomes immediately visible if we shape the division of the strophe into trios as a diagonal line:

---

[43] Three imperatives are visible; the fourth is virtually present in l.11b, thanks to the double duty of 'ask!'

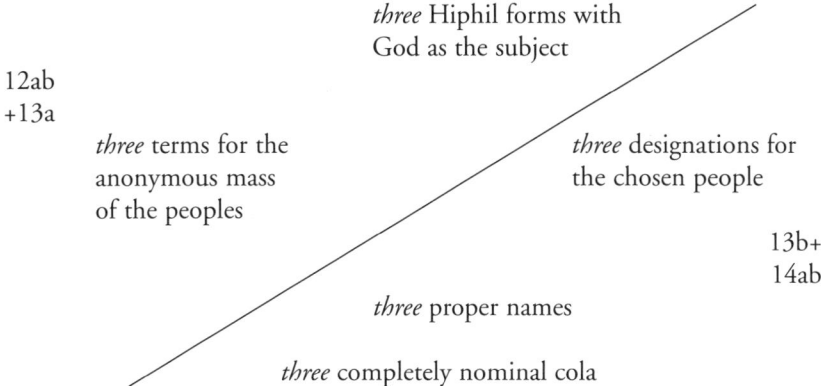

It is clear that the Hiphil has been used systematically. All the time God is the mighty subject, it is he who determines the appearance of the map of the world. The regrouping of the cola from three twosomes into two threesomes reveals which semantic axis is decisive/essential for this strophe: the opposition between on the one hand the nameless hordes, the mass of the peoples, and on the other the chosen people which has been called by name by God – with a variation on Deutero-Isaiah. The three proper names at the bottom right of the diagonal are all based on the pattern of the imperfect, and mention the partners of the covenant.[44]

Paradoxically, the similarities here mark the difference. The 'sons of' X nicely parallels 'the sons of' Y, but they are separated by the diagonal. The 'peoples' come from the same root as 'his people', but they are on either side of the diagonal. The two pairs yield the following equation: $b^e ne\ {}^{\flat}adam$ is to $b^e ne\ yiśra{}^{\flat}el$ as $ {}^c ammim$ is to $ {}^c ammo$.

The diagonal line runs through the central verse in the middle, coinciding with the caesura between l.13a and 13b, but bisecting the enjambment 13a > 13b. So how does the nominal part start? With a complement (l.13b) which nowadays is regularly 'corrected'. God fixed the bounds of the peoples, the colon says, 'according to the number of the sons of Israel.'

The compelling structure of threesomes on either side of the diagonal line, the division of the six cola into two trios and the semantic identity[45] of the terms in the equation formulated above crush the fashionable reading of 'celes-

---

[44] The imperfect forms *yahweh* and *ya'qob* are phonetically an apt continuation of the only finite verb, *yaṣṣeb*.

[45] The identity of the referents is the following: the 'sons of man' *are* 'the peoples' and the 'sons of Israel' *are* 'his people'.

tials' or divine beings (litt.: sons of gods) for בני אלים in l.13b, on the assumption, in itself understandable, that each territory or people has its own god.[46] This emendation of the text is inspired by a variant in the LXX ('angels of God') and two Qumran fragments (4Q). Unfortunately, this 'improvement' was made without first carrying out a decent structural analysis of the strophe. In this way, the organisation of the strophe is destroyed; moreover, the fact has been overlooked that as soon as we read 'celestials' in the central verse, all connection between v.8 and v.9 disappears and hence all logical basis for the conjunction *ki* which opens v.9, and which is truly motivating. Why indeed did God, when he was drawing the map of the world, draw it 'according to the number of the Israelites'? Why was that number normative for him? Answer: 'because his people are his portion'!

Finally and perhaps unnecessarily I note that the B-cola of ll.13 and 14 are organised chiastically so that not only the connection between 'number' and 'measuring-cord' becomes visible, but also and again the connection between (even the identity of) Israel and Jacob.[47] This, too, is an argument against changing the MT.

What, then is the number of the children of Israel? In this we have been prompted by Gen.46 - the text where the narrator, after the happy ending of Joseph and his brothers, can rise to the level of Jacob's *toledoth* and takes the crucial measure of the throng which accompanies the patriarch on his move to Egypt: seventy souls - and by Ex.1 (another strategic place in the sections of the Torah), but particularly, and nearer to home, by the book of which the Song of Moses forms a part: Deuteronomy itself, which in 10:22 says: 'Your fathers went down to Egypt seventy persons.'

This strophe is the first one in the narration, and consequently contains an important article of faith: it speaks of the election, and hence of the constitution of the people of God. Yet, the actual election is not related: the covenant is taken for granted and is the automatic norm for the activity which organises the map of the world. There are no verbs and consequently no actions in v.9 = l.14. Thus, the strophe is the first on the narrative road as this is where the history of the world starts. Via verse 9, however, the poet soon leaves this wide scope as

---

[46] Thus most recently Sanders, op. cit., pp.156-158. Further Skehan, CBQ 13 (1951) and JBL 78 (1959), Eissfeldt (1958), P. Winter in ZAW 67 (1955), D. N. Freedman, PPP p.123, S. Carrillo Alday, El Cántico de Moisés (Dt. 32), Estudios Bíblicos xxvi (1967), pp.143-185, P.C. Craigie (NICOT 1976) pp.378-379, S.A. Geller, The Dynamics of Parallel Verse, A Poetic Analysis of Deut 32:6-12, HThR 75 (1982) pp.35-56, J. Luyten, Primeval and Eschatological Overtones in the Song of Moses (Dt. 32,1-43), pp.341-347 of N. Lohfink (ed.), *Das Deuteronomium* (= BETL lxviii), Leuven 1985, A. van der Kooij in VTS 53 (1994), M. Rose, *5. Mose* (ZBK 1994) p.564 and 568, and others.

[47] This connection is further reinforced by another vertical line, that between גבלה and חלק in the A-cola.

his concern in reality is with the special relation between God and this one, tiny people.

The strophe gives an impression of compactness, and this is mainly due to the density of phonetic phenomena. Between the repeated *n-ḥ-l* which occupies the head and tail we soon notice the balance between *ḥlq* and *ḥbl*, and in between these *ya-* plus ayin and *yaᶜ-*. The beth with which the strophe opens appears five more times, and has been linked to the *nun* twice after l.12a, in the *bny* pair of the B-cola. Cola 12a and 13a rhyme on *-im*, the halves of v.9 rhyme on *-o*. This density adds extra force to the sensory effect of the strophe.

The diagonal organisation of cola into trios is one we shall find more often. Just like strophes 1 and 4 this strophe also contains three words per colon throughout.[48] The number three also governs prosodically, as there are only *Doppeldreier*. In the final verse the syntax is chiastic.[49] The order S + P / P + S itself bisects the positions of the two proper names: while the tetragrammaton forms part of the subject, Jacob is the predicate of the last colon.

The proportions of the two strophes in stanza II are as follows:

```
    str.4          str.5              S     +     L
   6+7=13         7+8=15
   9+9=18         7+8=15            3 + 3      3 + 3
     __+          6+6=12            3 + 3      3 + 3
     31             __+                        3 + 3
                    42
```

On the left, the numbers of syllables per colon, verse and strophe are given, and on the right the stresses in the short and the long strophe. The regularity here is considerable: metrically, the 3 + 3 symmetry dominates the entire field. The two verses of strophe 4 have practically the same number of syllables as the first two of strophe 5.

Strophes 6 and 7: stanza III

ובתהו ילל ישמן	ימצאהו בארץ מדבר	15 (MT v.10)
יצרנהו כאישון עינו	יסבבנהו יבוננהו	16
על גוזליו ירחף	כנשר יעיר קנו	17 (MT v.11)
ישאהו על אברתו	יפרש כנפיו יקחהו	18

---

[48] The exception confirming the rule is the monosyllable *ki* at the beginning of l.14. Compare this to notes 1 and 42 above.

[49] In the equally nominal verse about the Rock, l.5, the order of subject and predicate in the two cola is also chiastic, but inside out as compared to l.14.

Both these strophes are short and constitute a pair (stanza III), as they are being kept together by an impressive chain of verbs which are all of the narrative *yqtl* type. In four verses there are nine of these verbs, which means one more than the number of cola. In contrast, the strophes following in vv.12-14 (strophes 8-9), form a pair (stanza IV) which indulges in nominalising. In eleven cola these contain only five verbs, four of which are in strophe 8; they soon have to clear the stage for the most formidable chain of the poem, a series of nouns making up a an outrageous list of delicacies.

Strophe 6 has as many imperfect forms as cola, but they have been spread unevenly: the absence of a verb in l.15b is compensated by a twosome in the next colon, l.16a. The series as a whole exhibits a characteristic organisation of its own, thanks to the rhythm Qal / Polel + Polel / Qal. The chain has internal rhyme, as each form has the object *-hu*, 'him'.[50] Standing in a terrifying landscape, 'he' (the people) is threatened. The poet has found an apt expression for this, through a noun which also ends on *-hu*: the context is *tohu*, 'the chaos of howling wilderness'. The poet counters the danger of $y^e lel\ y^e šimon$ with the maximum assonance of $k^{e\prime}išon$. The sounds y^e- and *-on* then inspire him to the asyndetic duo of 16a which is based on the same conjugation, the Polel, and continues the y^e-, *o, n* and *-hu* sounds. The final line, ending on *-no*, reaches a physical intimacy: Israel has become the apple of His eye. In this way, the five terms of threat inundating l.15 are erased by the five terms of love and protection which completely fill l.16.

Strophe 7 is even more physical: nest, nestlings, wings and pinions. This is not surprising, as the main feature of this unit is its inspiration in the image of the eagle. An entire strophe here bears the stamp of the metaphoric, but the way in which this was done is complex. Formally, the beginning, 'like an eagle', is a simile. This comparison is directly connected to the end of strophe 6, as this ended on the simile 'like the apple of his eye'. Because of its position at the very beginning, the image of the powerful bird dominates line 17, the more so as the rest of the verse consists of 'only' two asyndetic relative clauses. Not until l.18a does the sentence core appear, and it is only there that the subject becomes clear to us: it is God. As a result, the wings and pinions of l.18 are true metaphors. God received those from the poet, so that the image of the bird hovers over the second verse as well and yet determines the strophe as a whole:

> Like an eagle who rouses his nestlings,
>   Gliding down to his young,
> So did He spread His wings and take him,
>   Bear him along on His pinions.

[50] The variation to be observed in the attaching of the suffixes, *-ehu, -enhu, -ehu, -enhu*, has also been motivated by the new prominence of the *nun*: from the end of l.15 until the end of l.16 the n occurs seven times.

There are even as many as five verbs here. Cola 17b and 18b repeat the preposition and chiastically place their predicates in-between. In this way, the strophe can end in a rhyme with the previous one: 'his eye ... his pinions'. Through maximum assonance, the verbs in the heart of l.18 turn back to the first word of the previous strophe and so contribute to the coherence of the stanza: *yimṣa'ehu ... yiqqaḥehu ... yiśśa'ehu*, God finds, catches, bears. The consistently maintained, if not total asyndesis governing the chain of verbs in this stanza suggests speed, effectual intervention and accuracy.

The linking of strophes 6 and 7 not only takes place via the similes on the boundary and the rhymes of their endings, but also by means of the sounds of ll.16b and 17a. With one exception, all consonants of 16b return in 17a, and this colon rhymes with the previous one (with *ʿeno*) through *qinno*. Finally, the strophes form a pair because of their graphic quality: there is a marked spatial aspect.

The proportions of both strophes in stanza III are as follows. In the left-hand column I give the numbers of syllables per colon, verse and strophe, and in the right-hand column the stresses for these two very lean strophes are shown:

str.6	*str.7*	S	+	S
8+8=16	6+7=13	3 + 3		3 + 2
10+9=19	9+8=17	2 + 3		3 + 2
—+	—+			
35	30			

Each of the strophes first has a short, then a long verse. The figures for the stresses reveal the compactness of these strophes: there are some cola now with only two stresses.

Strophes 8 and 9: stanza IV

ואין עמו אל נכר	יהוה בדד ינחנו	19	(MT v.12)
ויאכל תנובת שדי	ירכבהו על במתי ארץ	20	(MT v.13)
ושמן מחלמיש צור	וינקהו דבש מסלע	21	
עם חלב כרים ואילים	חמאת בקר וחלב צאן	22	(MT v.14)
עם חלב כליות חטה ודם ענב תשתה חמר	בני בשן ועתודים	23	

The space of the desert, its dangers and the deliverance by air determined the two strophes of the previous stanza. The strophes which together make up stanza IV answer this by stating the space and delights of the promised land. As I said earlier, the contrast is also marked by a restrained use of verbs and a clear preference for series of substantives.

Like strophe 5, strophe 8 contains three verses, and also employs three Hiphil forms which again have God as their subject. They are neatly arranged in a 'vertical' line, that is, in the A-cola. The balance with strophe 5 is a strong indication that we should resist the temptation to read another Hiphil in l.20b (= v.13b).[51] The Samaritan Pentateuch has such a causative form, 'he made him eat', and the LXX and the Targum presuppose it. This is a smoother text than the MT because it avoids a change of subject (from l. 20a to b and from 20b to 21a). I prefer the Masoretic text with its Qal as lectio difficilior. The responsion by the trio of Hiphil forms is probably part of a balance at a much higher level, being the number of verses and strophes throughout stanzas II-IV, as building-blocks for the eventual organisation of section II - more of which will be said later.

The three causatives of the A-cola still retain the object ending *-ehu*, as a continuation of the previous stanza. The last form (from *ינק) has to do with drinking. When they have finished their job, there is no sign of verbs for a long time - for as many as five cola, most of which deal with food and cattle - until the maverick v.14e (being a C-colon) again mentions drinking.

The deity proudly leads the way, a prominence semantically supported by the word 'alone'. Next, the nominal sentence l.19b turns out to have the task of explaining this בדד which makes not YHWH's activity but his uniqueness the focal point of the verse.[52] 'There was no foreign god with Him' - this anticipates the heart of the last section, where strophe 24 (= v.39) is devoted entirely to a self-revelation on the part of God. Colon l.61b is almost identical to l.19b, and states in the first person: 'there is no god beside me (*i.e.* like me).' To what extent the nominal sentence of l.19b serves l.19a also becomes clear from the chiastic semantics of the verse:

      yhwh   *badad*

      ʾ*en ʿimmo*   ʾ*el nekar*

A 'foreign god / not with him' - this may be translated as minus times minus is plus. This figure clearly shows the favourable quality intended for *badad*. It has everything to do with power and validity, and nothing with loneliness. The notion of 'foreign' anticipates the revulsion which in vv.16-18 becomes virulent

---

[51] A Hiphil in v.13b is read by O. Eissfeldt, Das Lied p.10, G. von Rad (ATD) p.137, P.C. Craigie (NICOT) p.380, M. Rose (ZBK 1994) p.564, Sanders pp. 167 and 169, and many others.

[52] The word order in v.12a is a signal in itself too: the verb comes only in third position; very different from the *yqtl* forms in vv.7-11 constantly playing the ringleader!

and forms the climax of the entire section. A piquant detail here is the fact that the uniqueness of the chosen people has been mentioned earlier in the text. The verse in question, together with the verse about God's uniqueness, revolves around the slim but compact central stanza III: verse 9 (which rounds off its strophe) and v.12 (which opens a strophe) adjoin and are outside vv.10-11 = stanza III.

The three verbs of v.13 are followed each time by a couple of nouns, 'the high places of the earth ... the produce of the field ... honey out of the rock', after which the final colon 21b is completely nominal, in preparation for strophe 9 = v.14. The quartet of cola in v.13 contains an evenly distributed quartet of $s^e mikut$ forms, with terms for land and rocks.

God makes an effort to wine and dine his people and the poet conveys this by inflating the hyperbolas. Israel does not get water from the cliff - satisfactory enough in Exodus... - but honey, and is even suckled on it. The momentous selection of the verb *ynq* entails the risk of God's treating his people too much like a baby. On the other hand, what else can you expect from someone who is *yldk*? Israel does not receive water from the rock, l.21b continues, but real oil. The word *šemen* has a disadvantage and an uncertain future. The drawback is that it fully alliterates with the $y^e šimon$ of strophe 6, so that the question arises if chaos will win after all in the patronised Israel. And 'uncertain future' I mean textually: the word 'oil', which here still pretends to be literal, returns in the fatal stanza V (= vv.15-18) as a strong anaphora heading the first pair of cola. It is used almost figuratively there, means as a verb 'to grow fat' and is highly incriminating, not for Israel, but... $y^e šurun$ (a beautiful nickname, but here used sarcastically).

The technique of exaggeration becomes completely clear in the (I would almost say) squared metaphors in v.14de. The final word of strophe 8 is not without venom. It is the only place in the poem where the word 'rock' is used literally.[53] The people stuffing themselves are more interested in what they can extract from a 'real' rock, than in the faithfulness of their Rock and the fact that their own self-respect depends on whether they can reciprocate with the same faith. Material considerations here override the spiritual idea of rock-solidity.

Strophe 9 is exceptional, as an enumeration, as a unit which contains four cola without predicate, and as a strophe containing a projecting C-colon. The verb in the C-colon does not affect the subject: the fact that this strophe has been stuffed like a sausage. In the same way, Israel is stuffed with delicacies. As the quartet of ll.22ab + 23ab is grammatically a series of objects and complements, and hence dependent on the sentence core in l.21a, the transition from

---

[53] In the other places, 'rock' is always a metaphor: a) in favour of the true God, v.4a, 15d, 18a, 30c, 31a ('our Rock' there), and b) for another god or gods in v.31a ('their Rock' there) and much more polemical in v.37b. Seven times in all.

strophe 8 to 9 is a drastic form of enjambment: the radical ignoring and traversing of a strophe boundary.[54]

The quartet 22ab + 23ab is no quadrocolon.[55] The structure of the pairs of cola is 'vertically' an even more marked parallelism than horizontally. The A-cola both have intracolon parallelism, which the B-cola clearly do not have. The A-cola both link herds and flocks, with the difference that l.22a employs the singular of the collective (*bis*), while in 23a this is explained by means of plurals.[56] The B-cola immediately manifest themselves as a vertical pair through the anaphora *ᶜim ḥeleb k-*.[57] A subtle shift, by the way, is the fact that in l.22b the fat still has a literal meaning, but has a more or less metaphoric function (meaning 'the best') in colon 23b which has left the animals aside and now talks about wheat. The metaphoric aspect is as it were squared or inflated by saturating one image with the other: 'with the fat of the kidneys of the wheat'. The metaphoric treatment is continued in a more moderate vein in l.23c which speaks of 'the blood of the grapes'.[58]

The alliterating series *ḥemʾat - ḥaleb - *ḥilb* (bis) *- ḥiṭṭa - ḥemar* cannot be missed, and just as the blood metaphor helps to keep the C-colon v.14e inside the strophe. This sentence also consists of four words, as do l.22a, 22b and 23b. This number may be considered a characteristic of this enumerative unit, as we find it in four out of five cola. The C-colon, which already strikes the eye by jutting out, becomes unique by suddenly starting an address: we unexpectedly

---

[54] A strophe boundary is ignored by the syntactic coherence once more in this poem, with all the force of l.64 (a conditional clause) on l.65 (main clause); a different situation is that v.30 is the content of the considerations indicated in v.29, viz. the words which should have been said by the enemies.
An interesting question arising from the enjambment: is the strophe division correct? Should not all the objects of v.14 together with v.13cd be kept together in one and the same strophe? In that case, ll.19-20 would be a S-strophe, and ll.21-23 a L-strophe plus C-colon. I do not adopt this division, on the grounds of a) the trio of Hiphil forms, which should remain intact, b) the four terms for landscape and rocks which are distributed evenly throughout v.13abcd, and c) because v.14 entirely concentrates on animals and goodies after that. The Masoretes made a similar decision with their verse division: they made v.14 into a *pasuq*.

[55] Contra Sanders, pp.(172-)175. The existence of quadrocola is doubtful in any case. The big question undermining them is: would such a quartet not simply be two bicola? See at this point my discussion of v.14.

[56] For instance, *baqar* is 'translated' as - note the double alliteration and the assonance - *bᵉne bašan*, while *ṣon*, small stock, is represented by 'goats'.

[57] Sanders, op. cit. pp. 174-175, thinks that just like the adjacent cola, v.14c is governed by עם חלב. That is a reasonable possibility. Its absence in 14c he calls an ellipsis, and considers the omission an argument in favour of a quadrocolon structure. I think that the ellipsis is rather an argument against a quadrocolon, and argues in favour of two bicola. For, if v.14abcd has been designed as a quadrocolon, two problems arise: a) why then should the poet repeat the עם חלב? And b) why does he not place it in 14c, instead of in 14d?

[58] This metaphor also occurs elsewhere (Gen.49:11, and a late echo in Sir.39:26) and is probably not original, but as old as Ugaritic poetry.

meet the second person. As stated earlier, this has to be viewed in the context of the trio of 2 masc. sing. perfect forms immediately below it, on the other side of the stanza boundary. The length of the verse and this second person indicate that the divisive force of this stanza boundary is above average.

The proportions of the two strophes in stanza IV are as follows:

str. 8	str. 9	L	S+
7+7=14	8+7=15	3 + 3	3 + 3
9+8=17	8+6+7=21	3 + 3	3 + 3 + 3
9+6=15	__+	3 + 3	
__+	36		
46			

Strophes 10 and 11: stanza V

Stanza V immediately distinguishes itself by being negative in literally every colon: reproachful, aggravating, incensed, etc. In this way, the fact is expressed that this couple of strophes is (both the climax, and) the anticlimax of the narrative section II. It is a reversal, a dénouement. Moreover, this reversal is marked very sharply by the difference nominal/verbal.

Whereas stanza IV only had a few verb forms in the beginning (i.e., strophe 8) and in principle was completely nominal in strophe 9, stanza V erupts in a baffling stream of verbs: no fewer than nine in strophe 10 and another seven in strophe 11.[59] The first verse, l.24, is a salvo of machine-gun fire. Here is the text:

שמנת עבית כשׂית	וישמן ישרון ויבעט	24	(MT v.15)
וינבל צור ישעתו	ויטש אלוה עשׂהו	25	
בתועבת יכעיסהו	יקנאהו בזרים	26	(MT v.16)
אלהים לא ידעום	יזבחו לשדים לא אלה	27	(MT v.17)
לא שׂערום אבתיכם	חדשים מקרב באו	28	
ותשכח אל מחללך	צור ילדך תשי	29	(MT v.18)

The formidable opening verse has a record number of verbs: they occupy five out of the six positions. The one word which is not a verb is $y^e\check{s}urun$. This word has been selected partially because of its sound. It is a station between the threatening $y^e\check{s}imon$ and the nearby $y^e\check{s}u^cato$, 'his salvation', which through an

---

[59] The nine verbs of strophe 10 all are predicates of main clauses. In strophe 11 this is different: there are only main verbs at the head (one: *zbḥ*) and tail (i.e. *tšy // tškḥ*); the other four are in asyndetic attributive clauses.

explicative genitive coincides with its nomen regens *ṣur* (the central metaphor of the Song). The fourth word ending on *-u* in this strophe, *ʿaśahu*, forms a word pair with *yᵉšuʿato* and extensively alliterates with it. The Rock is both his creator and his liberator, but Jeshurun will not have anything to do with it any longer. He has grown too fat himself.

The fat spills over from l.24 on all sides. It dominates this bicolon as an anaphora, and the other three verbs are all synonyms. The form *wayyibʿaṭ* means: 'he feasted'.⁶⁰ Usually this root is translated by 'kicking', but this meaning is hardly tenable, and worse, does not fit the context. The entire verse expressly aims at being the height of monotony, and in the form of a staccato at that, which assumes extra punch by changing to the second person in the B-colon. The importance to the poet of the trio of verbs which alone make up the B-colon becomes clear from the fact that in his preparatory Chapter 31 he has employed a synonymous trio of cramming oneself with food and growing fat, in v.20. He puts this series into God's mouth when he instructs Moses about the song, and God himself makes the link with the land of milk and honey, being spoiled, and idolatry.

The second verse of strophe 10, l.25, is determined completely by means of three parallel word pairs. It opens with two *wyqtl* forms which balance the two narrative forms of l.24. In l.24, with its five intransitive verbs, there was nothing but gorging and growing fat: no objects, no complements, no relation with God. This line, l.25, does regard the relation with God and uses two transitive verbs to put him aside. The sequel is extremely compact: asyndetically and in a chiastic arrangement two *yqtl* forms follow, still narrative, both taken from the Hiphil; they frame objects which are both plural but of different gender: masc./fem. In v.15 the people themselves were a singular, now a plural form. This small shift is not enough to exclude v.16 from the strophe.⁶¹ The poet has linked this verse to the previous one by means of various phonetic devices. There is not only the rhyme on *-hu* (l.25a-26a-26b), but also a string consisting of ayin, bet, ṭet and taw which among other things links up *yibʿaṭ*, *ʿabita* and *toʿebot*.⁶² In this way, the meanings of these censorious words merge with

---

⁶⁰ This meaning, in French 'se rassasier', has with good arguments been defended for the only other occurrence of the root, in I Sam.2:29, by Barthélemy *cum suis*, CTAT (1982) pp. 147-148. In my *Vow and Desire* (= NAPS IV), pp. 139 and 569-70 I also discussed this passage and presented new arguments, also taking into account Deut.31:20 (another trio of verbs about growing fat, this time a syndetic series) and 32:15.

⁶¹ If we disconnected v.16 it would be left dangling in the air. It would not have any link with v.17 with its negations and perfect forms, and there is no other instance of a one-line strophe in Deut.32, so that I do not want to isolate v.16.

⁶² L.25 also has a ṭet, a taw and twice an ayin. More alliterations: the combination sibilant + t/ṭ in ll.24a, 24b, 25a, 25b. This combination is continued in the strategic final line of the section, with *tśy* and *tškḥ*. The form *yaqniʾuhu*, as successor to *wayyeniqehu* in l.21a, has been placed exactly linearly in 26a.

each other. Moreover, the contents of l.25 and l.26 belong together as two sides of a coin: rejecting the one (true) God automatically implies accepting other gods. The following strophe calls them demons and gods, this one limits itself to pejoratives full of scorn: strangers, abominable practices.

Strophe 11 opens with a quartet of cola (in v.17) which abounds in plurals. There are four designations for the idols. The middle two, on either side of the caesura of l. 27, form the chiasm 'not god(like) - gods not'. The other two alliterate, *šedim* - *ḥᵃdašim*. Also, there is an exact quartet of asyndetic relative sentences.[63] The three negations may be supplemented by the negative meaning of 'come in recently'. In fact, there is only one main verb. It comes right at the beginning, 'they sacrificed', after which the four cola are filled with only appositions and subordinate clauses which move up further and further:

'they sacrificed to the demons
    which are not god(like)
        [to] gods
            which they did not know
                new gods
                      which have appeared only recently,
                          whom your fathers had not feared.'

At the end of this telescopic chain the second person appears in *-kem*. This prepares the way for the final verse of the section, the bicolon v.18 (= l.29) which forms part of the system of 4 + 4 + 4 morphemes for 'you' (sing.) on the boundaries of section II.

Just like the end of the previous strophe, the final verse arranges its syntax in a chiasm. The word Rock also appears again, as it did in l.25. The words of l.25a have identical meanings to those in l.29a. This may help us to interpret correctly the tricky *tšy* in l.29a. This imperfect deserves a minor adjustment, as many have proposed. To my mind, the best option is to read *tšh* = *tišše*, 'you have neglected'.[64] One is tempted to interpret this word as a continuation of the reprehensible *tište* of l.23c; one thing leads to another. The verb in l.28b I take as 'to dead'.[65] The syntax of l.29a is almost identical to that of l.19a which opened stanza IV: the deity in first position with an essential quality, only then followed by a verbal predicate. This time, however, God is not a powerful agent any more but the victim!

---

63   Besides the 'vertical' pair 'they did not know // they did not fear' placed chiastically between antecedent and subject, and the 'just arrived' of l.28a, the words 'not god(like)' of l.27a are also a relative sentence!

64   The BHS mentions this proposal, which is not exactly new, in its apparatus. The root, *nšy* = 'to forget', has now also been attested in Ugaritic. See HAL p.688, entry נשה, or already Ges.-Kautzsch § 75 s.

65   There are objections to connecting this *šʿr* (with a sin!) with the Arabic *shaʿara* (contra HAL IV p.1252, sub voce III שער). The Peshitta also has 'to fear': דחל.

The main contribution of the eleventh strophe results from its strategic position. It forms part of a well-founded inclusio, the components and meanings of which I have already discussed. The consideration in the present (demanded by strophe 4), the wisdom of the fathers and the fatherhood of the deity are wiped out by forgetfulness, by the foolishness which results from allowing oneself to be spoilt immoderately, and by idolatry. That is the outcome of the second section. The turn towards this anticlimax is reflected well in the many verbs of action. In strophes 5-8 God is an unceasing initiator and a powerful agent, he is the subject of the narrative chain of *(w)yqtl* forms. In strophes 10-11, Israel is first the thoroughly complacent subject of five intransitive verbs, and after that of seven transitive verbs which either mean forsaking (of the true God) or worshipping (of the wrong gods).[66]

The proportions of these two strophes are as follows:

str.10	*str.11*	L	+	L
9+9=18	9+7=16	3 + 3		3 + 3
8+9=17	8+8=16	3 + 3		3 + 3
7+8=15	6+9=15	2 + 2		3 + 3
―+	―+			
50	47			

The verse measures in the two L-strophes show a very regular pattern, 15 to 18 syllables per verse.[67] As regards metre, five out of the six verses again show the symmetry of two times three, just like all verses of the previous stanza; the chiastic verse 16 (= l.26) has the balance 2 + 2. So far we had only seen these figures for l.3, as a pleasant strophe conclusion; but what a difference in tone and power! With its machine-gun, the ternary principle now governs all details of the verse: not only does each colon consist of three words, but each of these words also has three syllables. A unique instance of well-sustained perfection.

Section II: review and summary
The section opens with two stanzas largely consisting of short strophes. The first strophe is set slightly apart because of the form of address and the corresponding tone, but on the other hand constitutes a suitable opening because of this. Next, there are three strophes which in various ways speak of the beginning of Israel. By way of the map of the world we end up at the one people in strophe

---

[66] The balance between God as subject in strophes 5-8 and Israel as subject in strophes 10-11 is remarkable: thirteen verbs for God (counting the two infinitives in l.12, but not the two imperfect forms for the eagle) versus twelve for the people (not counting the perfect forms of strophe 11).

[67] Their average fully corresponds with the averages found at the time by D.N. Freedman for the acrostic poems, in his study Acrostics and Metrics in Hebrew Poetry, HThR 65 (1972), now in PPP pp.69 and 76.

5, after which a very compact and graphic rendering of the election follows such as only a real lyricist can give. The images of the dangerous desert and the mighty bird remain on the reader's retina.

The following two stanzas are more directly involved with one another and more clearly manifest themselves as a couple. They need much more room than the previous couple. There are downright three L-strophes, and the one S-strophe tries to escape its shortness by extending itself through a C-colon. At stanza level there is the neat cohesion of being spoiled and corruption. This complementarity is simply but inescapably reflected in grammar and syntax. In stanza IV (strophes 8-9, vv.12-14) God is the giving subject with Israel, his grammatical object, at the receiving end. In stanza V (strophes 10-11, vv.15-18) Israel becomes partly the smug subject of intransitive verbs, partly the subject of relinquishing and apostasy, leaving God no other position than that of object.

It is attractive to read the four strophes according to the AB-B'A' pattern. Strophe 9 concentrates solely on the tasty morsels, which corresponds to the most striking characteristic of strophe 10, the hardly bearable stream of verbs meaning 'stuffing oneself'. Strophe 8, however, clearly looks at the relation God-people with its trio of transitive verb forms (always: he - Hiphil - him), and presents God as benefactor, as the bestower of the promised land. Moreover, there is already a verse declaring his uniqueness. This oneness of God's care and his matchlessness is now disgracefully answered in strophe 11, the unit dealing with idolatry (the downright denial of the uniqueness of the true God) and forgetting, which is an instance of completely mistaken retribution (remember *gml* in v.6!) and boils down to treason.

Stanzas IV and V are marked by striking opening and closing verses. The proper name proudly leading the way in l.19 and the anticipating statement of God's uniqueness form the beginning; the end answers by means of the third application of the Rock metaphor (supporting its second appearance in l.25b) and the remarkable quartet of you (sing.) forms as an incisive condemnation. The close relationship between the strophes in stanzas IV-V takes the form of a chiasm; this also affects the preceding text. The relation between stanzas II and III is less close, but as they remain outside the closed mould of stanzas IV + V when we read section II backwards, they are thrown together as the first half of section II.

Besides this division of four stanzas into four plus four strophes it is also possible, and even more necessary, to read the stanzas as a 3 + 1 series. Strophes 5-9, a long sequence of twelve verses, are completely devoted to the goodness, care and intense activity of the deity in favour of his chosen people. The end of the sequence is marked by the exceptional C-colon and the sudden appearance of the second person (before the winning post, in l.23c, and beyond it in l.24b). Next, the dramatic reversal in stanza V follows, whose six verses (strophes 10-11) speak of the response of the people colon by colon - nothing but corruption and apostasy. As stated earlier, this makes the stanza into the dénouement and the (anti)climax of the long, narrative section. This negative ending is the starting point and foundation for all subsequent difficulties - in other words, for section III.

The configuration of section II as 3 + 1 stanzas is confirmed at three levels. I now consider stanzas II-III-IV, the long, positive run-up to the shock. a) The compact and evocative centre of desert and eagle (strophes 6-7) is framed by L-strophes, each containing three Hiphil forms for the subject God. b) These touch on the centre by means of statements of uniqueness: first that of the people (v.9), later that of God (l.19). c) The length of the strophes in stanzas II-IV is as follows:

stanza II	stanza III	stanza IV
S + L	S + S	L + S

Such a symmetry alone cannot be proof of the three stanzas being a sequence, but it is an indication which ties in with the analysis of semantics and content. The section is rounded off by a stanza containing only L + L. Further down there is one more instance of a similar stanza, which of all things forms the end of the following section. This is stanza IX, containing strophes 20-21 (= vv.32-35).

Outside the boundaries of section II there is one more phenomenon which assumes those boundaries and confirms them at the same time. This is a ring of two verses which are positioned at exactly equal distances from section II. Both formulate the people's corruption, and both do so practically exclusively through nouns. The fact that they form a ring is confirmed by their mutual relation:

(l.6: ... *'emuna* ..)
l.7 Corrupt .. no children of his .. *mumam* / crooked, tortuous generation

l.32 they are a generation of perversions   /   children without *'emun*

We here see a chiasm which is formed not only by the words *banim* and *dor*, but also by the accompanying qualifications. The identity of blemish (*mum*) and unfaithfulness on the part of the people is contrasted with, and introduced by, God's faithfulness in l.6a. Whoever calls an entire generation 'sons' (and daughters, l.30b), presupposes fatherhood as a norm. This is God's fatherhood, not coincidentally one of the elements on the boundaries of section II responsible for inclusio.

§ 3. *The third section: four stanzas, ten strophes (vv.19-35)*

The poet allows Moses to fill just one more line with a narrative introduction, but after that God holds the floor for a long time. The articulation into levels of discourse is of strategic importance in Deut.32, and here the first major transition occurs. In principle, God speaks everything from vv.20 through to 35.[68]

The transition is marked by a collocation which we also find at the beginning of the fourth section.[69] This regards the verb which is essential to the quotation formula, אמר. Both here and in the next section it is combined with a double ראה (in stanza X: ll.57a, 58a, 61a). After section II God 'sees' (according to Moses, v.19) the corruption of his people and tells us what he proposes to do, after section III God 'sees' (according to Moses, strophe 22) the powerlessness of his people and tells us how this affects his stance.

Section III has a powerful division of its own, i.e. an internal organisation into two couples of stanzas:
- section IIIA = stanzas VI + VII = strophes 12-16 = vv.19-25,
- section IIIB = stanzas VIII + IX = strophes 17-21 = vv.26-35.

These halves have been systematically marked by the stem כעס. In the first place, this is already a key word as it occurs no less than five times in the range constituted by vv.16-27 in verses which are not exactly gentle.[70] The root has, however, an even greater weight which I would like to express by calling it a normative word. What exactly does the word כעס convey? Its semantic field harbours frustration, anger, annoyance, torment and provocation, and here it means all of those things. It has been placed at the beginning of the section halves to indicate the ground of God's actions, and thus puts its stamp on the entire section:
- God wants to destroy Israel because of the *kaʿas* it causes him
  (section IIIA)
- God decides not to punish his people because of the *kaʿas* the enemy causes him, and turns against the enemy
  (section IIIB)

This is why it is possible to define the halves of section III by means of a very simple pro and contra:
- IIIA : God is contra Israel (and implicitly pro the enemy),
- IIIB: God is contra the enemy and their illusions, so that eventually (in section IV) he will have mercy on his people.

---

[68] In principle, and moreover, almost everything. Only l.31 does not count, whether it is spoken by Moses or whether it is the writer's. Within God's speaking we shall shortly have to distinguish direct speeches of the third and even of the fourth degree.

[69] The verb כעס occurs in vv.16b, plus 21b and d; the noun occurs in v.19b and v.27a.

[70] The word is well known from various books of the Bible, among which Jeremiah, but the most relevant to us here is Deuteronomy and (its possible effects in) the Deuteronomistic Work of History: in Kings, *kʿs* is used *passim* as the most appropriate word for the condemnation of the kings from the Northern kingdom and some from Judah.

Section IIIA: stanzas VI-VII, strophes 12-16

Strophe 12 contains two cola for Moses, and four cola for God who as a speaker is introduced by *wayyomer* (the very last narrative in first-degree direct discourse, and the so very familiar quotation formula). His verses contain two verbal and two nominal clauses. The relation between these couples is that of intention (l.31) and the reason for it (l.32). The B-cola, and with these the verses, rhyme on 'their', the A-cola rhyme on 'them'.

מכעס בניו ובנתיו	וירא יהוה וינאץ	30	(MT v.19)
אראה מה אחריתם	ויאמר אסתירה פני מהם	31	(MT v.20)
בנים לא אמן בם	כי דור תהפכת המה	32	
כעסוני בהבליהם	הם קנאוני בלא אל	33	(MT v.21)
בגוי נבל אכעיסם	ואני אקניאם בלא עם	34	

In the first verse the poet avoids parallelismus membrorum. He manages this by employing a modest form of intracolon parallelism in both half verses. In l.30a (= v.19a) the last two actions of the narrative chain, *wayyar* and *wayyinʾaṣ*, are next to each other, around the proper name of God. The position of the tetragrammaton in the very first colon contributes to the delineation of the higher-level units: after all, the entire section III consists of reflections by this speaker. It can even be viewed as a long sustained soliloquy, since no addressee is mentioned.

In l.30b (= v.19b) there is another couple: 'his sons and his daughters'. They contribute to the mighty arcs which sustain the inclusio at the boundaries of section II, and at the same time collaborate with the word pair *dor* and *banim* from l.32 in keeping the three verses of ll.30-32 together as a strophe. As we have seen, line 32 is itself the counterpart of l.7. Because the two verbs in the A-colon are paired, and the reason for God's revulsion (torment and provocation) in the B-colon is served by a merism (sons/daughters), the absence of parallelism here implies the presence of enjambment. Next, the four cola of v.20 follow in which as many predicates are evenly distributed.

God starts off with two cohortatives.[71] 'I want to hide my face from them / I want to see what their 'end' is going to be.' They play an ingenious game with their objects. First, there is the paradox that there is not much to see for somebody who turns away his face. Next, there is *ʾaḥᵃrit*. The meaning of this root is ambiguous: 'after' may have been intended spatially as well as temporally. The

---

[71] A ל"ה form such as אראה cannot have the ending of the cohortative, but as a continuation of אסתירה it certainly is a cohortative.

primary meaning here is 'end': how is this perverse generation going to turn out? Badly, I will take care of that! But a spatial connotation comes up as well: the word *panim* reminds us of פנה, 'turn (towards)' and itself also means 'front side'. In this way, not only do 'seeing' and 'face' on either side of the caesura become connected, but also 'front side' and 'back side'. Moreover, there is a double alliteration and a complete assonance between the words *'astira* and *'aḥritam*, which form a ring around face/seeing. In this way, the result is a word play with a slightly naughty punch below the belt: a kick in Israel's backside.

One might be tempted to separate the introduction by Moses from the words spoken by God and accommodate it in a strophe of its own. The poet, however, has chosen his construction in such a way that such a separation would be wrong. Two diagonals connect the cola of l.30-31 with each other. The repetition of the verb 'to see' bisects the repetition of the fatal *min*. In l. 30b, this preposition is motivational, whereas its consequence is a *min* denoting separation in l.31a, 'away from...'. In this way, a chiasm chains the introductory verse to God's plans. The ideological effect of this is not surprising: if Moses' words (in l.30) are not already normative themselves, they still presuppose judgements which are entirely God's. So what then is the difference between one speaker and the other, as far as their scale of values is concerned?

The line about this 'generation full of perversions' - not a poetical plural, but a genuine one and hence much more venomous - is of great structural importance. We have already seen that it confirms l.7, and now deduce that Moses' verdict in l.7 was well-founded and anticipates the unfavourable diagnosis of the people by God here in l.32. This verse, however, will be balanced by a striking counterpart in l.45, a verse which in accordance with the sense of section IIIB (contra the enemy) condemns the other party, again in two nominal sentences.

These three verses make up an L-strophe with the rather regular pattern of 16-16-13 syllables. Their total is exactly the same as that of the only other L-strophe in the section, nr.15 (= vv.23-24), which with 14-14-17 syllables exhibits the same sort of regularity. Between these two L-strophes there are two S-strophes which also have the same length, with 32 syllables for both.

Strophe 13 shows its internal cohesion at first sight. This unit is an obvious instance of the tit-for-tat policy, but also of the symmetry between crime and punishment which goes with the concept of *talio*. The symmetry results in the front position of the forms 'they' and 'I'. As they are followed by finite verbs these forms seem redundant, but in reality they mark the symmetry of a diametrical opposition. What used to be the object now becomes the subject and vice versa. At the same time, this is the difference between past (including this day, in the speaker's view) and threateningly imminent future. Since the actions mirror each other completely, the verbs are repeated and thus become key words.

The symmetry raises the expectation that the complements mirror each other as well. This helps the reader to link $b^eh ablehem$ to $b^e goy\ nabal$; their three-fold alliteration is indeed eloquent. No wonder that in these B-cola the root k^cs frames it chiastically. To the stem hbl one might assign the same meaning as it carries in Qohelet: absurdity.[72] What the people prefer is indeed absurd; the way they insult their benefactor is beyond understanding.

In the A-cola the similarity of $b^elo\ 'el$ and $b^elo\ 'am$ cannot be missed. It helps us to understand what a non-people is, in spite of the fact that this non-people should be a genuine people which is to bring war and destruction to Israel, as a rod of God's anger. The point of contact of both these instruments seems to me to be 'disgrace': the disgrace of idolatry is punished by the disgrace of hastily assembled riffraff - something like a mercenary army - without internal cohesion, let alone a divine destiny such as Israel did receive in strophe 5.[73]

The verse structure - after the contrast they/I - is parallel in l.33, but chiastic in l.34. One subtlety remains: why did the poet in the one verse select the Piel and in the other the Hiphil for the two forms of extreme provocation?[74] Did he do this in order to indicate the difference in quality and legitimacy between the people and their God? There is also a phonetic aspect: the angry $'^ani$ which occupies the initial position is now also completely incorporated into the form $'aqni'em$, which is something the Piel cannot manage. The action completely envelops its subject, as an iconic sign of how God is totally enveloped within his anger.[75]

Strophe 13 is bounded by a quartet of morphemes for 'them'. Three of these are at the edges of the verses. This foursome makes the strophe match its predecessor. Another quartet is that of the imperfect forms which have God as a first-person subject and state his plan to intervene. Three of these are Hiphil forms.[76] So far, God has spoken four verses. These phenomena indicate that strophes 12 and 13 belong together in one stanza. The internal structure of stanza VII which follows confirms that the boundary between VI and VII comes after v.21.

---

[72] A good description of hbl is provided by Michael Fox in his *Qoheleth and his Contradictions*, JSOTS 71, Sheffield 1989.
[73] Note that it is this fifth strophe which just like strophe 13 employed the word pair גוי / עם.
[74] The question is all the more legitimate, as in v.16 the Hiphil was still used for the people, for the same crimes as mentioned here in l.33.
[75] Roman Jakobson at one time demonstrated a similar mechanism with respect to attachment, by means of a stylistic analysis of the famous election slogan *I like Ike*. Both object and subject are in the form of a verb - a fusion of love...
[76] We might even be justified in calling $'aḥritam$, on the basis of its phonetic correspondence with $'astira$, the fourth of a quartet of Hiphil forms! We would here be concerned with a pseudo-Hiphil, which by the way would not be too difficult to render in context by something like: 'I want to see how I can put them behind.'

Stanza VII (strophes 14-16)

ותיקד עד שאול תחתית	כי אש קדחה באפי	35	(MT v.22)
ותלהט מוסדי הרים	ותאכל ארץ ויבלה	36	
חצי אכלה בם	אספה עלימו רעות	37	(MT v.23)
וקטב מרירי	מזי רעב ולחמי רשף	38	(MT v.24)
עם חמת זחלי עפר	ושן בהמות אשלח בם	39	
ומחדרים אימה	מחוץ תשכל חרב	40	(MT v.25)
יונק עם איש שיבה	גם בחור גם בתולה	41	

This sequence of seven verses is clearly articulated into three units of 2 + 3 + 2 verses, in a concentric arrangement. The first unit, the four cola of v.22, is cosmic and as a whole serves one ominous subject: fire. The second unit consists of three verses and is itself arranged in a concentric pattern because the axis is utterly nominal and is surrounded by sentences with three transitive verbs. The subject of this strophe 15: plagues. Strophe 16 (= v.25) is another S-strophe and deals with war.

Strophe 14 contains four sentences with a common subject which however is only mentioned once: fire. After the start in l.35a (model X + *qtl*) it receives a chain of verbs of the *wyqtl* type, which each open their own colon and receive their complements from two spatial nouns.[77]

There are three levels in space: underneath (the Sheol in l.35b) and above (l.36b: the mountains), with 'the earth and its produce' in between. God's anger rages through the cosmos like a consuming fire. What, however, is his target exactly? I note that there is not one morpheme or syllable devoted to the odious people. This silence, almost an ellipsis, will prove highly relevant.

The first line is still inspired by the first person and has two times the long -i on either side of the caesura. The asseverative *ki* underlines the anger (*'appi*). The balance of the cola is supported by the double alliteration of *'eš* and Sheol, and the return of all the consonants of *qad^{e}ḥa* in *tiqad ... taḥtit*. Their quantities are symmetrical as well: 8 + 8 syllables, a total of 16. The second verse arrives at the same total by way of 7 + 9. Thus, strophe 14 has 32 syllables, which is exactly the same number as strophe 13.

Strophe 15 (= vv.23-24) now clearly presents the I as agent: the supplier of disasters. The middle verse is an axis, consisting exclusively of three nominal

---

[77] These *wyqtl* forms (leaving aside the two perfect forms of l.48 in third-degree direct discourse; the qtl forms of ll.62b and 64a do not refer to the past) are the very last narrative forms, and the last preterits in the poem!

twosomes. Should we distribute these words over the half verses as 4 + 2, or the reverse? The norm of the syllable count already points to the first option.[78] The decisive factor here, however, is the construction of the couples $m^eze\ ra^cab$ and $l^ehume\ rešef$: both are s^emikut constructions, both rhyme on -e, and both alliterate through the r- which marks the sinister pair of hunger and pestilence. Moreover, these couples are connected by means of an ingenious word play. Words on l-ḥ-m sometimes refer to both war and bread.[79] Here, the victims of the plague have not only been 'fought' by that disaster, but have also been 'devoured like bread', which is a rather nasty continuation of 'famine'. While the people are hungrily looking for bread, the pestilence has enough bread...

The syntactical position of the nouns in v.24ab is slippery. I am inclined to view the plurals as appositions to the 'them' which closes off v.23. In that case, the people *into whom* I shoot all my arrows are 'wasted by famine and consumed by pestilence'. Maybe the singular $qeṭeb\ m^eriri$, 'bitter destruction', already functions as an object to the following, besides 'the teeth of beasts'. In any case, the elements Rešef and Qeṭeb, reminiscent of a Canaanite god and a demon, provide this desolate strophe with mythical connotations.[80]

Verse 23 (l. 37) is structured by three word pairs, pattern abc-cab. Because the root *sph* is a highly improbable basis for the first word, I carry out a repunctuation in this verb and read it as the Qal cohortative of אסף: $\hat{}os^efa$, to be translated as: 'I will collect evils against them', where I interpret the preposition pregnantly and *in malam partem*.[81]

The last word of the strophe almost always carries connotations of death and mortality. All consonants of this ^cafar - phonetically, too, a successor to ra^cab which metonymically is linked to death - are already present in the first colon, and there are more phonetic correspondences between ll.37a and 39b. This is no coincidence, as the adjacent cola, 37b + 39a, put a ring of predicates around the pivotal verse which clearly are each other's counterparts: $^akalle\ bam\ ^ašallaḥ\ bam$. This opens the possibility for seeing arrows and teeth as a word pair around the centre. The creepy 'crawling things' of 39b, together with b^ehemot of 39a, being plurals, form a good successor to the 'evils' (ra^cot) in 37a.

---

[78] The large majority of cola in the Song contain 6-9 syllables. Very few (seven cola) contain 10-11 syllables, and there is only one colon with five syllables. Four is below par, and would occur in the A-colon if we structured l.38 differently.

[79] This for instance has been elaborately worked out through the name Bethlehem in I Sam.16 and 17 - see NAPS II pp.138, 152, 155. HAL distinguishes neatly between lḥm I and lḥm II, p. 500a.

[80] I do not follow the repunctuations by De Moor and Sanders (see for both Sanders, op cit. pp.193-198) who read the names of the demons, as transpires from Sanders' rendering: 'My Sucker (?) Hunger and my Warrior Rešep, and Qeṭeb, my Poisonous One'. These authors interpret the demons as the arrows God shoots in v.23.

[81] The Hiphil of *sph* is not attested, the Qal is itself transitive already, in the sense of 'to snatch away' (so that no Hiphil was needed for that meaning), and this meaning of the verb does not fit well here: God does not want to take away the disasters, but rather bring them.

The central verse of strophe 15 is a frightening enumeration. Strophe 16 has one, too. It consists solely of substantives, which two by two have been distributed over the half verses of l.41 and are linked by monosyllables (*gam .. gam .. ʿim ..*). There is only one verb in this strophe, at the beginning. Its subject is the sword as a metonym of the war. This concretum is assisted in the second half verse by another metonym, the abstractum terror, which makes the factors sword and terror into a word pair. One becomes an image of the other. In this way, they share their possibilities and intensify their impact. The predicate in l.40a does double duty, which is possible because both subjects are feminine.

The main formal principle of strophe 16 is the merism. In l.40 there is the pair outside .. inside. Its members seamlessly interlock – phonetically, this is suggested by the double *min + h-* – so that there is no escaping. The second verse also aims at completeness through merisms. The chain of victims comprises both sexes and all ages. The members of the merism in 41a cover society in a fifty-fifty division, to the binary accompaniment of a doubled *gam* and the sounds b..u-. The members in 41b, infant and greybeard, are the ends of a scale and comprise all ages in between without having to mention them. The final word[82] *śeba* is linked by means of rhyme and assonance to *ʾema* in l.40, and *baḥur* matches *ḥereb*. In short, no one is going to survive this war. The perfection of this announcement is realised down to micro level, because the figures for the syllables mirror each other and arrive at the same totals: 6 + 7 for l.40, 7 + 6 for l.41.

Stanza VII
A short review of stanza VII yields the following observations. There is a curious complementarity of subject and object in the short strophes surrounding the plagues. In strophe 14 the fire is given ample space with four predicates and the 'high' and 'low' domains, but there is not a single mortal to be found, nor anything to do with history. The unit is numinous in all respects and rather mythological in quality. In sharp contrast with this, strophe 16 presents as many people as possible through a double merism and encompasses them by means of the inside/outside. They are the grammatical objects, and from a pragmatic point of view the victims. The subjects are sword and terror. In this way, the strophe is undeniably that of the acts of war, but again no agent is indicated. The sword is shown as an independent factor, not as metonymy of its bearer. Thus, the war is presented as such, without anchoring it to a historical period or battlefield.

Strophes 14 and 16 have in common that in none of their colons God

---

[82] Usually, יונק is contrasted to זקן; the poet rejects this alliteration here and selects another root in favour of the rhyme between the two verses.

appears as agent or subject.[83] This form of avoidance, made the more conspicuous by the fact that the anger in strophe 14 is none other than God's and that the war in strophe 16 is expressly willed by him, itself is in radical opposition to the central strophe 15, where three verbal predicates refer to God and have the form of his first person. In this way, God after all becomes the central agent of the stanza.

Within the framework of God's speech, the mythological or at least cosmic strophe 14 also has a narrative character and is determined by four preterits. Yet, these verbs in the past tense cannot hide the fact that as soon as we have to do with the actual world of people down here, the stanza has the status of intentions proposed by the speaker, not deeds which he carries out or has carried out. The message of strophe 14 does not touch on people, they do not appear in the text of this unit. However, as soon as people come into view ('them'), starting from l.37a, there is no report but an announcement, a statement of plans. The images are terrible, but exactly how realistic are they? An answer to this question can only be given on the basis of a well-founded view of the next two stanzas (= section IIIB).

Section IIIA: review
The image of intentions, and of actions which are only being announced rather than reported, hardly changes when we survey the whole of section IIIA. In vv.19 and 21ab (= ll.30 and 33), God looks back on the recent past with sorrow and great frustration, and pronounces his judgement (l.32). In vv.20ab and 21cd (= ll.31 and 34) he decides on punitive action in the imminent future. The 'sons and daughters' of the first verse form a merism which co-operates with the merisms in the last two verses. Between these there are seven verbal I forms through which God announces his intervention.[84]

The prosodic picture for section IIIA is as follows:

VI)   L + S   VII)   S + L + S

       3+3   3+2   3+3   3+2   3+2
       4+3   3+3   3+3   4+2   2+3
       3+3   3+3

---

[83] This also holds for strophe 14, even though the fire comes from 'my nose'. The entire unit refers to that fire and specifically depicts it as an independently spreading force; this is why the four feminine verb forms are all dependent on the fire.
[84] The seven I-forms for God are the three from strophe 15, the two in l.34, and the two of l.31.

The two deviations from the norm of three ictuses per half verse in stanza VI compensate each other. In stanza VII the first strophe is completely regular. The second has the difference 4/2 in the middle which is related to the 2 + 1 twosomes of nouns. In the third strophe the balance is perfect, as 3+2 and 2+3 mirror each other.

When we next look purely at quantity by means of the fine measure of the syllable, we find that the two stanzas are much more regular than the metrical aspect can show. Section IIIa yields the following figures for its cola, verses and strophes:

stanza VI (two strophes)   stanza VII (three strophes)

str.12	*str.13*	*str.14*	*str.15*	*str.16*
7+8=15	8+8=16	8+8=16	8+6=14	6+7=13
10+6=16	9+7=16	7+9=16	9+5=14	7+6=13
7+6=13	__+	__+	9+8=17	__+
__+	32	32	__+	26
44			45	

It is remarkable that in almost every strophe there are two verses with the same number of syllables. In strophes 13-14 the totals in these pairs of verses are always the same, 16 per line. Only the third line of the two L-strophes dissociates itself from this strict regularity. It is also remarkable that these long strophes both have the same length, 44/45 syllables, adding up to 89. Between these two strophes there are two S-strophes which also have the same length, 32 syllables each. It should also be noted that the total for the three S-strophes is almost the same as that for the two L-strophes: 90 syllables. Thus, the twelve poetic lines together contain 89 + 90 = 179 syllables, which means an average of 15 syllables per verse.[85] With their three verses each, this average is exactly realised in the two L-strophes, 45 : 3 = 15.[86]

Section IIIB: stanzas VIII and IX, strophes 17-21

The text of strophes 17-19 looks as follows:

---

[85] The overall average for the Song: 1057 syllables in 69 verses = 15.3. If we leave aside the two tricola for a moment, we get a total of 1014 syllables for 87 bicola, and an average for the bicola of 15.134.

[86] This might explain the figures 13 and 17 which hold for the third lines (viz. ll.32 and 39) of the L-strophes 12 and 15. When we add them up they [prove to] contribute to the exact average: 13 + 17 = 30, which is exactly twice the average.

42 (MT v.26)	אמרתי אפאיהם	אשביתה מאנוש זכרם
43 (MT v.27)	לולי כעס אויב אגור	פן ינכרו צרימו
44	פן יאמרו ידינו רמה	ולא יהוה פעל כל זאת
45 (MT v.28)	כי גוי אבד עצות המה	ואין בהם תבונה
46 (MT v.29)	לו חכמו ישכילו זאת	יבינו לאחריתם
47 (MT v.30)	איכה ירדף אחד אלף	ושנים יניסו רבבה
48	אם לא כי צורם מכרם	ויהוה הסגירם
49 (MT v.31)	כי לא כצורנו צורם	ואיבינו פלילים

The very first word of vv.26-35 has far-reaching consequences. This אמרתי is a quotation formula by which the speaker God introduces himself. This means that what follows is a speech embedded in the speech of vv.20-25, which itself was embedded already. If we call this last speech soliloquy I, section IIIB should be soliloquy II. Neither has an addressee. The first monologue is a second-degree direct discourse, the second is of the third degree. In principle, it runs through to v.35, as out of the five strophes (numbers 17-21) the first two and the last two are definitely allocated to God as speaker. What happens in the central strophe is too complex to discuss at this stage.

The subject matter of section IIIB is an almost monotonous 'them'. In these 14 verses the nominal morpheme for this group occurs 14 times, the verbal morpheme 4 times.[87] God is now looking at the enemy, sees right through them, and draws his conclusions. The reverse side to all this 'them' is that Israel, which until very recently had been the target of disasters and war, hardly figures in the text anymore.[88]

It is not long before we hear the word which to God indicates a turning point: *kaʿas*! This is the second time this normative word is used in the form of a substantive, and just as in section IIIA it is positioned at the beginning, as a source of new torments and the considerations resulting from them. Together with the quotation formula this creates a parallelism at section level where the openings of IIIA and IIIB show a polar relationship. In IIIA God resolves to destroy Israel because of the *kaʿas* which it subjected him to, in IIIB he goes

---

[87] The suffix *-alem* or *-elamo* occurs 11 x, and the morpheme *-u* (the verb ending) is used four times in vv.27-29 (one might then also include the *-nu* in l.44a, but not the double *-nu* of l.49). The independent pronoun *hemma* is in l.45a, the form *-hem* in l.42a and 45b. A special position is occupied by the threefold *-am* in l.48: it refers to Israel, in the mouth of the enemy, so that we can either add it or not to our 18 cases.

[88] This should be said with two reservations: v.26 remembers the people for a moment, and in the central strophe 19 (= vv.30-31), which is exceptional in that it is fourth-degree discourse, the people are observed by the enemy and the author, respectively; more about this later.

back on that decision because he 'fears the *kaʿas* of the enemy'. God is plagued and annoyed by misunderstanding (*nkr) and the illusions which the enemy harbours about his initial victory over Israel.

This makes section IIIB into the passage in which an important and hazardous turn takes place, at the end of which God takes care of his inheritance. The perils of this phase and of the process of reflection are mirrored in the considerable variations between the arguments and the strophes, in the complexity of the levels of discourse, and in an astonishing play of reality and illusion (factual and counterfactual). The intricacies of this part of the text have proved too much for many commentators.

Strophes 17-19 (vv.26-31)
God's opening words in v.26 sound familiar because they are like l.31 (his first bicolon in section IIIA). This can be seen most clearly in the form *ʾašbita*, which through alliteration and full assonance is reminiscent of *ʾastira*. We will just have to conclude that God here repeats his intention to destroy Israel. This, however, will prove an illusion! In the opening line we cannot have a clue yet that already the poet is deliberately confusing us as regards reality and appearance.

Because of the elements aleph, pe and *-hem* the form *ʾafʾehem* seems to be a semi-acronym for God's first intention in section IIIA, *ʾastira panay mehem*, and the meaning of this obscure form will probably be just as unfavourable, in view of its context.[89] Verse 26 ends on *zikram*, 'the remembrance of them'. Much earlier the root *zkr* was used to open section II, and the connection between l.10a and l.42b which I make here is a first signal that we should ask ourselves whether sections II and III run parallel, and to what extent. The second signal is the fact that 'remember' in v.7 forms a word pair with *binu*, 'understand!' This same root is here also applied soundly, in strophe 18. And a third signal is the circumstance that the plural form *yomᵉru* occurs only here (in l.44a) and in l.11 (which means again: v.7). Their relation is polar: back in strophe 4 'telling' was desirable, its subject was the older generation, and the idea was that these elders would share their wisdom. Here, in strophe 17, the collective subject is the enemy, his 'saying' is undesirable – as indicated by the conjunction *pen* – and even feared by God, while its contents are foolishness, i.e. the illusion of their own power which is condemned by God. The polarity expressed by the repetition of 'lest/so that they say' can also be indicated as: historiography (about Israel's origin, by the elders) versus falsification of history (as regards the victory, by the enemy).

Before we cross the threshold of v.27a (= l.43a) we naively think we have

---

[89] The cohortative of l.42b helps us to read God's first imperfect as a similarly modal form. (This procedure, too, is the same as in l.31.) The etymology of *ʾafʾehem* is uncertain, but the context makes the rendering 'destroy' plausible. See also Sanders, op. cit., pp.202-203.

heard two cohortatives on God's part. The aspect of the opening verse, however, changes radically because of the conjunction *lule*, the notorious signal of the counterfactual. Suddenly we are forced to reconstruct the syntax of ll.42a-43a, resulting in: 'I might reduce them to naught, make their memory cease among men, if I would not fear the taunts of the foe, ...'.[90] What we have in l.42 are not two short, independent clauses any more, but the main clause (doubled by means of parallelism) of a compound sentence, which in l.43a is followed by a conditional clause whose counterfactual status in retrospect pulls in l.42. This is curious, as the two cohortatives suddenly belong to the counterfactual mode.

The 'fear' is followed by two dependent clauses governed by *pen*.[91] This conjunction indicates what God expressly does not want. He is now looking for a course of action which may prevent

> that their enemies judge amiss,
>   that they will say:
> 'our hand is triumphant,
>   and Y<small>HWH</small> has not wrought all this!'

Two-thirds of l.44 (the last seven words of strophe 17) consist of words on the part of the enemy which either are already being spoken (now, in the speaker's present, when Israel has already been defeated) or are about to be spoken, as an interpretation or evaluation by the enemy in which he is aware of his victory in battle. This again confronts us with an instance of embedding. In soliloquy II God quotes - maybe not even aloud - the enemies, which makes their words into a direct discourse of the fourth (!) degree.

Strophe 17 opened with one word in the second degree. Its body is a third-degree discourse and consists of slightly more than two verses in which two cohortatives and two *pen*-clauses are grouped around clause l.43a and the pivotal *lule*. The ending is in the fourth degree and contains two clauses spoken by the enemy.

The organisation of the strophe may be explained by means of a diagonal line of separation, in about the same way as in strophe 5. The division here is the difference between reality and (wrong) hypothesis. It is only too true that the enemy, the victim of complacency and misjudgement, will start to boast: the last three cola. This is why God decides to give his plans for destruction the status of a counterfactual: the first three cola. Obeying this dividing line in the middle there is a series of verbal forms in the first person for God in ll.42ab and

---

[90] This is partly the wording of the JPS. This translation even goes as far as employing a counterfactual of the past tense (might have reduced ... made cease ..); this might be pushing the cohortatives, already forced some way out of their direction, just a bit too far.

[91] Compare the use in Greek of the conjunction μη after φοβεομαι.

[92] The enemies a) are themselves a plural *ṣaremo* in 43b, b) twice receive an imperfect on *-u* in 43b + 44a, and c) have in their mouths a *-nu*, 44a.

43a, while there are plural forms for the enemies in ll.43b and 44.⁹²

The complacency and bragging of the enemy are curious things. What exactly is their reality content? When we do full justice to the language of strophe 17, essentially a gigantic period with its convolutions towards what God would want and what he even more strongly does not want, we have to say that the self-glorification is part of the extensive counterfactual. From a temporal point of view this means that God is just in time to prevent the boasting by reconsidering his position. From this same point of view it also means that God is predicting the self-exaltation, in which case the strophe takes on a proleptic aspect.

And yet this is not enough. The enemy's language is to God a real and substantial factor. The possibility that their bragging also takes place in reality (the present of the lyrical world evoked by the poem) deserves serious attention. And the decision that the self-glorification is not only part of the considerations in the hypothetical mode but is also at the same time an actual event, is facilitated for us by strophe 18. From that unit we may deduce unequivocally that the enemy 'have not understood their success' - a free rendering of l.46b. The exciting and surprising aspect about this verse, v.29 (= l.46), is that it has again been moulded in the language of... the counterfactual mode! We shall have to concern ourselves with the virtuoso dialectic of *lu* and *lule*.

Strophe 18 consists of two verses, the first of which is completely nominal and the second highly verbal, thanks to three forms with the enemy as subject. Semantically, the connection between the sentences is determined through the wise/foolish opposition, to such an extent even that the root *byn* appears as nominal in the first and as verbal in the second verse.

God now gives a diagnosis of the enemy. His nominal exposure of 'void of counsel and no understanding' is a strong reminder of the nominal diagnosis of Israel's foolishness in l.32. The parallel between strophe 18 and strophe 12 becomes definite and striking thanks to the repetition of the factor *ʾaḥᵃritam*, which there means 'their end' and here (the outcome of the battle =) 'their success'. The connection takes the shape of a chiasm-at-a-distance.⁹³ I underline the similarities, among which a word play between *bn* and *byn* and the balance *goy* // *dor*:

v.20	vv.28-29
I want to see their end:	ki goy ʾobad ʿe<u>s</u>ot hemma,
אחריתם	wᵉʾen ba<u>hem</u> tᵉ<u>buna</u>
ki dor tahpu<u>k</u>ot hemma,	אחריתם ya<u>binu</u>
<u>ban</u>im lo ʾem<u>un</u> bam	

---

⁹³ We have already seen another chiasm-at-a-distance: the cola of ll.7 and (again!) 32.

This type of parallel rhetoric saddles Israel, Moses' audience and the readers with the delicate question: what exactly is the difference between the chosen people and its enemies? So far they resemble each other painfully closely in stupidity!

The chiasm also offers positive suggestions: if you really want to be a child of God you will achieve understanding; if faith (*'emun*) is your principle you will not pervert matters (*hpk*), you will not forfeit good counsel and you will receive discernment (*t^{e}buna*).

At this stage of the analysis it is already clear that sections IIIA and IIIB are to a large degree attuned to each other thanks to the use of such key words as provocation, understanding and end. These large units of text form an antithetical parallelism: IIIA is contra Israel (and implicitly pro enemy), IIIB turns against the enemy (and is implicitly pro Israel).

The last verse of strophe 18 contains a deictic monosyllable, זאת, which in the shape of כל זאת rounded off the previous strophe. This is the demonstrative pronoun and it behaves modestly. From a rhetorical point of view, however, it is an understatement; it refers to an event which has been kept from us on purpose in section IIIA, and still is not described in plain terms here. It has to be - as we only gather from deduction, this time from strophe 19 - military combat from which the enemy has emerged the victor and Israel as the big loser. This *zo't* appears in the enemy's field of vision at the end of l.44 and brings him to a conclusion which denies the power of the true agent: 'it is not YHWH who has wrought all this!'

In strophe 18 the agent himself now also looks at this *zo't* and uses the linguistic mode of the counterfactual to state the reality of the enemy's stupidity. The verbal forms indicating the enemy multiply the long vowel of the crucial *lu* by four through their ending *-u*. 'If they were wise, they would investigate this / they would explain their success.' The enemy should have understanding, but they don't, and the fact of not-having-discernment has been shaped into the paradoxical form of the counterfactual mode.

The critical mass of strophe 17 was structured by the negative forms *lule - pen - pen - lo*. Strophe 18 follows and is completely negative, in l.45a via semantic means (see *'bd*), in 45b by means of a nominal negation, and in the whole of l.46 through the description of a virtual reality which has a priori been negated by *lu*.

Strophe 19 consists of three verses (ll.47-49, = vv.30-31), but is not a unit, as v.31 has a separate status as a kind of interjection. I first consider the quartet of cola in v.30. It has a regular structure of one verbal predicate per half verse. The Qal is used in both A-cola, the Hiphil in the B-cola. The unity of v.30 is elementary, since it is syntactic. The whole is a compound sentence - another one. The complex opens with a somewhat rhetorical question, 'how can one chase a thousand [men], and two put a myriad to flight', and then proceeds itself to answer the question in l.48, after the hinge of a cumbersome conjunction (*'im lo ki* ..), with the words: 'were it not that their Rock had sold them and YHWH had given them up'.

The question seems gnomic, if we take into account that this pattern of figures occurs elsewhere as well and that the figures themselves are hyperbolas with respect to the bloody reality of war.[94] Who is actually speaking here? Because of the third person for God in l.48 it is not an attractive option to consider the deity to be the speaker. Moses is out as well, as we cannot expect him to appear deep inside a third-degree argument, and he should have had an introduction of his own plus quotation formula. The only character which can function without an individual formula of introduction is the character immediately preceding. The fact that v.30 borders on v.29 indicates that the verses of pursuit and surrender are the words of the enemy.[95]

What to me is the decisive factor to indeed adopt this reading is a structural figure. If we allot this couple of verses to the enemy, we get a circular configuration of the stanza which gives full weight to the dialectic of factual and counterfactual. Around the nominal diagnosis of stupidity the words of the enemies now revolve in a *lule*-counterfactual (as part of the quartet 43ab + 44ab), and after the axis represented by v.28 in a *lu*-counterfactual which receives expression in the quartet 47ab + 48ab. In both cases their words are fourth-degree discourses.

The words of v.30 belong to the enemy and express the considerations they had or should have had.[96] Put differently: this compound sentence is the *content* of what v.29 called the correct 'understanding of their success'. In verse 30 the enemy spells out, upon further reflection (which does not actually take place), that 'the war is the Lord's' - to use David's words. Since this considera-

---

[94] The other passages grant the victory to Israel: Lev.26:8 and Josh.23:10; Is.30:17 puts the boot on the other foot again.

[95] The fact that the enemy does not receive an introductory formula here is no reason for alarm; in v.32, the return to God's discourse is not marked either, and neither is the momentary resumption by Moses in vv.36 and 43.

[96] Thus already Ehrlich, *Randglossen* II (Leipzig, 1909) p.344, and Eissfeldt, Das Lied Moses Deuteronomium 32 1-43 und das Lehrgedicht Asaphs Psalm 78 samt einer Analyse der Umgebung des Mose-Liedes, *in:* Berichte über die Verhandlungen der sächsischen Akademie der Wissenschaften zu Leipzig, Philologisch-historische Klasse, Band 104, Heft 5 (Berlin 1958). On p.12, Eissfeldt writes: "V. 30-31 führen Erwägungen vor, die Israels Feinde eigentlich anstellen müssten, aber zu ihrem eigenen Schaden nicht anstellen: Für Israels Niederlage gibt es gar keine andere Erklärung als die, dass Jahwe sein People dem Feinde preisgegeben hat." Thus also H.D. Preuss, *Deuteronomium* (Erträge der Forschung 164), Darmstadt 1982, p.168, and G. Braulik, *Deuteronomium II*, Die Neue Echter Bibel, Würzburg 1992, p.233.
As regards v.30 Eissfeldt is right, but not with respect to v.31. Patrick Skehan, who has marked off most strophes correctly, also seems to ascribe v.30 to the enemy: he puts it between quotation marks, CBQ 13 (1951) p.159.

tion is embedded in soliloquy II, God spells it out. And since God's speech is embedded in Moses' lecture, Moses spells it out for his audience, and since Moses is a character from the frame story, the narrator spells it out for his audience. A fourth-degree discourse is embedded deeply, but the advantage of this rhetorical type of Chinese boxes is that the speech functions at four levels, with a continually shifting claim to reality corresponding to the continually changing level of communication.

The ring of the double counterfactual around the diagnosis of stupidity is all the stronger because these two quotations from the enemy finally confirm that something terrible has happened in the meantime: Israel has actually and seriously been damaged by losses in battle. In l.44b the enemy denies that all this has been the work of YHWH (this is the nightmare God does not want), in l.48a on the contrary the enemy confirms (with imaginary understanding) that he was granted victory by the God of Israel. This polarity is also an indication that v.30 does contain the words of the enemy, just like l.44. At sound level, the illusion of *yadenu rama* receives a counterpart in *ṣuram mekaram .. hisgiram* in l.48a. For the Israel of the 'narrated' (and at the same time lyrical) world, that is the people in the text whom Moses addresses, it is ironical and embarrassing that the enemies give recognition to God and formulate his power in an exemplary fashion, but at the same time it is a relief that this understanding on the part of the enemy is imaginary and that God turns against them.

Verse 31 cannot have been spoken by God any more, and because it is some sort of commentary or explanation of v.30 and hence situated at this deep level of embedding, it cannot have been spoken by Moses either. The enemy, too, is out; here an Israelite voice speaks about the true Rock and 'our enemies'; these must be identical with the enemies in l.43.

The two statements in the verse, in nominal sentences, are dry and not very poetical. The shift which makes 'their Rock' in l.49a into another person than the one in 48a, is not very elegant. The verse impresses me as an interjection, intervention or interpolation. I ascribe it to the author, and therefore I will put it on yet another level: a zero-degree discourse, which is a kind of explanation in the margin. I read v.31b as a wish, 'let our enemies judge [for themselves]'.[97]

Stanza VIII
The glory of this group of three strophes, in their circular alternation long-short-long, results from the paradoxes created by the dialectic play of reality versus language in the counterfactual. Now that we have deduced from v.27d and v.30 that a disaster has indeed occurred which has greatly damaged Israel, we can conclude that the self-glorification of the enemy in strophe 17 is real - but

---

[97] Compare Sanders p.214, 'our enemies may be assessors', accompanied by an extensive discussion (pp.215-221) of the problematic פלל. A good alternative ('accountable') has been advocated by Adele Berlin, On the Meaning of *pll* in the Bible, Revue Biblique 96 (1989) pp.345-351.

it is clothed in the sustained counterfactual of a period. The paradox of the real disguised as the counterfactual is the same as in the sentence where God admits to being afraid of the enemy's taunts. That fear is real, just as the taunts have already become a fact, and the *lule* of l.43a cannot truly undermine this reality any more. The completely imaginary thus arises from the wish in v.26, which God abandons at the moment when he expresses it once more. I would like to wipe out Israel from the face of the earth, he thinks, but at the same time he knows he will have to drop this plan as there is something even more momentous, something he absolutely cannot bear.

In v.30, too - the main point of strophe 19 - fact is clothed in fiction. The enemies should realise that it is God who decides the outcome of the combat, but they do not. Their considerations are already negated in advance, as they have been introduced as non-existent by the framework of the counterfactual set up in l.46. However, while the considerations are negated by being non-existent, at the same time they exist and are totally true as well. The imaginary cannot obstruct truth. What is more, the mode of the imaginary, or the counterfactual, through the effect of the paradoxical adds the more impact to the proclamation of God's decisive power.

Because of the repetition of the quotation formula and of words with great capacity such as 'result' (אחרית) and 'provocation', stanza VIII has become the counterpart of stanza VI. Their relation is still partly complementary, in as far as the terms of Israel's defeat occur in both. The antithesis, however, is stronger, as God sees himself forced to change his attitude contra Israel radically and end his punitive policy. The people's depravity (in strophe 12 it is especially faithlessness, but stupidity is not altogether absent) is replaced by the wickedness of the enemy, mainly stupidity and self-aggrandisement, strophe 18. Both stanzas excel in studied avoidance: they carefully refrain from revealing any concrete place or time, or the name of any enemy or tribe of Israel, as though from the outset they were intended as a provocation of modern exegetes who at all costs want to be able to date texts scientifically.... And yet, it is this very avoidance which is essential to the aims and character of this didactic poem. In order to remain effective, the last thing this poem wants is to be locked within one specific horizon of origin.

The proud interjection of v.31 marks the end of the stanza. I conclude this paragraph with its metrical representation, and its measures in numbers of syllables.

st. VIII) L + S + L

2+3   4+3   3+3
3+3   4+2   3+2
4+4   3+2

This diagram creates the impression that the prosodic regularity of the stanza is much less than was the case in the previous stanzas. Because of that it is useful to add our quantitative measurements:

str.17	str.18	str.19
6+8=14	8+7=15	7+9=16
7+8=15	8+7=15	8+6=14
9+8=17	__+	8+8=16
__+	30	__+
46		46

The averages per colon and per verse show only minor deviations, so that we still have a fair regularity here.

The second and last stanza of section IIIB consists of two strophes of three verses dealing with venom and vengeance, still in relation to the enemy. I will first print the text.

Strophes 20 and 21 (vv.32-35)

ומשדמת עמרה	כי מגפן סדם גפנם	50	(MT v.32)
אשכלת מררת למו	ענבמו ענבי רוש	51	
וראש פתנים אכזר	חמת תנינם יינם	52	(MT v.33)
חתם באוצרתי	הלא הוא כמס עמדי	53	(MT v.34)
לעת תמוט רגלם	לי נקם ושלם	54	(MT v.35)
וחש עתדת למו	כי קרוב יום אידם	55	

Strophe 20 is the only one out of the total of 27 which really is completely nominal. Thus, the unit is incapable of expressing time. This timelessness lends the strophe an highly static character. The fact alone that not a single verb is to be found raises a formidable obstacle for the type of exegesis which holds that the strophe is a prophetic announcement of punishment to the enemy, maintains in the same breath that this punishment is the antecedent of *hu* at the beginning of strophe 21 (in l.53a), and then necessarily has to insist that the punishment (in its material form of the poison described in strophe 20) is what is stored in the treasuries of the Lord. As there is no verb in the strophe, there is no agent either, let alone a powerful or divine I; a new problem for the exegesis mentioned above. Its stock does not go up either because of the fact that the final strophe of the section, vv.34-35, is in essence also purely nominal.[98]

Before I develop more arguments against this interpretation, I will give a description of this strophe 20, = vv.32-33 (= ll.50-52). The subject matter consists exclusively, almost monotonously, of a comparison wine/poison. The grammatical subjects of he three A-cola are in order: 'their vine - their grapes - their wine'. This triad covers the whole of viticulture by naming its significant stages (plant > fruit > drink). The A-cola present their subjects, the B-cola follow obediently by only presenting variations. All this is underlined by a careful application of assonance and alliteration. The main phonetic chain runs as follows: -*dom* becomes -*dmot*, followed by -*mora*, -*emo*, *ro*- -*lot* m^e*rorot* -*lamo* -*mat*. In l.52 t and n are frequent. In l.50b/51b -*ot* for the fem. plural occurs three times.

An asseverative *ki* opens the strophe and marks its start. Next, the origin of the enemy's vine is pointed out. The reader might think for a moment that this is meant literally, as he now hears of Sodom and Gomorrah. These geographical names, however, indicate the spiritual origin rather than the literal, as they are themselves emblems of wickedness.

Then follow two verses (ll.51-52) which contrary to l.50 have no enjambments as each of their cola is an independent clause. The four cola of ll.51-52 make up a closely-knit quartet; they all deal with poison. There is a connecting diagonal thanks to the repetition of *roš*, which first immediately precedes the caesura and then comes immediately after it. On the intersecting diagonal we find the nouns of *mrr* and *ḥmt*. These two terms already occurred in strophe 15. The correspondence is as follows: the plagues and the poison which there had to be brought in by God in order to torment Israel, are by nature present in ample abundance in the enemy's territory, and symbolise his depravity. The message to Moses' audience is: whoever wants to refresh oneself with the enemy's drink - mainly spiritually, I would think - will fall victim to poison.

The careful construction of this sustained nominality is also reflected in the smoothness of the quantitative level. The verses have 7+7, 7+8 and 7+7 syllables. With one exception all cola have three stresses.

Could the 'he' introduced in strophe 21 (= *hu*, l.53a) refer to 'their wine', as some people think? I can well imagine barrels of wine being stored in God's treasuries. There are, however, more arguments against this connection than have been mentioned earlier. First, I find it hard to believe that God would store their wine. The hypothesis that this refers to wine (= poison) *for* them is linguistically possible (as an objective genitive), but practically far-fetched, among

---

[98] Essentially strophe 21 is also nominal, because a) the passive participles in l.53 are nominal predicates, b) as a parallel of the adjective *qarob* the participle *ḥaš* in l.55b is one too, and c) the only finite verb form of the strophe, *tamut* in l.54b, is between brackets in as far as it is only part of an attributive clause.

other reasons because strophe 20 provides a good description of wine-making. And secondly: because it is exactly this strophe which sets up the vine-grapes-wine chain, it is not desirable to separate the last element of the triad and declare only this the antecedent of *hu*. Or conversely: it is not necessary and not correct to just forget about the vine and the grapes for the purpose of making the connection 'wine-he'. It is natural to interpret 'their vine and their grapes' as elements from the enemy's landscape, i.e. as pars pro toto for their viticulture. If we leave the chain intact, we will be forced, in the interpretation which I criticise, to place not only the wine, but the complete scenery with vines and bunches of grapes in God's storerooms; which is a laboured, even nonsensical idea. Finally, I find that the concept of 'punishment' cannot be located anywhere in strophe 20.

What, then, is the meaning of the strophe of vine and wine? The poet forged the chain in order to then add the point that this type of viticulture yields venom. He says this in order to disqualify the enemy as such. In short: these vineyards and their poisonous produce are a metaphor for the enemy himself. Israel would do better to stick to 'the foaming wine' of Palestine, as that was given to them by God himself: strophes 8 and 9.

Strophe 21 is almost completely nominal, still, and God here concludes his argument about the enemy. Here he himself comes on stage again, as in contrast to the previous strophe this unit contains morphemes for him. For the first time after three strophes these are even first-person morphemes. There are no real actions here yet, but the avoidance of these indicates the lull before the storm.

The speaker God turns back into himself, to what is in store, to what lies ready in his treasuries. What may this be? The pronoun *hu* of l.53a refers to it, but what it means exactly can only be reliably determined when we view the strophe structure clearly. This is prescribed by a diagonal.

This strophe is the third instance of a diagonal traversing the heart of the unit, so that the six cola are arranged into two threesomes, independent of the fact that their prosodic face is one of three bicola.[99] The first triad is completely nominal, and its content is dominated by somebody who is indicated by the morpheme 'me/my' in every colon. Any other person is absent. The second triad is mainly nominal,[100] its contents the fate of 'them' who in every colon are indicated by the morpheme *-am*, and again no other person is present. Moreover, the second series is characterised by expressions of time in every colon.[101]

---

[99] The two other strophes containing the diagonal dividing three bicola into two threesomes were vv.8-9 (strophe 5) and vv.26-27 (strophe 17).

[100] About the verb in l.54b and the participle in l.55b see note 98.

[101] The temporal terms: in l.54b the word 'time' itself, in l.55a 'day' and in 55b 'the impending things' (thus the translation in BDB), 'destiny' (JPS).

The first verse shows the obvious balance of two passive Qal participles, *kamus // ḥatum*, while 'with me' in the A-colon is soon specified into 'in my treasuries'. In the meantime, the poet keeps us in suspense about the subject during one whole verse (who or what may *hu* be?), while at the same time he teases us by means of the combination *hᵃlo*, which usually presupposes an affirmative answer to what it introduces - the question following *hᵃlo* is almost always rhetorical. In l.54a the solution is finally given. Whereas the 'me' in the two cola of l.53 followed the *qatul* form, the order is reversed in 54a, so that *li* is in front and two nouns rhyming on *-m* follow. They form a couple (maybe even a hendiadys?) within one colon, balance the passive participles which also rhyme on *-m* and were spread over two cola, and afterwards slide into the subject slot: this is what God has up his sleeve, vengeance and retaliation! The pronoun *hu* was their proleptic representative.

The coupling of the adjectival clause 54b, which at the same time implies enjambment from the A-colon to the B-colon, indicates how closely the second triad is connected. The sounds *li -qam -lum* of the crucial pair 'vengeance and recompense' also prepare the way for the sequel, where we are presented with *lᵉ-, tam- , -lam* (54b) and in l.55 *ki qa- , -om, -am* and *lamo*. The weight of *naqam wᵉšillum*, however, exceeds their strophe. They are key words because they anticipate the foremost strophe of action against the enemy (vv.41cd-42, = strophe 26), where they appear both, and the final strophe, in whose centre **nqm* is subjected to a remarkable doubling. In this way, they mark a parallelism between the end of section III and that of section IV. The culmination of section III, the notion of retaliatory action, becomes an act and reality in section IV.

In the second threesome of cola of strophe 21 there is for the first time a sign of weakness on the part of the enemy. Their slipping feet, a metonym of defeat, provide a contrast to their 'high hand' of l.44a which was a metonym of victory. This opposition itself builds a beautiful inclusio delineating section IIIB. In the colon which follows, 55a, there is again a structural signal. The word *qarob* which here refers to the destruction of the enemy was also used at the end of section II and there revealed, in the strophe which pre-eminently dealt with Israel's apostasy, the unreliable new-fangled idols - the numina which the reader associates with the enemy. The 'close' of v.17 represents defectiveness and rot, the 'close at hand' of v.35 on the other hand betrays the inescapability of what has been decided.

The final verse (l.55) is both conclusion, because of its motivating *ki*-clauses, and anticipation: what lies ready here will explode in the heart of section IV. With the words 'the day of their calamity' it is at the same time the counterpart of the 'end' in strophe 12. At the beginning of section III God was curious to know how his people 'would fare' if they were shorn by his punishing hand. At the end of the same section the tables have been radically turned. God has decided against the continued destruction of his people, and now announces the ruin of their attackers. By the way, here, too, there is no explicit (or even prophetic) announcement of an action: there is no person who is subject of a transitive verb which as a predicate announces impending punishment. God coolly refers to what has long been decided and what, almost as a ready-to-use parcel, is waiting in the storeroom of his celestial palace. And in the same way as God saves something for the enemy, the poet saves the actual verses of punishment for his last section. The sentences of action, with God himself as I and subject, with his arrows drunk with blood and the enemy's scalp, have been reserved for strophes 23-26, God's last speech.

The proportions of stanza IX are much more regular than those of the previous one:

	strophe 20	*and 21*		*strophe 20*	*and 21*
syllables:	7+7 = 14	8+7 = 15	stresses:	3 + 2	3 + 2
	7+8 = 15	6+6 = 12		2 + 3	3 + 3
	7+7 = 14	6+7 = 13		3 + 3	3 + 3
	___+	___+			
	43	40			

Review of section IIIB = vv.26-35
God's reflections in this part of the text concern the enemy. He fears their self-glorification, diagnoses ignorance, probes how poisonous they are, and checks his own gun room to see what he has got ready for the enemy. At this point he does not yet betray how he plans to deal with them, and this reticence contrasts with the unsavoury details of IIIA which discussed Israel's punishment.

The text consists of five strophes. The middle strophe is a peak of complexity, with its unmarked fourth-degree discourse and its zero-degree interjection, and as part of an astonishing play of appearance and reality. Around this central unit (strophe 19) there are strophes 18 and 20 which both screen the enemy for their qualities: ignorance and poison. Around this ring, yet another ring is made by strophes 17 and 21.

These outside units of IIIB both deal with destruction: that of Israel is suddenly cancelled, that of the enemy looms on the horizon. The powerful first person, for God as subject, only occurs in this ring. In strophe 17 (the first person of) God is three times subject of a finite verb, while the enemy tries to eliminate him as a decision maker, through the proper name *yhwh* (l.44b).[102] In

---

[102] I put the quotation formula אמרתי between brackets here; we are concerned with the soliloquy containing 3x an imperfect 1st pers. sing. for God.

opposition to this triad there is a threefold 'them' which is in rhyming position and consistently refers to Israel.[103] The strophe which concludes the section also has a systematic structure of three versus three. The arrangement here, however, is linear, with 'me/my' as the only person in the first three cola, and 'them' as the only person in the second trio of cola. By now the 'they' are not the afflicted Israel any longer, but have become the enemies.

The concentric articulation of the five strophes is beautifully delineated through the contrast between the strong hand and the slipping foot. This opposition has the potential of a narrative path: the developments unfold themselves, and God cannot watch much longer how the enemy triumphs. In section IV he cannot resist intervening in favour of his heritage, which he does with his mighty... hand.

Review of section III as a whole
The section as a whole comprises two halves of two stanzas and five strophes each. Almost imperceptibly the length of the strophes has increased. In IIIA there still were three short strophes, in IIIB this number has shrunk to one. The subject of both halves and the radical turn in the centre of III (i.e. immediately after strophe 16) are clear: God's anger is directed first towards his renegade people, but he sees himself forced to stop that campaign and prepare himself for the attack on the enemy.

Both collectives have exasperated, irritated and provoked God; in one word, they have brought him considerable *kaʿas*, which not surprisingly is the normative word at the base of both IIIA and IIIB. The parallelism in the start of these text passages goes even further, past the well-known stations of 'end, outcome' and the nominal diagnosis of faithlessness, stupidity and poison. At the end, the sounds of *ʾedam* echo the rhymes on *ʾema* and *šeba* in strophe 16.

The correct demarcation of section III is supported by a parallelism with section II. Both start with 'your father' and 'his sons and daughters'; the root of the last word, **bn*, is a counterpart to **byn*, understand, which in strophe 4 is required of the young audience. There is also the keyword 'generation' at the beginning of II and III. Within III, the motif of 'understanding' is unfavourably elaborated in strophe 18.

The two sections end on categories of time. Moses ends on the negative note of the transience of the idols, in order to strengthen his attack on the apostasy, God ends on a negative note with his preview of the enemy's ruin. While Moses is devastated and concludes with a condemnation of the people who forgot their God, God in section III ends with what he keeps in store for the enemy; that will certainly not be lost. The forms *zkr* and 'they say' (recommended, by Moses) of strophe 4 (i.e. at the start of section II) are the counterparts of *zkrm*

---

[103] The enemy twice gets an imperfect plural on *-u*, and one *-nu* in the quotation.

and 'they say' (not desired, by God) at the beginning of section IIIB (strophe 17).

One last reflection about the contents. Its most striking aspect is a double-faced tactic of hiding and revealing:
1) in section IIIA, which after all provides us with unmistakable images of a horrific punishment of Israel, we are not given any confirmation that the people are actually struck; after the cosmic strophe 14 this unit only speaks in the mode of announcement and intentions. The poet refrains from returning the floor to Moses after God's soliloquy and does not wish to assure us through Moses that illness and war have indeed been raging.
2) The reverse side of this veiling belongs to the contents of section IIIB and means that from the data of stanza VIII the reader has to deduce for himself that Israel has indeed been struck. We have to conclude this from the ring around strophe 18 (God's analysis of ignorance on the enemy's part): the ring made up by two quotations from the enemy's speech. It is actually from the very two speeches in the deep embedding of fourth-degree discourse that the reader has to discover that Israel is indeed at the brink of ruin. Put in yet another way: it is only the enemy who furnishes us with that information! Not even the actual enemy at that, but a) the feared (of l.44) and b) the imagined (of ll.47-48 = v.30). It is not God who owns up to this, in second or third-degree direct discourse, nor is it Moses who is willing to assume his role of narrator one more time and convey the fatal information in the form of a report (a quasi-narrative stanza for instance) to his audience.

Thus, we can only speak of Israel's defeat from the moment when God started his turn towards forgiveness. The lyrical world of Deut.32 does not offer us a direct view of wounds, blood and victims among the chosen people. This forms a polar opposition to the expressive language in the heart of section IV where the enemy will be suffering heavily.

§ 4. *The fourth section: two stanzas, six strophes (vv.36-43)*

Short preview of section IV
This section consists of an envelope spoken by Moses (two short strophes, vv.36 and 43) and the body: four strophes containing God's second speech; this time, his discourse has a clear address, i.e. 'you', even though this is not revealed in the quotation formula.[104] The structural analysis shows that the six strophes have been grouped into two stanzas of three strophes each. Their order is S-L-S and S-L-S, which already suggests that the two threesomes have been closely attuned

---

[104] The address nevertheless becomes morphologically visible in the text, thanks to the two suffixes -*kem* in l.60 and the 2nd person plural of the imperative in l.61a; so, in two different strophes the audience is explicitly addressed.

to each other. The end of stanza X is marked by l.62 in its quality as a tricolon, a rare occurrence in the song as we have seen.[105]

The first half of section IV, the tenth stanza, parallels the start of section III through the return of a remarkable collocation. In the same way as the initial strophe 12 contained 'he said' (the quotation formula in its most familiar form, *wayyomer*) for God, with around this two examples of his 'seeing' (one report, one spoken by God himself), there appears in stanza X 'he shall say' for God, on the brink of the central L-strophe, with around this a new 'he sees' in l.57 and the exhortation 'see now!' of God to his people in l.61a. The three forms making up the chain, *yir'eh - we'amar - r^e'u*, are this time not concentrated in one strophe, but have been distributed evenly over the three strophes of stanza X.

The parallelism goes even further. The collocation at the beginning of section IIIA was succeeded by a form at the beginning of IIIB which puts the speaker God himself on the threshold, אמרתי of l.42a. The collocation of seeing and saying in the first half of section IV (i.e. stanza X) is succeeded at the start of the second half, in stanza XI, by the form ואמרתי which again is spoken by God himself, l.63a. The one perfect form, 'I said', introduces a third-degree direct discourse which is soliloquy II, the other perfect (consecutive), 'I shall say', introduces soliloquy III. This is also a third-degree speech, and one of special power: an oath by God which occupies the rest of the strophes 25-26 (nine cola!).

The ויאמר of v.37a as quotation formula marks in first instance the satire on the idols which fills the L-strophe 23, but goes even further, to the self-revelation in v.39 (= strophe 24). The ואמרתי of v.40b marks the oath and introduces the text in which God explicitly states his awesome power and unleashes it on the enemies. This quotation formula also covers two strophes. Out of the nine cola occupied by the oath and its elaboration, six are in L-strophe 26, and we shall see that this unit itself forms a striking counterpart of the polemics in strophe 23.

Stanza X = strophes 22-24 (vv.36-39)
The new strophe, v.36, is instantly determined by a change of voice and anaphora. Suddenly, God is again spoken *of*, so that we will have to ascribe this unit to Moses. The repetition of *ki* plus *yqtl* form characterises the lines. The word pair 'his people .. // his servants' returns in l.68, at the moment Moses has the floor for the last time, and is one of the most important elements which turn the strophe pair 22 + 27 into an inclusio.

How should we interpret the particle *ki* which opens ll.56-57? Could it be

---

[105] I remind the reader that the only other tricolon, l.23, also marked the ending of a stanza, at an extremely delicate moment (the transition from being spoiled to corruption).

the conjunction and have a temporal meaning? If we follow this option, the result is a very long, compound sentence which transcends the strophe boundary and only reaches the sentence core in l.58a: 'when YHWH vindicates his people ..., when he sees how powerless they are, he will say... [then follows strophe 23, jeers for the competitors].'

Passing the strophe boundary is no recommendation to begin with, but what really decided me against adopting this interpretation of *ki* is the fact that the information of strophe 22 in such a sentence has as it were been demoted to the status of secondary considerations because it has been relegated to a subclause. It is much too important for that. The statements of v.36 without doubt deserve full attention and so should have their own independent sentences, because their content is new. For the first time in about twelve strophes we read something favourable about the relation between God and his people. This is the result of the about-face in God himself. The favourable aspect itself is the reverse of God's verbal attacks on the enemy in section IIIB.

I read *ki* as an asseverative particle, which here underlines good news. The turn against the enemy is at the same time a turn towards the people, and this last about-face is here called vindication and compassion. The contrast with section IIIB is indicated by a parallelism. At the beginning of IIIB there was the hand of the enemy with his illusions, raised high; here we find the exact complement: the vanished hand (*yad*, l.57a, = power) of the humiliated Israel. The strophe prepares us for the fact that God will exert himself on behalf of his people; a three-fold 'my hand' in the central strophes 24-25 of section IV is the image and the metonymy of his all-encompassing power. A reading of *ki* as meaning 'truly' fits in with its function as anaphora.

Until recently the duo *'aṣur w^e'azub* has been a formidable crux.[106] Now at last a good solution to this puzzle is available. The words are probably a hendiadys, and mean 'ruler and helper'.[107] Thus, the B-colon states that Israel has lost its leaders, and that fact is the counterpart of the power that 'has gone' according to the A-colon. The couple עצור ועזוב balances the words 'people' and 'servants' of l.56. The complementarity of leaders and subjects is present, and we hear the well-sustained alliteration with the ayin.[108] And finally, there is a pho-

---

[106] The third volume of HAL, which appeared in 1983, offers no fewer than six proposals with respect to this duo, p.824a-b. Further see the next note.

[107] The welcome solution to the crux is provided in a long article in ZAW 101 (1989), pp.85-112, by Shemaryahu Talmon and Weston Fields: The Collocation משחית בקיר ועצור ועזוב and its Meaning. The authors derive the forms from *'ṣr* II and *'zb* II, and interpret the *qatul* pattern here in an active sense. Their translation 'ruler and helper' excellently fits the prophetic statements in Kings contra dynasties such as Achab's, and here as well, taking into account the parallelism with *yad* = power in l.57a.

[108] Note also the fact that five words start with the yodh (four of these of the pattern *yqtl*), and that *ki* occurs three times.

netic link with the conclusion of section IIIB, where the pair חתם/כמס occurred. On our way to the rest of stanza X I print the text of its three strophes:

	ועל עבדיו יתנחם	כי ידין יהוה עמו	56 (MT v.36)
	ואפס עצור ועזוב	כי יראה כי אזלת יד	57
	צור חסיו בו	ואמר אי אלהימו	58 (MT v.37)
	ישתו יין נסיכם	אשר חלב זבחימו יאכלו	59 (MT v.38)
	יהי עליכם סתרה	יקומו ויעזרכם	60
	ואין אלהים עמדי	ראו עתה כי אני אני הוא	61 (MT v.39)
ואין מידי מציל	מחצתי ואני ארפא	אני אמית ואחיה	62

Strophe 23 is easily recognisable as a unit because of its genre aspect. It is a satire about and against the idols. The polemic starts with a question about 'their gods' in l.58, then takes an excursion in l.59 by suspending a double attributive clause (marked by אשר) to an antecedent (which?), and with l.60 ends on a response to the question 'where?'. The speaker, God, seems to start off with a speech to himself, as he accords the people 'only' a third person (*their* gods) and keeps this up in l.59 (whose *z^{e}bahemo* rhymes with the *^{e}lohemo* immediately above it). His final verse lashes out at the gods with deadly sarcasm by defying them.

This challenge to the competition is the point of the strophe to such an extent that it is not only an answer to the question posed by the speaker himself, but also changes the direction of the address. God now directly speaks to his faithful, with a double *-kem*. The relation between l.58 and l.60 is not only based on the question-answer pattern, but also on their terms of space and protection. The notion 'where?' and that of 'refuge' (the verb *^{h}sy*) receive chiastic counterparts in the verb 'to help' and the noun *sitra* (lit.: hiding, but in the sense of protection, hide-out) which the sarcasm exposes as an illusion.[109]

The God who is called the true Rock, at three levels, now assigns the proud metaphor to the competition in his own words, but not because he cares one jot for their stability or existence. If we listen closely, we understand that with l.58a he primarily wants to cover the point of view of the naive and faithless members of his people. In the pivotal line, they are characterised as those who take food and drink, in the form of sacrifices and libations, to the idols. This cannot possibly have any favourable connotations any more, after the stuffing and gorging which Moses reported in section II. We might even interpret this feasting as the offshoot or point of the revelry in strophes 8-10. The people, who

---

[109] The two u-sounds of l.58b are answered by the three u-sounds of l.60a: *yaqumu w^{e}ya^{c}z^{e}rukem*.

received such bounty from their own God, have become corrupt because of this spoiling, started to follow other gods and now in turn stuff these idols inside the framework of the cult. The image of the despised rites is now introduced by God in his mockery. The link with section II is made, among other things, through חלל, the root which there occurred three times in one strophe, during the climax of the spoiling (the enumeration of strophe 9).

Who actually is the antecedent of the double ᵃšer-clause of v.38ab? Is it the gods who eat and drink, or the mortals who make sacrifices to them? This ambiguity can hardly be solved, as from a purely grammatical point of view it can be both the idols and their misguided Israelite worshippers. The relative pronoun can link up with 'their gods .. the rock' (option 1). The construction then becomes as follows: first we have the interrogative main clause, short and nominal, next three relative clauses with a change of subject after the first:

'where are their gods, [where is] the rock
   1) where they take refuge
   2) [the gods] who eat the fat of their sacrifices
   3) and who drink the wine of their libations?'

In this interpretation we see the gods feast. The possessive suffix may refer to the people who are bringing sacrifices, but it may just as well refer to the gods as those who acquire the food and enjoy their due. The alternative means that the digression of l.59 provides more detailed information on the people who worship the idols:

'where are their gods,
[where is] the rock where they take refuge,
[they] who eat the fat of the sacrifices for them [= the gods]
and drink the wine of the libations [which are their due]?'

Here it is the people who throughout the series of relative clauses remain the subject and hence eat and drink, and the suffix 'them' has become an objective genitive. This interpretation is not impossible, but runs less smoothly, and focuses a bit too much on the people in a strophe which aims at false gods. For this reason I still prefer the first reading. The wine which now forms part of the false cult might well be just as poisonous as the wine discussed in strophe 20...

Strophe 24
This unit is unique: it is the self-revelation of God which is finally granted to the audience, and is almost hymnic in its celebration of the uncontainable power of God through, among other things, two merisms strongly reminiscent of the compact centre of the Song of Hannah. This is the theological point of

gravity of the composition. For the first time, God here addresses the people directly, and although it is not the very first time the pronoun 'I' occurs in the text, the ʾ*ani* of strophe 24 receives a unique emphasis. It is the first and only word which is immediately and asyndetically doubled; it is reinforced in the remarkable statement 'I am he', which might also have been said by Deutero-Isaiah, and which means something like 'I am the tops', I am the True One.[110] The first person here is the dialogic counterpart of the 'you' of the address.

The reverse side of 'It is me [i.e., your true refuge and the true Rock]' with its double אני is a double negation which occupies cola 61b and 62c. Each element of these nominal sentences has its counterpart, which results in maximum parallelism:

w*ᵉ*ʾen   ʾ*e*lohim   ʿimmadi

w*ᵉ*ʾen   miyyadi   maṣṣil

Conjunction and negation lead the way. The form אין alliterates with the pronoun אני.[111] Next, a chiasm follows, with on one diagonal the evident assonance ending on 'me/my', and on the other the coinciding of saviour and deity. When we now merge the head and tail of the nominal predicating in strophe 24, the conclusion must be that the true God is incomparable as he is the only powerful one. The comprehensiveness of his power is demonstrated through the merisms life/death and wounding/healing of l.62ab. To their verbal predicates the form אני has twice been added, in a quasi-redundant fashion. Hence, the pronoun once more occurs twice in l.62 which is no coincidence.

What God shows us by means of 'see now!' is the reverse of what was reported in strophe 22. There, God saw the futility of his people, now they are allowed to witness His power. There is also a strong link with strophe 23, to such an extent that I consider strophes 23 and 24 an antithetical pair. The one unit argues the weakness of the gods, through the detour of scorn and challenge, the other unit posits the power of the real God with maximum directness.

We now have an image of stanza X as a whole. Each of its three strophic parts represents a new phase in the development of an argument. Moses brings up the total impotence of the people (strophe 22); God continues by deriding the a pri-

---

[110] Just like the poet of Jud.5, Deutero-Isaiah is also fond of instant duplication, as his opening נחמו נחמו in 40:1 immediately shows. Compare for the double אני Is.48:15 (and 43:11, 25 and 51:12 which has the long form אנכי repeated), and for the predicative combination of הוא and אני Is.43:10, 13 and 48:12. The same poet uses the sentence 'and there is none other' passim as the reverse of the self-revelation.

[111] This S-strophe contains eight words in all which use the aleph-in-first-position in reference to God and/as the first person; I do not count the nominal negation (*bis*) here, but it does play its part.

ori unreliable help or power of the gods (strophe 23), which is a good leg-up to strophe 24, where God confidently, overwhelmingly and very directly expresses his unstoppable power to the people themselves. Now there is hope that God will extend his strong hand (l.62c) in support to the now powerless hand (l.57a) of his people. All this comes nicely together in a symmetry of 2 + 3 + 2 verses which is exactly copied by the next and last stanza.

The metrical proportions are regular:

stanza X	S	+	L	+	S⁺
	3+3		3+3		4+3
	3+3		3+3		3+3+3
			2+3		

The lengths of the cola only show a regular pattern in strophe 22; they amount to a figure which we will find again in strophe 27, 2 x 15 = 30. Remarkable in the other two strophes are the facts that there are two cola of 10 syllables, that l.59a is rather noticeable with its ten syllables, and that the S-strophe 24 because of the addition of the C-colon almost reaches the length of the central L-strophe. All three strophes end on an 8 + 7 combination.

str.22	str.23	str.24
7+8=15	8+5=13	10+8=18
8+7=15	10+6=16	8+8+7=23
__+	8+7=15	__+
30	__+	41
	44	

Stanza XI: strophes 25-27 (vv.40-43).
These three strophic units also contain 2 + 3 + 2 verses. Their contents and structure prove that this is no coincidence. There is an obvious link between strophe 27, as verses by Moses, and strophe 22, and in the middle of the L-strophe there is a verse which will prove to be the virtuoso complement of v.38ab. However, let us have the text first:

ואמרתי חי אנכי לעלם כי אשא אל שמים ידי	63	(MT v.40)
ותאחז במשפט ידי אם שנותי ברק חרבי	64	(MT v.41)

ולמשנאי אשלם	אשיב נקם לצרי	65	
וחרבי תאכל בשר	אשכיר חצי מדם	66	(MT v.42)
מראש פרעות אויב	מדם חלל ושביה	67	
כי דם עבדיו יקום	הרנינו גוים עמו	68	(MT v.43)
וכפר אדמתו עמו	ונקם ישיב לצריו	69	

Strophe 25.
The last stanza is closely linked to what went before by means of strophe 25. Strophe 24 ended, by way of negation and *ʿimmadi,* in a negative colon about 'my hand' *(miyyadi),* and is now answered by a strophic unit with two positive cola about 'my hand', l.63a and 64b. These sentences function as an inclusio and so should mark the strophe. They couple the hand with two elements which make the positive turn even clearer: heaven and judgement. So, God starts at his own dwelling and points to the justice he will bring to the earth. The poet beats the abstract noun into a fully operative factor by presenting it as something the deity can literally grip. In this way, the law almost becomes the sceptre he wields.[112]

The second element linking this strophe to the previous one is the word *ḥay*. Before, God was the Lord of life and death, now he emphasises the fact that he himself lives for ever. He states this in v.40 in the most binding linguistic formula available: an oath. Raising his hand to heaven is the required gesture which must accompany this.

The form ואמרתי, a perfect consecutive which as a continuation of אשא and its asseverative *ki* is a solemn assurance, constitutes the last quotation formula of the Song. From l.58 through to l.63a God's words were a second-degree direct discourse. From l.63b through to l.67 (i.e. in vv.40b-42) God speaks in the third degree. Although no address is mentioned, I hesitate to call this speech a monologue. At this point in the argument, God's long series of future tenses in strophes 25-26 functions as a promise of liberation to his people, and with the gesture of the oath God addresses, as it were, the open space. In the spirit of verse 1: the heavens should also hear this binding statement, because God will not go back on this speech, which does not address the enemy and yet is a declaration of war in their direction.

God first says: 'I live for ever.' With this 'I' , this time even in the long form אנכי which is unique in the poem, the speaker also makes a close link with his self-revelation. As the strophe containing the oath, and as a statement about

---

[112] The verb אחז, 'to grip, to hold', here governs its object through the preposition *bᵉ*, and the hand is the subject. In this way the words surrounding 'judgement' transform that word into a concretum.

'my' exuberant life, this unit simply belongs on the same level as the previous one. We count no less than seven times the ending -*i* governed by the first person.[113] Yet, something strange is going on. God starts, but is this the exordium? His words in l.63b are very similar to the usual introductory formula by which an oath is introduced, but they are different.[114] What follows is also a deviation, as it does not start with the oath particle כי or even אם.[115] First, there is a period which occupies no fewer than four cola and even ignores the strophe boundary (ll.64-65), then another quartet of cola as a smooth continuation in ll.66-67, and this entire sequence is governed by imperfect forms through which God announces the battle. This is why I am not sure at all whether here we can still speak of the introductory formula plus - clearly separated - the contents of the oath. Maybe the words 'I live for ever' are themselves the contents of the oath which God swears in the presence of the cosmos, and the rest is a concrete elaboration of this. There, God will prove the validity and power of his existence ('life') by presenting himself as the actual Lord of life and death, which for strophes 25-26 means: sowing death and destruction by waging an actual war against the enemy.

Be this as it may, the significance of strophes 25-26 is the fact that in one specific respect they are the climax of the poem: they are the last long speech (strophe 27 is 'only' a coda), they are a speech by God, and their meaning is: action! God is now really going to make a move, and a dangerous one at that, which he prepares explicitly and in two ways by a) granting his people the strophe of self-revelation and pronouncing this by way of introduction, and b) pronouncing the strophe of the oath.

Strophe 25 is itself a quartet of cola, with on the one diagonal the repeated 'my hand', and on the other one two perfect forms in the first person, that is, forms rhyming on -*ti*. There is a hidden word pair which we notice when we see 'lightning' - the metaphor governing 'my sword' - directly below 'heaven'. The connection illustrates the fact that God, who lives on high, not only makes heaven into a witness of his oath, but also engages in battle from heaven, with a heavenly attribute. The word חרבי rhymes with ידי and is semantically connected with it, among other things via metonymy. Because of these kinds of cross-links l.64 belongs to l.63. The verse at the same time concludes its strophic unit, in spite of the fact that it provides clauses dependent on the main clause of l.65 (in the next strophe!). By the way, this implies a drastic form of enjambment: a link across the strophe boundary.

---

[113] I put it like that, because the -*i* once is part of the afformative of the perfect, occurs once in the asseverative *ki*, and the remaining five times is always the suffix.

[114] The preamble to an oath is of course either *ḥay ʾᵃni*, or *ḥe nafši*, or *ḥay (ʾᵃdonay) yhwh*. See Waltke & O'Connor, Biblical Hebrew Syntax, § 40.2.2, or Joüon-Muraoka § 165.

[115] Note: the אם which opens v.41a (= l.64a) is a temporal conjunction, not the 'if' belonging to a formula of self-imprecation ('May God punish me, if I do this or that').

Strophe 26 (vv.41cd and 42).
Is the strophe boundary really situated between l.64 and 65, so that we deviate here from the Masoretic verse division? We consider the structure of this strophe.

Lines 65 and 66 open almost anaphorically, with the Hiphil forms *ʾašib* and *ʾaškir* in front. In their B-cola the verb moves to second position. The predicates in ll.65-66 are regularly distributed over the four cola. These are all imperfect forms for the speaker, taking into account that in the last form of the chain, in l.66b, he has a metonymic representative: again the sword. The final verse (l.67) picks up *middam* from the middle, treats its preposition as anaphora and provides a concrete and bloody image of the war by consisting exclusively of nominal complements. Lines 66-67 show a maximum parallelismus membrorum, as the words of each colon (always three) have their counterparts in the adjacent colon. The preposition *min* is always partitive and works against the enemy.

The central verse functions metonymically in two directions. God is here represented by his weapons (which alliterate, *ḥiṣṣay* and *ḥarbi*), and through synecdoche the enemy is reduced to flesh and blood. The surrounding verses, however, abound in terms for the enemy himself, so that they form a ring. The enumerative scene in l.67 is the nominal illustration of l.65 with its transitive verbs and dénouement of reprisals. We here recognise 'vengeance' and 'retaliation' as the words which occupied the strategic position at the end of section III, in strophe 21 (and v.35). The hell which there was ready to receive the enemy has now materialised. As a rendering of vengeance the strophe has a sensual quality which it derives from various phonetic patterns. A resh occurs five times, and there are ten labials (each consonant from *baśar* returns in 67b). L. 67b contains 3 times -o-, and the het creates the harsh series arrows - sword - pierced via alliteration.

In the central verse (l.66) God makes his arrows drunk with the blood of the enemy. The drinking implied in this image forms a word pair with the eating on the part of the sword in the B-colon. This pair, however, we have also met in the previous stanza. The pivotal line of strophe 23, which is at the same time the axis of stanza X, mentioned eating and drinking. We discover that the pivotal line of strophe 26, which at the same time is the axis of stanza XI, constitutes the chiastic continuation of that line.[116] The connection is extremely meaningful and based on opposition. In strophe 23, the powerless idols ate and drank the food and wine presented to them by the misguided Israelites; here, the weapons of the real God eat and drink (the flesh and blood of) the enemy who denied the power of this deity. Seeking refuge under the wrong rock (*ṣur*, l.58)

---

[116] This observation of pivotal lines is a strong argument in favour of the decision to take the gods (rather than the people) as the subject of l.59.

is now opposed to God's vengeance on the enemy (*ṣaray*, l.65), and the semblance of protection (*sitra*, l.60) is now contrasted with the grim fate of the enemy, *šibya* (l.67).

The last unit, strophe 27, returns straight to the first-degree discourse, because this is where Moses speaks his coda. Its structure is extremely tight. The quartet of cola is a composition following the AB-B'A' pattern, as there are four sentences held together by diagonals. Each sentence occupies a colon and contains a verbal predicate. The repetition of 'his people' in final position (of ll.68a and 69b) occurs on one diagonal. The other diagonal not only contains the rhyming antithesis *ᶜabadaw* versus *ṣaraw*, but exists primarily thanks to a special application of contiguity[117]: the first verse ends on the verb with which the second verse starts, *yiqqom - wᵉnaqam*. This repetition of the root is very meaningful, as it demonstrates that this one action of God's is double-edged: pro Israel, contra the enemy. One belongs to the other. Revenging oneself on the enemy is revenging the blood of one's servants. This has its consequences for the other crosswise axis: with this war, God brings reconciliation to the land, and in this way Moses can now gather the peoples - whose number and territory had been determined 'according to the number of the Israelites'! - and exhort them to cheer. A word play encompassing the entire poem reveals to us that its sound reaches from high to low: their *harninu* evokes of its own accord a *haʾzinu* by the heavens and the listening of the earth. A nice balance of the oral and the auditory in exordium and coda frames the composition.

The tight structure of the strophe makes tinkering with and fashionable 'improvements' of the text on the basis of LXX and Qumran fragments unnecessary and undesirable. This is brought home to us even more forcibly when hobbyists want to read 'his sons' in l.68b, instead of 'his servants'.[118] This spoils the firm inclusio which links strophe 27 to the other couple of verses by Moses, strophe 22. Not only does the word pair people/servants from v.36 return at the end, but there is also a synonymy-plus-word play at a distance. God's *nḥm* in favour of his servants, which Moses announced in v.36 on the threshold of section IV, materialises at the last minute in a concrete and bloody way as *nqm*.[119] Line 69a is clearly the complement of the colon which opened the previous strophe (l.65a). The blood (*dam*) rhymes with *ᶜam* and prepares the way for *naqam*.

---

[117] This device for contiguity also occurs in Isaiah 45:1, the second verse of which ends on אפתח with the next verse starting with לפני.

[118] Contra Skehan (BASOR 136, 1954), Eissfeldt (1958), Wright (Festschrift Muilenburg, 1962), Sanders (1996) and others.

[119] The same word play נקם - נחם (this time not 'at a distance', but) within one verse is for instance also found in Is.1:24cd. What the words have semantically in common is the notion of satisfaction.

Stanza XI and section IV.
This stanza, too, makes three steps. The first one is covered by strophe 25, which is characterised by the seriousness of the oath and the drawing of the sword as the instrument of justice. The second step is strophe 26, which is completely devoted to the war and exclusively directed against the enemy. This makes the unit into the fulfilment of what was in store in strophe 21, and into a compensation to the strophe about war against Israel (strophe 16). In the third step the sense of all the bloodshed becomes clear, when Moses reverses the concept of *nqm* like a sheet of paper and shows that in this way, country and people are revenged and granted atonement. This strophe primarily speaks in favour of God's inheritance.

This stanza mainly leaves the floor to God himself and shows him to be the character who, after a lot of pain and much deliberation, is ready to make the final choice. The double edge to this - pro Israel, contra enemy - is that of dispensing justice. The one party gets a yes, the other a no.

The proportions of stanza XI require little comment. Metrically strophes 26-27 are very regular, while v.40 has a remarkable B-colon. Its four stresses may be matched with the two of l.65b. Thus these two figures only serve to underline the norm of three stresses per colon. The syllables show a largely similar picture.

	stresses			syllables		
	S	+ L +	S	*str.25*	*str.26*	*str.27*
stanza XI)						
	3+4	3+2	3+3	8+11=19	7+8=15	7+7=14
	3+3	3+3	3+3	8+ 8=16	6+7=13	8+8=16
		3+3		__+	7+6=13	__+
				35	__+	30
					41	

'Improving' verse 43 to form a unit of six cola is an intervention which negates the striking symmetries of the section. The purely quantitative balance of the three plus three strophes, S-L-S plus S-L-S, or in other words 2+3+2 and another 2+3+2 poetic lines, becomes eloquent thanks to the much more important links between the two stanzas as created by style and content. There is a tight ABC-C'B'A' pattern. The outside ring already manifests itself by belonging to Moses; as first-degree discourse it is set off from its surroundings. There is also, however, the obvious repetition of 'his people .. his servants'. Inside this, the two L-strophes form a ring by deriding the gods and celebrating God as a warrior, respectively, the most striking detail being the correspondence between their pivotal lines, about eating and drinking as a false cult versus the drinking and eating to be done by the weapons of the Lord. The main relation between strophes 23 and 26 might well be that of futility and power, in about the same way as between strophes 22 and 24. In the heart of section IV there is the ring C-C' in which God uses the strongest terms of commitment: self-revelation and swearing an oath. At word level there are the repetitions of 'I' and 'my hand'.

The ring structure finds a striking confirmation in the number of syllables in Moses' few strophes. They have exactly the same total: thirty syllables. The one strophe has a 7+8 and 8+7 balance, the other strophe divides these figures horizontally, as 7+7 and 8+8. The totals for strophes 24 and 26 do not fit into the ABC-C'B'A' pattern, but are also identical (41 syllables). This has become possible by the surplus colon in l.62 (the ending of v.39).

Chapter 4

The Song of Moses in Deut.32 as a whole

§ 1.   *The argumentative structure at three levels.*

In this paragraph I will raise the question how the articulation of the whole contributes to structure and argument of the poem. The first level which deserves attention as a factor in the argumentative structure is that of the strophes. I will start with a short review.

The description of the poem has been completed in Chapter 3, so that we have a fair idea of the Song as a whole, and the question of what exactly constitutes the unity and cohesion of every strophe will hopefully be a productive one. Are the determining factors matters of form or of content? Intrinsic or extrinsic structures? Boundaries or cores? Because of the extent of the study in the previous chapter I can now limit myself to the main issues when addressing these questions; I will mention only two or at most three factors or aspects per strophe.

In sections I and II Moses speaks eleven strophes. Strophe 1 is characterised by its character of introduction and opening, and by the interweaving of two quartets of terms. Strophes 2 and 3 manifest themselves by respectively being favourable towards God in hymnic language, which is mainly nominal, and by referring pejoratively to 'you', the people, in the manner of an accusation.

Strophe 4 is another opening, taking into account the imperatives, and belongs to the genre of an admonitory exhortation. After this, a narrative sequence starts. In strophe 5 it is the content which is unusual - the map of the world containing all peoples versus the one people of YHWH - and its exact delineation through inclusio. The short strophe 6 pictures a barren landscape and presents the initiative of the deity in four *yqtl* forms. The short strophe 7 is dominated by the bird-metaphor and five *yqtl* forms. In strophe 8 (just as in 5), the powerful God receives three Hiphil forms; he leads the people to the promised land. Strophe 9, being a massive enumeration of goodies, has an extremely nominal character, and the first C-colon juts out. Strophe 10 is very unfavourable towards Jeshurun by means of nine disapproving verbs; the point here: being fattened is being corrupt. Finally, strophe 11 is distinctive through its subject matter: idolatry as the obverse to forsaking the true God.

In the third section, with its two halves, God is the speaker; we follow his tormented deliberations and inner reversal. It falls to strophe 12 to prepare for this. God turns away from his people, because of the *kaʿas* (provocation, torment) done to him. The symmetrical form of strophe 13 has been inspired by, and shows the balance of, the concept of *talio*. Strophe 14 is characterised by its content: fire throughout the cosmos. A concentric structure keeps together strophe 15 as a unit of plagues. The stylistic device of the merism determines 16 as a strophe of war.

Strophe 17 signifies a dramatic turnaround in God himself. His speech (containing a counterfactual) and the words of the enemy and their illusions (a factual!) demarcate the unit; again, *kaʿas* is the starting point of a development. Strophe 18 has a nominal/verbal balance and turns on having/not having understanding. Strophe 19 presents the true understanding in the counterfactual; the image of Israel's defeat is drawn in fourth-degree direct discourse. Strophe 20 is completely nominal, and its subject matter is so rich in synonyms as to be almost monotonous: wine is poison. In strophe 21 'my' returns for God. The subject here is that the enemy's downfall has already been decided, and (just as in strophe 5) the structure is diagonal: three cola in favour of God, three contra 'them'.

The last section is marked by two short strophes by Moses which form a frame. In strophe 22 we see an anaphora, and the subject is God's taking pity on his weakened people. The other half of the frame, strophe 27, exhorts to jubilation about God's vengeance, which is double-edged: for his people, against the enemy.

Within this frame, God speaks four more strophes. Unit 23 is striking because of its genre and subject: it is a satire directed against the weakness of the idols. Strophe 24 directly addresses the audience, is of the genre of self-revelation, and is replete with *ᵃni* and power. Strophe 25 presents an oath, which via enjambment moves to God's last strophe, 26, dominated by terms for the enemy and his defeat; God explains his actions as a warrior.

This survey of strophe structure shows that these units have taken shape in highly divergent ways and by means of very different devices. Often, the subject matter makes it possible to quickly pin down a unit (#2, 3, 5, 9, 11, 14, 18, 20, 23, 26). A number of times it is the aspect of genre (#1, 4, 10, 23-25, 27). Striking stylistic and structural devices such as inclusion, the use of key words, foregrounding of a morphological category (for instance the Hiphil), the variation nominal/verbal or symmetrical patterns occur regularly: # 4, 5, 7, 8-10, 15, 16, 20. Three times, we have seen a diagonal structure in a long strophe: units 5, 17 and 21.

Before I continue my argument I here give the complete Hebrew text, on two facing pages, to provide the reader with a comprehensive view of the poem.

The numbers in brackets on the far right indicate the strophes, the numbers one column to the left of these indicate the Masoretic verses, and the numbers in italics denote the poetic lines (i.e. the verses in a literary sense). The Roman numerals on the left-hand side indicate the stanzas.

VII	ותיקד עד שאול תחתית	כי אש קדחה באפי	35	22	(14)
	ותלהט מוסדי הרים	ותאכל ארץ ויבלה	36		
	חצי אכלה בם	אספה עלימו רעות	37	23	(15)
	וקטב מרירי	מזי רעב ולחמי רשף	38	24	
	עם חמת זחלי עפר	ושן בהמות אשלח בם	39		
	ומחדרים אימה	מחוץ תשכל חרב	40	25	(16)
	יונק עם איש שיבה	גם בחור גם בתולה	41		
VIII	אשביתה מאנוש זכרם	אמרתי אפאיהם	42	26	(17)
	פן ינכרו צרימו	לולי כעס אויב אגור	43	27	
	ולא יהוה פעל כל זאת	פן יאמרו ידינו	44		
	ואין בהם תבונה	כי גוי אבד עצות המה	45	28	(18)
	יבינו לאחריתם	לו חכמו ישכילו זאת	46	29	
	ושנים יניסו רבבה	איכה ירדף אחד אלף	47	30	(19)
	ויהוה הסגירם	אם לא כי צורם מכרם	48		
	ואיבינו פלילים	כי לא כצורנו צורם	49	31	
IX	ומשדמת עמרה	כי מגפן סדם גפנם	50	32	(20)
	אשכלת מררת למו	ענבמו ענבי רוש	51		
	וראש פתנים אכזר	חמת תנינם יינם	52	33	
	חתם באוצרתי	הלא הוא כמס עמדי	53	34	(21)
	לעת תמוט רגלם	לי נקם ושלם	54	35	
	וחש עתדת למו	כי קרוב יום אידם	55		
X	ועל עבדיו יתנחם	כי ידין יהוה עמו	56	36	(22)
	ואפס עצור ועזוב	כי יראה כי אזלת יד	57		
	צור חסיו בו	ואמר אי אלהימו	58	37	(23)
	ישתו יין נסיכם	אשר חלב זבחימו יאכלו	59	38	
	יהי עליכם סתרה	יקומו ויעזרכם	60		
	ואין אלהים עמדי	ראו עתה כי אני אני הוא	61	39	(24)
	מחצתי ואני ארפא ואין מידי מציל	אני אמית ואחיה	62		
XI	ואמרתי חי אנכי לעלם	כי אשא אל שמים ידי	63	40	(25)
	ותאחז במשפט ידי	אם שנותי ברק חרבי	64	41	
	ולמשנאי אשלם	אשיב נקם לצרי	65		(26)
	וחרבי תאכל בשר	אשכיר חצי מדם	66	42	
	מראש פרעות אויב	מדם חלל ושביה	67		
	כי דם עבדיו יקום	הרנינו גוים עמו	68	43	(27)
	וכפר אדמתו עמו	ונקם ישיב לצריו	69		

I	ותשמע הארץ אמרי פי	האזינו השמים ואדברה	1	1	(1)
	תזל כטל אמרתי	יערף כמטר לקחי	2	2	
	וכרביבים עלי עשב	כשעירים עלי דשא	3		
	הבו גדל לאלהינו	כי שם יהוה אקרא	4	3	(2)
	כי כל דרכיו משפט	הצור תמים פעלו	5	4	
	צדיק וישר הוא	אל אמונה ואין עול	6		
	דור עקש ופתלתל	שחת לו לא בניו מומם	7	5	(3)
	עם נבל ולא חכם	הליהוה תגמלו זאת	8	6	
	הוא עשך ויכננך	הלוא הוא אביך קנך	9		
II	בינו שנות דור ודור	זכר ימות עולם	10	7	(4)
	זקניך ויאמרו לך	שאל אביך ויגדך	11		
	בהפרידו בני אדם	בהנחל עליון גוים	12	8	(5)
	למספר בני ישראל	יצב גבלת עמים	13		
	יעקב חבל נחלתו	כי חלק יהוה עמו	14	9	
III	ובתהו ילל ישמן	ימצאהו בארץ מדבר	15	10	(6)
	יצרנהו כאישון עינו	יסבבנהו יבוננהו	16		
	על גוזליו ירחף	כנשר יעיר קנו	17	11	(7)
	ישאהו על אברתו	יפרש כנפיו יקחהו	18		
IV	ואין עמו אל נכר	יהוה בדד ינחנו	19	12	(8)
	ויאכל תנובת שדי	ירכבהו על במותי ארץ	20	13	
	ושמן מחלמיש צור	וינקהו דבש מסלע	21		
	עם חלב כרים ואילים	חמאת בקר וחלב צאן	22	14	(9)
	עם חלב כליות חטה ודם ענב תשתה חמר	בני בשן ועתודים	23		
V	שמנת עבית כשית	וישמן ישרון ויבעט	24	15	(10)
	וינבל צור ישעתו	ויטש אלוה עשהו	25		
	בתועבת יכעיסהו	יקנאהו בזרים	26	16	
	אלהים לא ידעום	יזבחו לשדים לא אלה	27	17	(11)
	לא שערום אבתיכם	חדשים מקרב באו	28		
	ותשכח אל מחללך	צור ילדך תשי	29	18	
VI	מכעס בניו ובנתיו	וירא יהוה וינאץ	30	19	(12)
	אראה מה אחריתם	ויאמר אסתירה פני מהם	31	20	
	בנים לא אמן בם	כי דור תהפכת המה	32		
	כעסוני בהבליהם	הם קנאוני בלא אל	33	21	(13)
	בגוי נבל אכעיסם	ואני אקניאם בלא עם	34		

The Song of Moses is so long that the separate verses cannot feasibly be considered the building-blocks of the argument. For the basic building blocks we have to climb up one level of text units: that of the strophes.

The strophes are the first layer of building bricks which have been used to construct the poem as a rhetorical performance and text of persuasion. My aim is to do them justice as elements of reprimand and persuasion by summarising them here as succinctly as possible. In this way, they appear one by one as small steps in an unfolding argument.

Moses speaks, sections I and II.
(1) I offer you useful insights!
(2) God is faithful and just,
(3) but you are corrupt and repay good with evil!
   (4) Ask your forefathers:
(5) Jacob is the heritage of the LORD.
(6) He has chosen him as the apple of his eye and
(7) taken him with him, protected, like an eagle.
(8) He took him to a land of milk and honey and
(9) spoiled him with all sorts of delicacies.
(10) Grown fat, Jeshurun neglected God and
(11) forsook him: worshipping idols turned into forgetting God.

God speaks, sections IIIA and IIIB.
(12) Because of this provocation I turn away from them,
(13) I shall repay them in kind!
(14) Fire rages through the cosmos,
(15) I shall send them disasters and diseases,
(16) nobody will escape the horror of war.
   (17) The enemy's pride is an even greater torment.
(18) They do not realise
(19) that it is YHWH who delivered Israel into their hands.
(20) In reality, their produce is poison, and
(21) their defeat is close at hand, my vengeance lies ready in the store room.

God speaks, section IV (with Moses speaking the introduction and conclusion)
(22, M) God takes pity on his weakened people.
(23) Your idols are a fake protection.
(24) Look closely: *I* am the powerful one, Lord of life and death
(25) and I swear that I will engage in battle:
(26) I am going to revenge myself on the enemy!
(27, M) Celebrate God's vengeance on the enemy, to save his people!

This sequence of small steps already has a clearly discernible internal logic. Because of the length of Deut.32, however, the number of strophes itself is still so large that the overall structure is not immediately apparent. At this point, we get assistance from the fact that the strophes have been grouped into twos and threes. In this way, the poet, being a master of structure, has created eleven stanzas. The level of stanzas may now also be tested for internal logic. I here give the contents of the stanzas as summarily as possible, concentrating on their contribution to the argument and granting them their own summary as much as possible by repeating only few terms from the sequence discussed above.

Moses:
I   My useful lesson is about this theme: your treachery and faithlessness is opposed to the faith and honesty of God.
II Look in the book of history: God appointed Jacob to be his heritage.

III He found him in the desert and protected him,
IV   took him to the Promised Land and gave him a wonderful life.
V   But Jeshurun stuffed himself and became corrupt, so that he started to worship idols. You (sing.) have forgotten your divine Father!

God:
VI   I will punish the provocation on the part of my corrupt children.
VII I will torment them with disasters and war.
VIII But wait, the enemy's illusions are even worse.
IX   They are poison, and their downfall is inescapable.

God: [after the strophe by Moses indicating His turnabout]
X   Your idols are powerless, I am the powerful!
XI   I swear I will revenge myself on the enemy by war.
     [Moses' final strophe is about vengeance and reconciliation]

The contents of the various stanzas are not all equally important, and the same holds for the strophes. I will therefore point out some focal points here.

The most important stanzas are the following:
- stanza I, because of the exposition in strophes 2 and 3, and the sharp contrast between them which will provide considerable dynamics and generates a narrative path;
- stanza V as the dénouement of the history lesson: idolatry and forsaking the true God;
- stanzas VI and VIII, as here God formulates his enormous frustrations and decides to take disciplinary measures, first against Israel, then against the enemies;

- and finally, the heart of section IV (i.e., stanzas X and XI), especially strophes 24-26, because of the solemnity of the renewed revelation and its consequence: starting off the campaign for the destruction of the enemy with an oath.

The outline of the argument probably manifests itself most clearly at the next, *still higher level,* that of the *four sections*. First I want to note here some considerations regarding the delineation of units.

When the poet creates a sequence of six units, for instance strophes, he does not need to mark every textual unit in order to get a clear articulation. It is sufficient to give units 2, 4 and 6 a clearly recognisable internal structure or delineate them by means of clear boundary markers. What remains between the strophes the reader can then easily accommodate in units 1, 3 and 5.

A good example of this type of economy is section II. This large unit has been decisively marked through the complementarity of father and children, and we have seen how this image of the relation between God and his people is supported by the notions of old/young, understanding/ignorance and remembering/forgetting which in lexical form also appear on the boundaries, and through the careful employment of the second person. By this one ring structure or inclusion, however, the poet marks four boundaries and serves three sections, as its components not only provide the borderlines of section II, but also the final boundary of section I and the threshold of section III.

The correct articulation of Deut.32 is to a large extent determined by the careful use of the verb 'to say'. It occurs eight times, in two pairs and in a quartet. One pair goes to Moses, the other is about speaking with/without understanding on the part of the collectives 'the people'/'their enemies'. These four instances contribute to the delineation of (always the beginning of) sections I, II and IIIB.

The quartet goes to God, and may be divided into pairs in two ways: a) there are two preterits (ll.31a and 42a) versus two *wqtl* forms (in ll.58a and 63b, that is, both at the heart of section IV). According to the other division (b), the two third-persons forms (ll.31a and 58a) alternate with those of the first person for God, ll. 42a and 63b. In both cases, however, all forms of אמר occupy strategic positions: at the beginning of sections IIIA, IIIB and IV. The forms in the centre of section IV are important for the demarcation of ever deeper embedding. The two forms for God in the third person (the narrative form of l.31a and the future of 58a) are moreover each surrounded by a couple of forms of the verb ראה (three with God as their subject, the fourth spoken by him to the people as an index of the climactic strophe of self-revelation), and with these form an exact collocation.

Therefore, the strategic positioning of the verb 'to say' covers all sections (including the halves of III). This is not surprising, as this verb is at the same time the main index of the complex and sophisticated play with ever deeper embedding of speeches. This system of Chinese boxes has to wait until section

III, but realises its true potential in its second half and together with the other play, that of reality and truth versus counterfactual expressions, creates surprising effects.

Other boundary markers for sections, less striking but no less sophisticated, are - as we have seen - the repetition of קרב (at the end of section II and the end of section III), and of the root זכר in active (l.10) and passive combination (l.42b) with the people of Israel (at the beginning of sections II and IIIB). On the way to the section in which God's hand holds sway there is the inclusion of IIIB by the high hand of the enemy misleading himself, versus the slipping foot as the metonymy of their downfall in the near future. Next, section IV follows with the completely impotent 'hand' (= power) of the people (l.57a) and the triple mention of God's decisive hand.

These forms of careful demarcation are not there for nothing. They go hand in hand with the considerable articulatory power of the sections. The argumentative structure of the Song in its quality of compelling discourse is determined most strongly by the contribution of the four sections.

What exactly does the network of these large textual units say? I see a consistently maintained thematic, covered by the both simple and powerful pair good/evil:

- Section I contains the exposition which contrasts God's goodness with the faithlessness and corruption of His people.
- Section II refers back *in extenso* to what went on before; the long account of the election by God, his guidance and exceptional care is followed by the cruel reversal, and the disappointment about the people forsaking Him and turning to idols. In this way, three stanzas extensively prove God's goodness, and the one climactic stanza (V) proves the unfaithfulness of His people. Moses knows how to document his discourse!
- Section III consists of dramatically contrasting halves because of God's reversing his position. In IIIA, the punishment God has in store for Israel implies a certain usefulness of the enemy, as an instrument of His anger. In IIIB God recoils from the consequences: the conceitedness of the enemies becomes too much for him. The enemy's even greater depravity - 'the poison' - forces him to turn around, and God takes the road towards grace for Israel. He contains his anger, and keeps its power in store for the other party. Implicitly, God is about to show his conciliatory side to His people.
- Section IV also divides good and evil very clearly. God comes to Israel's aid, and compresses his anger and power into the explosive mixture of warfare which is to destroy the enemy. Even the coda (strophe 27) with its double use of נקם presents in unambiguous terms the two sides, good and bad, of the retaliation which God finally executes. The jeers for the idols, and the image of war at the cost of the enemy are contrasted to what forms the very heart of the last section: the triumphant words of self-revelation and the oath in favour of Israel.

In this way, all sections serve the well-sustained theme of good and evil. With their clear demarcations, the sections are the most important units as regards structure and articulation of the massive argument.

After this consideration of structural and discursive aspects I will discuss one more major issue, the studied avoidance of historical facts. In the long article by Eissfeldt – not the most obscure representative of the historical-critical school on this continent – of 1958 the reader is confronted with a titanic struggle to pin down the date of the poem. The author asks himself which war is meant in the middle of the Song, when the young Israel gets trounced. He totally disregards here the delicate hermeneutic consideration that the lyrical world and the situations evoked there do not need to have the same mode of existence as 'historical reality'. Eissfeldt keeps tugging and pulling at the text until he thinks he has discovered that the war in question must have been the early wars against the Philistines, about which there are stories in I Samuel.

Unfortunately, these contortions go too far. They pass over a striking characteristic of the text, which should serve as a red traffic light to the historical-critical scholar and here deserves reconsideration. The text avoids any concrete indication of a historical situation. An enormous difference with Ex.15! There is not a single name of a neighbouring people here, not a single hint of politics, not a trace of a specific historical situation. Not even names such as Egypt and Canaan occur. All this means that the poem refuses to be pinned down in this way, for which there are in turn good rhetorical, communicative and thematic grounds.

The express avoidance of any historic context whatsoever is a signal not to lock the text within the horizon of its origin – to be constructed by us – and its first audience. This is because this speech indeed sets out to be a 'lesson' (insight, wisdom: לקח) and is just that. This instruction has been given in lyrical form, which means in that form of language which is the most complex and hence the most meaningful. At the level of the lyrical world itself – the multicoloured and dangerous world, that is, which has been evoked by the verses – the lesson is directed towards and meant for Moses' audience and their issue. At the level of author, text and reader audience this instruction has been passed down to and is meant for the audience of contemporaries which the writer (maybe also the author of Deuteronomy) hoped to reach, and after that for future generations.

The lesson has been put in such terms as to be applicable to every generation. Consequently, what is important here is not the evaluation of a concrete lapse of the people, fixed at a specific date, at all, but a lecture delivering the warning that every generation is threatened by corruption (its own) and by apostasy, and as a result also risks punishment (from God). With that, the Song exhorts to reflection: every generation in Israel (and then, every reader willing to imagine himself in that position) is here made conscious of their elected status (as God's favourite), of the adage resulting from that: *noblesse oblige*, and of the accompanying pitfalls of being spoiled, moral laziness, etc., and hence of their own responsibility in the face of God.

This universal scope does not differ from that in almost every Psalm: those poems, too, have been made in such a way that each generation of believers, pilgrims and participants in the cult can identify with the feelings of gratitude or anger, exaltation and relief, misery and powerlessness which are expressed in the various genres. And in that case, concrete hints or references to historical circumstances are not wanted. The poem of Deut.32 fits in well with the book it forms part of. Just like Moses' long admonitory sermons and the rules of law which occupy the main part of the book, the Song wants to sound a serious warning for times to come. The historical, actual readers of the book will have little trouble to project themselves into the audience presumed in the lyrical world; this will be easy because, as believers, they are the heirs of the canon, or because of the effect of their imagination.

These insights on the thematic and communicative object of the poem cannot be very surprising for whoever receives the poem within its context. The reader who slowly and with concentration digests chapter 31 of Deuteronomy finds that it is not necessary any more to look for an original genre definition for the song. Everything (regarding character and function of the Song) has already been perfectly expressed there. This was done by somebody who was either himself the author of all of Deuteronomy (both paraenesis and poetry), or an editor responsible for Ch.31, who felt so congenial to the poem that the difference between him and the writer is not visible or effective any more. The author of Ch.31 was obviously inspired by the poem. This can be seen most clearly in v.20 of the paragraph 31:16-21 (the speech in which God presents the poem to Moses, after which he gives him the practically unique instruction to record the text in writing). In imitation of the awesome gunfire of synonymous verbs of 32:15, especially the asyndetic trio of the B-colon, the author produces a similar trio of verbs about growing fat and conceitedness; this is the striking sequence ואכל ושבע ודשן, followed by a verb, ונאצוני ..., which is to return in 32:19 as an indication of God's horror at the apostasy.

What, then, does the writer say of the poem? He calls it עד, a warning and testimony for future generations, and that is what it is. 'This poem shall confront them as a witness, since it will never be lost from the mouth of their offspring.' We have been relieved of the necessity to bend over backwards in order to pin down the genre. The author leads us in the interpretation, and he knew very well what he was doing. He has God define it in advance: 'this poem may be My witness against the people of Israel.'

I conclude this paragraph with a page-length table showing the articulation and most of the proportions of this long poem.

proportions of Deut.32

strophe #	1	2	3	4	5	6	7	8	9	10	11	12	13	14	15	16	17	18	19	20	21	22	23	24	25	26	27
S/L	L	L	L	S	L	L	S	S	L	S	L	L	L	S	L	S	L	S	L	L	L	S	L	S	S	L	S
verses	3	3	3	2	3	2	2	3	2	3	3	3	2	3	2	2	3	2	3	3	3	2	3	2	2	3	2
cola	6	6	6	4	6	4	4	6	5!	6	6	6	4	6	4	4	6	4	6	6	6	4	6	5!	4	6	4
words	19	21	22	13	19	11	12	20	19	16	19	21	13	14	20	13	21	14	20	18	19	15	18	18	16	17	13
syllables	46	39	49	31	42	35	30	46	36	50	47	44	32	45	26	46	30	43	40	30	44	41	35	41	30

	stanza I = 3 strophes	stanzas II-III = 4 strophes	stanzas IV-V = 4 strophes	stanzas VI-VII = 5 strophes	stanzas VIII-IX = 5 strophes	stanzas X-XI = 6 strophes
	INTRO = Moses' exposition	SECTION I Moses narrates	SECTION II	SECTION III speaker God considers pros and cons		SECTION IV M God acts M
	3 x L	4 x S and 4 x L		4 x S and 6 x L		4 x S and 2 x L

§ 2. *Patterns and proportions.*

Strophes and strophe structure.
In the case of a very long poem, such as Deut.32, some statistical processing and consideration of proportions become relevant. The table shows that the poet created twelve strophes containing two verses and fifteen strophes containing three verses. The short strophes have been indicated by S, the long strophes by L. They have not been combined on the basis of a simple pattern which is the same throughout the poem. Yet, some regularity may be discerned, especially at section level.

There is some significance in the fact that the opening section contains only L-strophes. Their total results in a careful balance of three times three verses. The distribution of the 12 S-strophes is remarkable. Each of the sections following the exposition contains four of them. This makes three quartets. In section II there is another balance also involving four L-strophes, but in the section which aims to be 'problematic' and presents us with the convoluted and tormented deliberations on God's part (i.e., section III) the L-strophes gain a majority: six of them. In the first half of sections II and III there are already three S-strophes, combined with 1 and 2 L-strophes respectively. This leaves only one S-strophe each for the second half of sections II and III, surrounded by 3 and 4 L-strophes respectively. In other words: these body sections first maintain a certain speed with their succession of short strophes; this is slowed down half way along when the longer strophes start to dominate. Both in section II and in section III this is related to the increase in number and seriousness of the problems.

The arrangement of S-strophes and L-strophes in section IV is beautiful. The symmetrical alternation S-L-S plus S-L-S is the harmonious base of the concentric ABC-CBA arrangement of these two stanzas, with their inclusio (Moses speaks strophes 22 and 27 whose lengths are exactly identical), their virtuoso axis (lines 59 and 66 as the centre of the central L-strophe), and their polarity of powerless idols versus the power of the true God.

We get a clear idea of the extent and range of the strophes by drawing up a scale running from short to long. Below, scales for both series are given. Words differ so much in length that they can be only a very rough and hardly serviceable measure. The (pre-Masoretic) syllables are a considerably more accurate measure, but in a number of strophes their figures are not quite certain. The figures for the stresses are much more tentative; however, I will give them, so that the reader may get some idea of the relations between words and stresses, and between syllables and number of stresses.

S-strophes

number:	16	7	22	27	18	4	13	14	6	25	9	24
syllables	26	30	30	30	30	31	32	32	35	35	36	41
words	13	12	15	13	14	13	13	14	11	16	19	18
ictus	10	10	12	12	13	12	11	12	11	13	14	16

The fact that strophes 9 and 24 are at the top of the scale is no coincidence, as these are S⁺ strophes: they stick out by containing an extra C-colon. These two strophes do not have four, but five cola each, and this total bridges the gap to the (bottom of the) next scale, that of the L-strophes with six cola each.

The broad centre of this S-scale indicates that most two-line units contain 30-35 syllables; this is the case in ten out of the twelve strophes.

L-strophes

number:	2	21	26	5	20	23	12	15	19	1	8	17	11	3	10
syllables	39	40	41	42	43	44	44	45	46	46	46	46	47	49	50
words	21	19	17	19	18	18	21	20	20	19	20	21	19	22	16
ictus	18	17	17	18	16	17	19	17	16	16	18	19	18	19	16

The number of words varies from 16 to 22; the variation in stresses is even smaller, from 16 to 19. The figures for the syllables show a remarkably even distribution, they very gradually increase from 39 to 50. It is also remarkable that the increase in the first row of figures, those of the syllables, is not reflected at all by the rows for words and stresses. A scale which was not based on the increasing number of syllables, but for instance on the numbers of stresses, would show a totally different order of strophes.

The structure of the strophes.
What can we expect from the short and long strophes in terms of possible balance, pace, closedness? I will first discuss the S-strophes.

Strophe 4 is perfectly balanced because of its four imperatives, evenly distributed over the four cola; at the same time, however, there is a repetition of clauses and predicating in the second verse (l.11), so that this contains the centre of gravity.

Strophe 6 alternates the nominal/verbal balance. The first verse contains only one verb, followed by five nouns (complements), while the second has an asyndetic series of three verbs plus one s^e*mikut*. Strophe 7 is very regular, as in principle it has one verb and one noun plus suffix 'his' per colon.

Strophe 9 has an extra fifth colon, containing the only verb, but for the rest there is a nice balance in the basic quartet, thanks to the symmetries of the long enumeration; each colon has three stresses. The equilibrium of the verses in strophe 13 is evident and reflects the perfection of the vengeance. It is based on pairs such as present/past, they/I. Strophe 14 is tranquil in spite of the raging fire, thanks to the identical subject and the regular distribution of predicates plus spatial terms. Strophe 16 leans towards the front, thanks to the only verbal predicate, but the balance is nice because of the systematic use of the merisms.

Strophe 18 shows a balance resulting from the alternation of the nominal (no understanding: factual) and the verbal (understanding, in the counterfactual). Strophe 22 lends its verses about equal weight, as the anaphora already leads us to suppose. The chiasm of l.56 (P + O / O + P) and God's mercy on the people are followed by a motivation: the situation of 'no power' and 'vanished leaders' occupies a double object sentence.

Strophe 24 again creates a balance through the alternation of the nominal (l.61, another double object clause) with the verbal (again a double 'I' and 2 + 2 verbs); the projecting C-colon is a nominal clause which does not disturb the balance because it is very similar to l.61b. Strophe 25 balances neatly thanks to one verb per colon, always in front, a lot of inner rhymes on -*i* and a repeated *yadi* on the diagonal. Strophe 27 arranges its two *Doppeldreier* by means of a rigorous chiasm, which guarantees an almost perfect balance.

Looking back on the complete series I note that many strophes want balance, for instance numbers 9, 13, 14, 22, 25 and 27 - that already constitutes half of the S-strophes - and that optimum balance occurs in 13, 14 and 27. When the weight is clearly distributed unevenly, the point of gravity is usually situated in the second verse. In those cases, we find an acceleration, or more movement, or more action: see #4 and 6, a borderline case in 7, and compare 18 and 24. On the other hand, we may also get a decrease in pace; thus for instance the grim strophe 16 (and compare its counterpart contra the enemy, the L-strophe 26). A delay of a considerably more friendly nature we also find at the end of the L-strophes #1, 2, 5.

The structure of the L-strophes.
When three verses need to be filled, there are other options and rules. For Deut. 32 I distinguish about five situations.

a) We have seen three strophes which by means of syntactical and semantic devices have cunningly changed their binary character. They have arranged their three times two cola as two times three; thus strophes 5, 17 and 21. In this way, a diagonal division bisecting the centre of the strophe creates balance.

b) There are L-strophes which employ an obviously central line. This is clearly the case with nos. 1, 15, 23 and 26. With nos. 3, 10, 12 and (again) 17 this is less clear but still defensible as an ordering device. The pattern with a verse as axis combines well with the ABA' pattern for the three verses, but this co-operation is not necessary.

c) A number of strophes arrange their three verses as single + double. The Masoretes have led us in this observation, as they distinguished several times between one versus two poetic lines per *pasuq*. This is immediately clear in the first section, where three times they are absolutely right in recognizing the rhythm 1 + 2 in every strophe. Strophe 8 is another example: two nouns start off the A-colon and are supported by the nominal clause which completes the first verse, verbs govern the quartet of cola which follows. The rhythm of single + double also operates in vv.19-20 = strophe 12 (narrative introduction + two verses for God who starts to speak), and for strophes 17, 21 and 26 the pattern single + double is defensible. (The principle does not combine well with model b in strophe 23, with its clear concentric arrangement.)

d) The reverse model has been employed as well, in strophes 5, 11 and 19 - independently of the probability that the Masoretes were not regarding the strophic units as such. The coupling of vv.8-9 (double + single) covers the syntax (a long verbal sentence in ll.12-13, followed by two short nominal clauses in 14ab). In vv.17-18 four cola deal with the false gods, followed by two cola who complain about forgetting the LORD and re-introduce the second person. Verses 30-31 are slightly separate, as v.31 = the single line 49 presupposes a shift of speaker and zero-degree discourse.

e) Only one L-strophe remains which will not fit any of the models a-d; this is the extremely regular, highly synonymous and completely nominal strophe 20 about wine and poison.

Figures for the eleven stanzas.
I will first present a scale containing the figures for all stanzas. This series runs from short to long and is based on the syllables as measure of length.

stanza no.	III	II	VI	IV	IX	V	VII	XI	X	VIII	I
syllables	65	73	76	82	83	97	103	106	115	122	134
words	23	32	34	39	37	35	47	46	51	55	62
stresses	21	30	30	32	33	34	39	42	45	48	53
cola	8	10	10	11	12	12	14	14	15	16	18

The differences between head and tail are here about the same as those between the shortest S-strophe and the longest L-strophe. The longest stanzas are more than twice the size of the shortest. The difference in half verses says the same: from 8 to 18 cola. The middle group, ranging from 10 to 15 cola, still shows a difference of 50%.

The stanzas also obey the quantitative principle of 'two or three'. There are

six stanzas containing two strophes each, and five stanzas containing three strophes.
This is the scale for the long stanzas:

no.	VII	XI	X	VIII	I
syllables	103	106	115	122	134
words	47	46	51	55	62
cola	14	14	15	16	18

These are the stanzas containing seven to nine verses. Stanzas I (coinciding with section I) and (the stanza in which God turns around, with a complicated embedding of discourses) are especially long.
This is the scale for the short stanzas:

no.	III	II	VI	IV	IX	V
syllables	65	73	76	82	83	97
words	23	32	34	39	37	35
cola	8	10	10	11	12	12

We had already seen that stanza III is short but sharp, about the election and the eagle. When we leave this stanza aside for the moment, the variations in length are not enormous: from 10 to 12 cola, 32 to 39 words. When we look at the syllables, stanza V suddenly proves deviant. This unit has virtually the same number of words as stanza VI, but there the words contain twenty syllables more. It is this stanza which brings the dénouement of section II, with words which are both angry and long.

Chapter Five

The poem of Job 3: its structure and numerical perfection

Once more, I begin a chapter by presenting the text under discussion in the full rendering from the Jewish Publication Society of America. The poem Job 3 is printed here in seven strophes. In v. 10 I have altered the grammatical subject "it" in "He", and in v. 8b I render the infinitive form with "to rouse".

¹Afterward, Job began to speak and cursed the day of his birth.
²Job spoke up and said:

strophe

³Perish the day on which I was born,
    and the night it was announced, "A male has been conceived!"
⁴May that day be darkness;   1
    may God above have no concern for it;
        may light not shine on it.
⁵May darkness and deep gloom reclaim it;
    may a pall lie over it;
        may what blackens the day terrify it.

⁶May obscurity carry off that night;
    may it not be counted among the days of the year;
        may it not appear in any of its months.   2
⁷May that night be desolate;
    may no sound of joy be heard in it.
⁸May those who cast spells upon the day damn it,
    those prepared to rouse Leviathan.
⁹May its twilight stars remain dark;
    may it hope for light and have none;
        may it not see the glimmerings of the dawn.

¹⁰For He did not block my mother's womb,
   and hide trouble from my eyes.
¹¹Why did I not die at birth,
   expire as I came forth from the womb?
¹²Why were these knees to receive me,
   or breasts for me to suck?

³

¹³For now I would be lying in repose,
    asleep and at rest,
¹⁴With the world's kings and counselors,
   who rebuild ruins for themselves,
¹⁵Or with nobles who possess gold
   and who fill their houses with silver.
¹⁶Or why was I not like a buried stillbirth,
   like babies who never saw the light?

4

¹⁷There the wicked cease from causing agony;
   there rest those whose strength is spent.
¹⁸Prisoners are wholly at ease;
   they do not hear the taskmaster's voice.
¹⁹Small and great alike are there,
   and the slave is free of his master.

5

²⁰Why does He give light to the sufferer
   and life to the bitter in spirit;
²¹To those who wait for death but it does not come,
   who search for it more than for treasure,
²²Who rejoice to exultation,
   and are glad to reach the grave;
²³To the man who has lost his way,
   whom God has hedged about?

6

²⁴My groaning serves as my bread;
   my roaring pours forth as water.
²⁵For what I feared has overtaken me;
   what I dreaded has come upon me.
²⁶I had no repose, no quiet, no rest,
   and agony came.

7

§ 1. *Job 3 according to its various forms of regularity*

The poem in chapter 3 is for various reasons unique within the Book of Job. It is set apart because of its consistently maintained tone of anger, despair and bitterness. It is unique because of the well-maintained theme of the death wish. It even more deserves to be called exceptional, however, on two other grounds; the one discursive, the other poetical.

The discursive reason for this poem to stand out is that it still remains outside the construction of the book as a debate between the hero and his friends.[1] It precedes these painful conversations, and this fact will only be done full justice if we recognise the programmatic value of Job 3.

The poetical reason why Job 3 is unique within the book is an aspect of verse and strophe construction. Throughout the book, the poet only uses strophes consisting of either two or three lines.[2] In chapter 3, however, strophes containing four poetic lines occur next to three-line units.[3] I interpret this aspect, for which I account in § 2, as our first indication that in this poem quantity should receive more than its usual share of attention.

During my own study of Job 3 I did not pay any attention to numbers and proportions until a fairly late stage, for the simple reason that in dealing with poetry counting and measuring are less important than feeling, weighing and interpreting. The structural analysis of the poem, however, resulted in an increasingly more compelling confrontation with various forms of regularity, and in the necessity to pay systematic attention to proportions. What I then discovered is to me so surprising and intriguing that this time I will open a chapter with a paragraph full of figures. Job 3, I found, is a gold mine of numerical perfections.

---

[1] The construction as a debate runs at least until ch. 26, or, in a less economical view, through to ch. 31. After that, the fourth friend, Elihu, comes forward, who is introduced by the prose of 32:1-5 and then speaks verses through to ch.37. However, he does not receive a reaction from Job anymore, since God is the next speaker. God speaks chs.38-41 and receives a short reaction of repentance from the hero, 42:1-6, after which the prose framework takes over and completes the book (42:7-17).

[2] This assertion only has the status of hypothesis and probability, as it is based on my own extensive, but not exhaustive investigations. It is, however, to a large extent confirmed by the best inquiry into strophe division, stanzas and poems available at the moment: Pieter van der Lugt's *Rhetorical Criticism & the Poetry of the Book of Job*, Leiden 1995. On the basis of extensive observations up to and including ch. 39 this author recognises only two-line and three-line strophes; see for an overview his pp.457-459. For God's final poem now see my next note 3.

[3] Van der Lugt finds seven four-line strophes in the literary unit 40:7-41:26. These are the only units in the entire book to contain that many verses. The question may justifiably be asked, however, whether these groups of four verses may not be broken down further into pairs which then are the actual strophes. A homologous question one level down is whether so-called quadrocola actually exist; I myself suspect they do not, cf. my note 55 *supra*, in Chapter 3, where I put the question: should a quadrocolon not be read as two bicola?

Anticipating the results of my structural analysis, I here take the position that Job 3 is a well-integrated poem containing three stanzas and seven strophes, and that these strophic units alternately contain three and four verses. As this alternation is the hallmark of the poem, I accord to each strophe the label S or L, short or long. The central stanza comprises three strophes; stanzas I and III, on either side of it, each have two strophes:

Strophe #	1	2	3	4	5	6	7	totals
S/L	S	L	S	L	S	L	S	
verses	3	4	3	4	3	4	3	24
cola	8	10	6	8	6	8	6	52

The division into cola of the 24 verses is beyond dispute. It is generally agreed that the beginning of the poem, in keeping with the seriousness of the speaker and his situation, has been reinforced. This concerns verses 4-6 and 9, all tricola. This means that in Job 3 there are 20 bicola, and four verses containing a projecting third colon, i.e. the surplus made up by a C-colon.

The first stanza has been set in the mode of malediction, and consists of two strophes which each have been reinforced with two of these extra cola. In the first strophe, the speaker turns against the day he was born, vv.3-5. The second strophe goes back even further in time by elaborating on v.3b and turning against the night he was conceived, vv.6-9.

The second stanza comprises 3 + 4 + 3 verses, all bicola, and is concerned with death and the quiet in Sheol. It remains within the counterfactual mode throughout. Strophe 3 is vv.10-12, strophe 4 is vv.13-16 and strophe 5 is vv.17-19. In the final stanza, the speaker ends up in his current reality: bitter complaint in vv.20-23 (= strophe 6), fear and unbearable pain in vv.24-26 (= strophe 7).

The correct division into strophic units has already been glimpsed more than a century ago, and defended once more in this century, but has not had many followers due to a lack of argumentation.[4] Two factors have had a disruptive effect and have wrong-footed almost everyone. Many scholars are of the opinion that the why-question in v.11 signals a new beginning - a mistake - and further, many commentators succumb to the temptation to 'improve' the poem by moving up v.16 three places.[5]

---

[4] J.G. Stickel, *Das Buch Hiob*, rhythmisch gegliedert und übersetzt, Leipzig 1842, already has the alternation of 4 and 3 verses; Franz Delitzsch, *Das Buch Iob*, Leipzig 1864, 2nd ed. 1876 [= Keil-Delitzsch IV.2], saw the poem as a series of 8-10-6-8-6-8-6 cola. In this century only E.J. Kissane, *The Book of Job*, Dublin 1939, offers the correct division.

[5] Thus recently still Van der Lugt, p.50-51, and earlier NEB, Dhorme (Paris 1926), and De Wilde (OTS xx, Leiden 1981). Verse 16 has also been placed after v.11: thus Duhm (Freiburg 1897), Skehan (in CBQ 23, 1961) and NAB. Even more ruthless is Fohrer (KAT 16, Gütersloh 1963), who deletes v.16.

Still, Stickel, Franz Delitzsch and Kissane were right. A thorough structural analysis, also covering the level of the stanzas, may prove this and draw the interpretative consequences. Although I will start with a series of numerical analyses, we will see that already at this stage observations concerning structure and subject matter are indispensable.

A. *From the whole to the parts.*
The total number of cola, 52, may be divided into 26 + 26, as Freedman has pointed out.[6] The relevance of this division into halves is immediately proved by an observation concerning semantics and verse structure. The first and the second series of 26 cola end on the 13th and 26th verse respectively, which show a polar relation:

| verse 13: | ישנתי או ינוח לי | כי עתה שכבתי ואשקוט |
| verse 26: | ולא נחתי ויבא רגז | לא שלותי ולא שקטתי |

While the large majority of the cola in this chapter have one or no verbal predicate, these verses stand out by containing 2 + 2 verbs.[7] They are supported in this by the opening verse[8] and the adjacent verse 25, which in this way contributes to the reinforcement of strophe 7 as the climax. One quartet dreams of total quiet, the other rudely disrupts this illusion.[9] They represent the opposition of counterfactual versus harsh reality.

There is also a numerical aspect which supports the division into twice 26 cola. The poem contains 192 words. This is an even number, so that the middle of the chain does not consist of one word, but a couple; these are # 96 and 97, which respectively close off the first half of the sequence of words and open the second half. This turns out to be correct: #96 is the last word of v.13 and #97 is the first word of v.14. In this way, their positions exactly reflect the division into 26 + 26 cola.

The number of verses in Job 3 is 24, which seems to hint at two times twelve. Is this correct? The division of the poem into twelves is not the most important one, but is confirmed from various quarters. The first dozen, verses 3-14, obviously contains more words and cola than the second half, as a result of the reinforcing of stanza I with four C-cola. The second dozen covers vv.15-26. Both the number 24 and the number 12 are in first instance supported by the fact that the speaker refers to himself 24 times in the poem. The distribu-

---

[6] David Noel Freedman, "The Structure of Job 3", Biblica 49 (1968) pp.503-508, now reprinted in PPP, p.323-328.
[7] Two more cola containing two verbs are vv.11b en 22b.
[8] Incidentally, the syntactical relations between the four verbs in v.3 are different from those in vv.13 and 26. The two cola of v.3 each have a verb in a main clause plus one in a relative clause.
[9] The correspondence is mainly based on the repetition of נוח + שקט, which is supported by the synonymy of שכב and שלו.

tion of these 24 forms is very uneven, but this makes it all the more relevant that these references are spread over the two halves of the poem as roughly 12 + 12: there are twelve morphemes for 'I' in vv.3-14 and eleven in vv.15-26, to which I add *gbr* = *gbr*.[10] Both halves start with an isolated morpheme of the first person (in v.3a and v.16a respectively), but end in a dense cloud of them (strophe 3 and strophe 7, respectively).

The symmetry of 12/12 verses is not threatened by the expansion into tricola in stanza I. The dividing line between the twelves, situated between v.14 and v.15, bisects the exact heart of the central strophe 4, which itself shows a concentric design, and hence presupposes the strict regularity of alternating S and L in the seven strophes.

The number twelve we also encounter in other ways. The four tricolic verses state: four times three is twelve cola. This might be a coincidence, but for the fact that the correct division into stanzas and strophes recognises the numbers three and four as an organising principle:

strophes #2 + 4 + 6   = three L-strophes = 12 verses = 26 cola
strophes #1 + 3 + 5 + 7 = four S-strophes   = 12 verses = 26 cola

The end of this diagram is a surprise, as we are again confronted with the number 26, which now proves no longer a product of purely arithmetic or linear bisecting, but a structural entity, based on the correct articulation of the composition.

The long strophes state: three times four is twelve, and the short strophes state: four times three is twelve. Consequently, at the level of verses and cola the L-series and the S-series have exactly the same length. And when we measure the series with the much finer measures of words and pre-Masoretic syllables, the difference is negligible:
- the three L-strophes: 95 words, 213 syllables
- the four S-strophes: 97 words, 211 syllables.

Measuring the units which are not linear, but which are indicated by the articulation of the composition, also shows that the expansion of verses in the beginning, by means of C-cola, does not disrupt the poem. The tricola do not disturb the balance, as their strophes have been incorporated organically into the system of alternating 3/4 verses. Although there are four of them, they also form pairs. One pair (the C-cola of vv.4-5) reinforces the first strophe, the other (the C-cola

---

[10] Out of the 24 times Job mentions himself, there are 23 morphemes for 'I' or 'me/my'. These places are, in the first half: an imperfect in v.3a; in strophe 3 three times the suffix, three imperfect forms of the 1st pers. sing., and one perfect form ditto; next, two times *-ti* with perfect forms in v.13, once *li* and once the 1st pers. imperfect. In the second half of Job 3: 1x imperfect in v.16a, then nothing until strophe 7 which contains ten I-forms (5x *-ti* with the perfect, 5x the suffix). The *gbr* in v.23 coincides (after interpretation) with *gbr* in v.3b, thus providing the 24th self-reference.

of vv.6 + 9) the second. This now means that they have been evenly distributed over S and the L-series of strophes.

There is another manifestation of the number twelve and its double. The final strophe contains in its three verses 5/3 + 4/4 + 4/4 words, 24 in all. Several levels down, this total reflects both the number of verses (as a figure for the entire poem), and half of that. The point of this is that strophe 7 is the climax of the poem, and in various respects the dénouement of the titanic struggle the speaker is having with his position as a victim. The climax can also be discerned in the fact that the first-person singular morpheme occurs no fewer than 10 times in the final strophe.

Besides multiplying three by four, we may also add them up. This yields the number seven, which has also seen a lot of service in the Hebrew Bible. Three plus four strophes makes seven, and one level up there are three stanzas. These figures for the initial and programmatic poem of the book of Job remind me of the chapter which opens the books of Samuel. I Sam.1 consists of seven sequences, grouped into three parts according to the pattern AA' / BXB' / CC'.[11] They too contain a climax, but in this case outside their own chapter, as they are governed by the 7 + 1 pattern which I see at work in I Sam.16 and elsewhere.[12] The climax consists of poetry: the Song of Hannah, which itself is programmatic for the books of Samuel, and which as regards composition and thematic matter belongs to chapter 1, functioning as its key-stone. Now, this poem has seven strophes, which have been accommodated into three stanzas as 2 + 3 + 2 units. Of these strophes four are short and three are long, according to the yardstick we have encountered in Ex.15 and Deut.32 and which probably is also normative for the whole of Job: S-strophes of two lines and L-strophes of three lines.[13]

B. *From the parts to the whole*

There is an even finer measure than that of words: the numbers of syllables. We are in the fortunate position that doubtful forms such as לך (one or two sylla-

---

[11] See Chapter 1 of my *Vow and Desire* (= NAPS IV, 1993), pp.2-4 and 73. After an introduction and iterative background in Shiloh (AA', vv.1-8), the plot opens with Hannah's vow, the conversation with the mistaken Eli, and the birth of Samuel (BXB', vv.9-20, 296 words), after which delay (Hannah versus her husband) and the delivery of the child to Eli in Shiloh form the conclusion (CC', vv.21-28). Nota bene: only after finishing the analysis of this structure did I count the words; I then found the first and third parts to contain exactly the same number of words, 119 each.
[12] See for the 7 + 1 pattern the subject index at the end of *Vow and Desire*.
[13] *Vow and Desire*, Chapter 1, § 3 contains the detailed analysis of the Song of Hannah and the account of the figures mentioned here: pp.73-111.
The long poem II Sam.22, David's Song of Thanksgiving as king, contains 19 S-strophes (consisting of 2 verses) and 5 L-strophes (consisting of 3 verses). The Song of Deborah contains, in the correct colometry (see my article in the Festschrift Milgrom) 11 strophes of two verses, 5 strophes of three, 3 strophes of four verses and one strophe of only one verse; no alternating of two lengths here.

bles?) do not occur in Job 3, so that counting the pre-Masoretic syllables will not present insurmountable problems.[14] I have included a detailed table in the Appendices to this book.

There is something very special about the syllable figures. I will start with the phenomenon which immediately strikes the eye: the surplus formed by the projecting C-colon. The four instances of it in the first stanza are all nine syllables long. Arranged in pairs, they add a surplus of 18 syllables to both the first and the second strophe.

As a C-colon can only exist by the grace of a preceding A plus B-colon, and is carried by this combination, I will call the A + B-cola of verses 4-6 and 9 (together with the bicola vv.3 and 7-8) the base of those strophes. I will label the C-cola E for Excess. The figures for the base show a striking correspondence with the figures for the completely bicolic strophes which follow, both for S and for L:

	stanza I		stanza II			stanza III	
strophe #	1	2	3	4	5	6	7
base	46	65	46	65	46	65	55
plus E	+18	+18					
	64	83					

Strophes 3 and 5, and the base of their opposite number strophe 1, all have exactly the same number of syllables. And this threesome of equal length is followed by another trio of exactly the same lengths! These are the three L-units, strophes 4 and 6, and the base of the opposite number strophe 2.

Another remarkable aspect is the fact that the number 9, characteristic for the 2 + 2 C-cola (with their label E), plus its double 18 function as links by which the numbers are connected in even more ways. Nine bridges the gap between the number 46, which occurs three times for S-strophes, and the figure for the only remaining strophe 7, the climax, containing 55 syllables. In this way, the entire chain of S-strophes is interconnected.

[14] In the table at the back of this book the reader will find the figures for the syllables per word, colon, verse and strophe. In the case of Job 3, reconstruction of pre-Masoretic length is considerably less problematic than usual. All that is necessary is reduction of 22 segholates (sing. without suffix, including *mym* and *'yn*) to their monosyllabic base, the dual ending in v.12 (*bis*), the apocope **yihy* (*bis*) and 3 ḥataph-vowels going back to zero (the cases of furtive pataḥ are not disrupting). There is only one point I am not sure about: how many syllables does הממלאי in v.15b contain? Applying virtual elimination twice (as in the Masoretic *ham-dab-rim*, instead of *hammᵉdabbᵉrim*) results in three syllables - not enough, I think - while five syllables is rather a lot. I will adopt a middle course here and assume four syllables.

157

When we now go back from the end to the beginning, the number 9 again forms a bridge, since 55 + 9 = 64, and this last figure is the total for strophe 1. And what is the position of strophe 2 in these sequences, with its total of 83 syllables which seems rather an unruly number? This unit is not only the first L-strophe, but as a component part of stanza I has also been reinforced with a double E (the C-cola of v.6 and v.9). If we now subtract the length of this surplus (9 + 9 = 18 syllables) from the total, we arrive at exactly the base number for the series of L-strophes: 83 - 18 = 65.

We had already met the totals for the S-strophes and L-strophes, 211 and 213 syllables respectively. However, we can now also observe their components:
- the S-strophes contain (46 + 18) + 46 + 46 + 55 syllables, a total of 211,
- the L-strophes contain (65 + 18) + 65 + 65 syllables, a total of 213.
Both series are dominated internally by the differences introduced by 9 and its double. I compare this to an earlier result: the two series of strophes contain exactly the same number of cola — 26.

At the level of word counts there are also clear connections between the strophes. The surplus of strophes 1 and 2 consists of 7 and 8 words. When we subtract those numbers from their totals 29 and 37, we obtain the figures for the bases of strophes 1 and 2: 22 and 29. I compare them to the figures for the other strophes:

	S	L	S
stanza I	*strophe 1* 22 + 7 = 29	*strophe 2* 29 + 8 = 37	
stanza II	*strophe 3* 22	*strophe 4* 32	*strophe 5* 22
stanza III		*strophe 6* 26	*strophe 7* 24

We now see that also as regards numbers of words the base of strophe 1 exactly equals the totals for strophes 3 and 5, and differs little from strophe 7. The total for strophe 1, that is base + E, is a figure which itself forms the base of strophe 2. With its great bulk of 10 cola, 37 words and 83 syllables the strophe in which darkness and night are combated with even more darkness is of course the longest of all. The trio of L-strophes steadily diminishes throughout the poem, while the quartet of S-strophes slightly expands at the end.

§ 2. Structural analysis of strophes and stanzas.

The unity of the first stanza is based on a merism and the special treatment this receives. The merism is formed by 'day' and 'night', which each get a strophe. It is no coincidence that they are also the very first word pair of the poem, in the bicolon which opens the poem, v.3.

Day and night are here very much involved with each other. This has two effects. As a pair, they are the foundation of the parallelismus membrorum of v.3, which is the only poetic line in the initial strophe to contain two instead of three cola. For a moment this even tempts us to interpret the first verse as an independent strophe.[15] The close relation between day and night also has the effect that each of the two strophes contains the word for the complement. In the strophic unit dealing with the day, which is an S-strophe and contains the phrase 'that day' once, the word 'night' occurs once; in the strophic unit dealing with the night, which is an L-strophe and contains the phrase 'that night' twice, the word 'day(s)' occurs twice.

So, night penetrates into day and day penetrates into night. What does this form of interrelation mean? The poet here pulls an extraordinary trick. The polarity of night and day is also that of darkness and light, and as such constitutes one of the most spectacular dualities of the universe, and of our world. It is also the first dichotomy which is made and manipulated by the Creator in Gen.1. In Job 3 the hero is now allowed by the poet to make a titanic effort at eliminating this elementary polarity.[16] In his anger and despair Job fights the day of his birth in his first strophe using a multitude of terms for darkness. Within this unit, we can still think that he is presupposing the day/night duality and in that sense respects it. But then we get to strophe 2, in which the speaker combats the night of his conception. He does not curse it by means of its opposite (what, after all, could that be?), or forms of its complement, but rather with ... even more darkness: so much darkness that that night vanishes completely from calendar and history. And if necessary, the despicable means of magic must be used.

But, the reader of Job 3 is asking, surely this is impossible and illogical, and moreover totally unrealistic? Certainly, however fanatical Job's aspirations here, they are doomed to failure. But exactly that message is the main characteristic of Job 3. In every stanza, this poem is occupied with unique exercises in real versus unreal, and with the tensions between the empirical and the counterfactual mode. The speaker tries to make the impossible come true by means of verbal and poetical contortions.

Finally, the unity of stanza I also manifests itself quantitatively. It is only here that tricola are used, and as we have observed and measured from close by, the C-cola are distributed in pairs over the 'day' and 'night' strophes. What remains is the question of what is the significance of this reinforcement, and whether it

---

15   Thus Van der Lugt, op. cit. pp.50-51. One of the signals, however, which already belie such a decision is the inclusio of strophe 1 by means of the singular יום (3a...5c).
16   Hartley devotes an excursus to this and speaks of a counter-cosmic incantation, pp.92, 101-102.

makes sense to have the tricola next to each other in the day strophe, while the two tricola of the night strophe are not adjacent and appear as an envelope around the two central bicola? In order to answer this question I descend to the level of the separate strophes.

Strophe 1 (vv.3-5).
The measures of three and four, which I found determined the strophe lengths in this chapter by exception, are immediately visible in the lengths of the cola:

	v.1	*v.2*	*v.3*
words	4 + 4	4 + 4 + 4	3 + 3 + 3

These figures relativise the difference between bicolon and tricolon. While the one tricolon is determined by the number 4, in the middle of the strophe, the other shows the regularity of three times three. This is the final verse, which in this way has almost exactly the same length as the initial verse.

One of the main characteristics of the language here is the fact that each colon is a syntactic unit, each time with a verb as predicate. There are three characters. In the first verse, and only there, we have the speaker. In the first colon he is still an 'I', but in a certain sense his identity soon fades into the anonymous 'a man'. This happens in the second colon, i.e. the entity where the first shadow of darkness already looms. The second character is God, who appears in v.4b. The distribution of his presence in the poem is remarkable, but the exegetes do not realise this because of their delusions about the organisation of the poem and misconception of v.10.[17] The deity occurs in three places in Job 3, always in the first strophe of a stanza, as the subject of an action: vv.4b, 10ab and 20a + 23b. In all three cases a negation taints the act: by means of the jussive in v.4b Job orders God not to do something, in v.10 Job is both despondent and indignant about God's having neglected to stop his birth, and in v.20 his indignation has increased to such an extent that he presents God as the raiser of obstacles. The reproachful question of v.20 is the reverse of the affirmative v.10.

The third character in strophe 1 is the darkness. The many terms which the poet employs for it lend the unit a massive synonymy. In five cola, darkness clearly rules.[18] Each time it is deployed against one and the same day: 'the day I was born'. In his first verse Job does not speak of the physical phenomena of day and night which appear every 24 hours, but of unique and existential entities: the day of my birth and the night of his conception. For this, he goes back in

---

[17] Scholars are almost united in thinking that the night is still subject in v.10a - erroneously - and slightly less united in including v.10 with the first stanza. A sound structural analysis will easily show that v.10 opens stanza II (and strophe 3).

[18] The five cola in question are vv.4a, 4c, and 5abc. This count presupposes and confirms the decision that in v.5c the root *kmr* is used, instead of *mrr*.

time. The temporal sequence of v.3a + b runs counter to the chronology of life. Job does not literally state that he was born during the day and conceived during the night; he introduces the merism of day and night because he wants to speak in more fundamental terms. He enters on an embittered fight against life itself, and the merism enables him to immediately penetrate deeper into the day/night polarity, or transform it into the light/dark polarity which is more emotional and has a greater potential for symbolism and connotations.[19]

The first verse serves the entire first stanza, since its balance of day and night is promoted to the balance of the two strophes which make up stanza I. In this way, it performs a programmatic function. Yet, at the same time, the verse is also part of the day strophe. Several signals support this arrangement. Each verse in strophe 1 contains the singular *yom*. The elimination of the day of [Job's] birth is echoed by 'the eclipses of the day' which close the strophe.[20] This inclusio is the envelope containing the various manifestations of darkness swallowing that doomed day. Finally, there is the emphatic positioning of *hayyom hahu* in the front position of the second verse. After v.3b which spoke of the night, this is a corrective signal, indicating that the subject still is the day.

The marked jussive of v.4a is followed by two prohibitives in 4bc. A parallelismus membrorum is not immediately visible in this verse; still, there is one, although hidden in intertextual depths. I read the contrast of day and darkness in 4a and the action by a demanding God in 4b against the background of Gen.1, and recall that the first speech in the Bible was accorded to God when he said: *y^{e}hi 'or*, and then called this light 'day'. If we now link this first act of creation to Job's complaint, we see how the speaker here tries, with the power and evanescence of his lyric, to make an opposite gesture by saying that the day should be darkness (here, too: *y^{e}hi*) and that 'God above' should dismiss it.

The light (*n^{e}hara*) not shining 'upon it' in 4c has a parallel in 5b, where a dark cloud (*^{a}nana*) should dwell (*škn*) 'upon it' - about the opposite of what the Rabbis pictured for the Shekhina. One strophe further down we find the sequel, with another jussive and the alliterating *r^{e}nana*: 'let it not rejoice'.[21] The image of the cloud in v.5b may also be meant as a contrast to the cloud which in Exodus is a manifestation of God's presence near, and protection of, the people setting out.

---

[19] The fact that day and night in v.3 should not be interpreted literally may also be deduced from the verse which, as the opening line of strophe 2, counterbalances v.3. In v.6 the speaker says that 'that *night*' (6a) ... 'should not be among the *days* of the year' (6b). Only in the eyes of a pedant could this be considered a logical inaccuracy.

[20] At the phonological level this is supported by alliteration of the predicates: the sequence y-b-d in 3a is counterbalanced by y-b-ṭ in 5c.

[21] The line which so connects 5b to 7b suggests that there may also be a connection between 5a and 7a. This might be the fact that an original *ṣalmut* nicely assonates and alliterates with the equally negative *galmud*.

The delineation of strophe 1 is confirmed by parallelisms appearing at strophe level. The second strophe even exceeds its predecessor by two cola. This creates yet more room for extensive synonymy. While strophe 1 managed two jussives plus the negation אל, strophe 2 has got four. In strophe 1 there is one *hayyom hahu*, in strophe 2 has *hallayla hahu* twice. The three syntactic units dealing with darkness, which occupy as many cola and fill v.5, receive a clear counterpart in the tricolon v.9, which also speaks of darkness three times.

This parallelism of the final verses also yields a strong argument in favour of reading *kimrire yom* (5c) to mean 'eclipses of the day'. The reduplication of the third radical of **kmr* is answered in 9c with a more extensive reduplication, in *ʿapʿappe šaḥr*. This latter form of *sᵉmikut* nicely balances the *kokᵉbe nišpo* of 9a, which also show a reduplication.[22] There is more weight in the semantic observation that these 'eyelids of the dawn' contrast the 'eclipses of the day', but in fact say the same because of the introduction of the negation in v.9c. The number of syllables in the final cola 5c//9c is exactly the same.

Strophe 2 (vv.6-9).
The numbers three and four remain interesting when we count words per colon:

	v.6	v.7	v.8	v.9
words	4 + 4 + 4	5 + 4	3 + 3	3 + 3 + 4

The numbers of words per verse are 12, 9, 6 and 10. The outside verses are the longest; no wonder, as these are the two tricola. The bicolon v.7 hardly differs from the average of 4 words per colon which was maintained in v.6, as a continuation of strophe 1. Verses 8 and 9ab contain short cola of three words each. The final v.9c returns to 4, in order to attain the syllable total 9 for the C-colon.

The quantitative aspect of two bicola being surrounded by two longer verses is no coincidence. It forms part of an organisation based on the ABBA pattern, which also governs the remaining two L-strophes. Here, too, there is a hermeneutic circle at work: the pattern presupposes the correct division of the poem into strophes, but at the same time confirms it. If the poem is divided incorrectly, the well-maintained systematic structure in the composition of the long strophes 2, 4 and 6 cannot be retrieved. The verses indicated by B all refer to collectives, to a human character in the plural.[23]

---

[22] To what extent reduplication may be exploited by the poet and elevated to the rank of a stylistic device, is demonstrated beautifully by Job 16:16. There we come across one of the two other occurrences of 'eyelids', and with the word preceded by a reduplication in the A-colon: פני חמרמרו מני בכי / ועל עפעפי צלמות. Job dixit!

[23] This is evident in vv.14-15, with their five masculine plurals, four of which rhyme on -*im*; also in vv.21-22 with their anaphora on *ha*-....-*im* and their function as a digression with respect to 'the bitter in soul' of 20b.

At the core of strophe 2 the people are implicitly present not before v.7b, in the act of jubilation. In v.8, however, they become visible in the text, in two morphemes of the masculine plural. The people 'who curse the day' are those who 'are ready to rouse the sea monster'. Both actions are directed against life itself, and hence I think that the *yom* of v.8a (and 5c) may be interpreted as 'life', in a metaphoric expansion.[24] The author of the book has prepared us for this in his introduction to the first poem. In v.1 he writes that 'Job cursed his day', and this 'day', too, should be interpreted rather broadly.

Verses 6 and 9 form a ring of tricola. They contain two times two construct state combinations. The cola 6b and 6c put two negative imperatives around it in a crosswise arrangement. The chiasm is continued in such a way that vv.6 and 7 belong within the same strophe. The אל יבא at the end of 6c receives a successor אל תבא at the beginning of 7b, while 6a and 7a contain the broad anaphora 'that night'.

Verses 8 and 9 also form an excellent team. Our ears are quick to tell us that, as there is a carefully maintained sequence of words with aleph/ayin, long o, and resh linking all cola: *'or^{e}re* and *'orer, kok^{e}be, yom* and *'or*, and a negation of *yir'eh* which just like 9b does not give the light much chance. In the centre there is the connection between vv.7 and 8. The positive aspect of jubilation as an oral act is crossed out, and replaced by the negative oral act of damnation and the sinister rituals of magic. Job does not say that he himself is a conjuror, or the inciter of a mythological monster, but he does want to employ those sorts of people to further his cause. The content of v.8a is little different from that of v.5c, which at the auditory level is expressed by the remarkable phonetic correspondences.[25]

In v.6, the night of his conception is struck off the calendar in a magical-omnipotent gesture.[26] In v.9 the destruction is presented in a different form. A night, for instance that of my conception, proves to exist only in as far as it is marked off from what is different. If after such a night no light appears – as v.9 wants to have it – and hence night is not relieved by the following day, darkness will not end and the night cannot be determined anymore. In v.9 a kind of vanishing trick is played, and in this way the speaker manages the impossible: abolishing the polarity of light and dark.

---

[24] The revocalisation of *yom* (day) into *yam* (sea) in v.8a, executed by various exegetes (among whom Gunkel, Albright [in JBL 57], Pope [AB ad loc.], Good, Michel), is unnecessary and completely wrong. Most recent authors are correct: Habel, Hartley, Alonso Schökel, Clines, Van der Lugt.

[25] The cola start off rhyming on *yqtl* in the plural plus object *-hu*. The gemination of the r in 'cursing' neatly corresponds to the reduplication of the third radical of *kmr* in 5c, and the endings of the cola are identical: *yom*.

[26] In v.6 I read, as do many others, the form *yeḥad*, 'unite', from the root יחד or אחד.

In the second strophe there is a balance of positive and negative imperatives: there are five commands and five prohibitions.[27]

The balance in the first stanza, already created by the merism distributed over two strophic units, is reinforced by more forms of equilibrium. Both strophes contain five cola which are either full of darkness, or turn against the light. The 'I' who tries to cancel his birth in strophe 2 invokes the help of professionals to spirit away 'his day'. We have indicated various semantic links, and even at sound level there are symmetries.[28]

Stanza II = strophes 3-5 = vv.10-19.
We now reach the exclusively bicolic part of the poem. This means that the ten verses of stanza II consist of 20 cola. They have been distributed 6-8-6 over the three strophes the central stanza consists of, being the only stanza to contain three strophes. Even the word totals have been distributed symmetrically over the strophes: 22-32-22, just like the syllables (46-64-46).

Strophe 3. The boundaries and the unity of this strophe are implied in the subject matter (linking death to birth), the recurrence and frequency of the first person singular, and the fact that each of the six cola mentions a part of the body. This last series is moreover articulated into two threesomes, following the pattern ab - aa - bb as distributed throughout the tricola. The letter a here represents the singular of the word 'womb', while b indicates a dual form: my eyes, knees, breasts. The strophe starts with a *ki*-clause which occupies an entire colon and ends with a *ki*-clause of half a colon. As in strophe 1, each colon has a verbal predicate.[29] There is hardly any enjambment.[30] In each of the three verses, however, double duty is employed.

The strophe is also characterised by its tone – of reproach and accusation. In v.10 Job is still speaking positive quasi-constatations, but the other four cola are dominated by the rhetorical question 'why', which almost always is the vehicle for reproach and indignation. The interrogative itself is in front position three times.

[27] The five commands: two are marked jussives, in 7a and 9b, three are unmarked (modal imperfect forms): 6a, 8a, 9a. There are also five prohibitions if we can include ואין of 9b (which is indeed a wish of Job's): four of these are introduced by the prohibitive אל, in 6bc, 7b and 9c.
[28] While the y occurs eight times in strophe 1 and thirteen times in the second strophe, the totals for the phonemes l, long o and long u are exactly the same: l occurs eleven times in both strophes, o nine times, and u six times. The object suffix appears four times in each of the two strophes.
[29] Strophe 2 contains only one colon which is not an independent syntactical unit, v.8b. This means that there is enjambment in v.8.
[30] I use the word 'hardly' because the phenomenon of double duty (the negation in v.10a, the word 'why?' in v.11a and the perfect in v.12a) is responsible in each of the three verses for a very slight enjambment.

The start at v.10 is usually misinterpreted. Due to a misleading division of strophes, v.10 is taken to refer back to the foregoing, so that the night becomes the subject of 'to close'. Hence the usual translation: '*it* did not block my [mother's] womb.' This is unlikely in any case, for three reasons. If we want to have the night as antecedent we have to refer back to v. 7a, passing no fewer than 5 syntactical units with very diverse subjects. The fact that there is a stanza boundary after v.9 does not argue in favour of such a jump. And thirdly, this reading would imply a sloppy handling of metaphors. The first colon speaks of 'the doors of my [mother's] womb'. This in itself is already a crass image, not very ladylike I would say. If it were now supposed that these doors could be opened by the night, we would have a problematic squaring of a metaphor, as becomes clear when I put the seemingly childish question: how is the night supposed to do this? Has it got a monkey wrench or a set of keys?

I myself approach the matter positively by asking the almost rhetorical question: who was the only character in the Hebrew Bible who could open and close a woman's womb? And then I immediately remember the stories of Leah, Rachel and Hannah, who only had children because the deity opened their wombs.[31]

God is the subject of the entire v.10, but as a subject he is governed by an ellipsis in this opening line of the stanza. Exactly the same is going to happen in the first verse of stanza III: v.20, where nobody doubts that God is the subject. The least hazardous way to recognise God as the subject of v.20 is to anticipate: when one skips to the final verse of that strophe, there is an explicit אלוה in v.23b.

The reference to v.23 is no coincidence. God is there responsible for the actions *str* and *skk*. This pair of verbs is itself a chiastic successor and counterpart to the two in v.10, *sgr* and *str*.[32] So, God has two terrible omissions on his conscience according to the speaker: first, in the ante-natal stage, he omitted to block my mother's womb, so that this wretch (עמל, v.20a) entered life, and now (strophe 6) he fails to grant me free access to the peace of the grave, vv.22-23!

These observations enable us to refine the previous contention that God occurs in three passages. God is explicitly mentioned in v.4b and v.23b, and in between he appears as an active agent twice more, but then subject to an ellipsis: in v.10 and in v.20. The meaning of the ellipsis is Job's being engaged in a veiled attack on God; and indeed it is God who is responsible for the miserable state the speaker is in. As to this, the narrator of Job 1-2 has confided in us and not left us in any doubt. By hearing about the wager between God and Satan

---

[31] In the actual texts both פתח and עצר / סגר are used, with בטן and usually רחם as the grammatical object: Gen.20:18, 29:31, 30:2, 22, I Sam.1:5,6, Job 32:19.
The interpretation that God is the subject of v.10 is considered by Michel p.59, and is also found with Kissane, pp.14 and 17, and Tur-Sinai p.60 - hats off!

[32] N.B. at the phonetic level: the samekh hardly occurs anywhere in this chapter, but it does appear 2 + 2 times in the predicates of vv.10 and 23!

we have superior knowledge. What we know, the hero does not know: that he is the victim of a horrible test.

Verse 10 not only has close connections with v.23, but also with its opposite number v.20, with which it forms a chiasm. The correspondence between 10b and 20a may be shown word for word.[33] And the life which has been given to the bitter in soul (20b) links up with not blocking the womb in 10a. The positioning of both verses is of structural importance: both v.10 and v.20 open a stanza.

Strophe 3 contains seven morphemes for the first person singular. The contents may be summarised as follows: I wish I had been stillborn, Job says. The sequence of sentences in vv.11-12 corresponds to the natural chronology of the beginning of human life. In 11a he wishes to have died in the womb, in 11b immediately after birth.[34] In v.12a we see how the child is received on the mother's knees, and in 12b the baby is suckled. If we now return to v.10 we see that this verse is separate as to the temporal aspect, by being both earlier (through 10a) and later (through 10b) than its successors. In 10b we meet the grown-up, discerning man who rejects his misery, but 10a may even go back further than the birth, and offers a hypothetical resistance to the conception. If this is correct, the opening of stanza II is connected to the first verse of stanza I, which also manipulates chronology and in v.3b mentions the conception.

The rhetorical force of strophe 3 is caused among other factors by the fact that two inimical forces are linked in an oxymoron: birth, i.e. giving life, and death. This can be seen most clearly in the contact, if not the clash, between the words of the pivotal verse 11. There, 'womb' is right next to 'I died', and 'expire' immediately follows 'come from the womb'. The double oxymoron subtly echoes a syntactical decision which typifies this strophe. We find a form of consecution in the verbs, with the scheme *qtl ... (w)yqtl* and occurring, as does the phenomenon of double duty, in all three verses.

Much of what has been formulated here remains hidden if the verses are grouped in the wrong way. The main factor responsible for erroneous strophe divisions is the fact that readers have been magnetised by the interrogative 'why' in v.11a and have 'recognised' it as a strophe marker. Closer observation, however, shows that this recognition is unnecessary and incorrect. The word למה occurs 9 times in the book of Job and is in the majority of cases anything but strophe-initial.[35] This in contrast to the use of 'why' in the Psalms.[36]

---

[33] The reproach 'why does he give' of 20a semantically corresponds to the bitter discovery 'he did [not] hide', while 'light' goes with 'my eyes' and עמל (in 10b substantive, in 20a adjective) is repeated.

[34] N.B. The preposition *min* in v.11a still means 'in', but in v.11b, governed by the verb יצא, it means 'from'.

[35] The word למה only occurs in speeches by Job himself, and in 3:11, 9:29, 13:24, 19:22, 27:12 and 30:2 it is *not* the beginning of a strophe, in both my view and Van der Lugt's. An initial/intro-

Strophe 4.
The correct delineation of this unit is also hampered by zealous exegetes. They move v.16, usually to a position three lines earlier, and so wreak havoc. The move is not necessary, and the ABBA pattern of this L-strophe disproves such a measure.[37] The outside lines of the quartet of verses refer to the hero and contain mainly singular forms, the inside two teem with plurals. These vv.14 + 15 are connected by the anaphora ʿim .. ʿim in their A-cola, and moreover by ha + participle + ending -im in their B-cola.

The word which best expresses what torments the speaker is *rogez*: agony, turmoil; it occurs both in v.17a and in v.26b (as the very last = definitive word!). That is why Job here wishes rest and quiet for himself. Hence I would think that the image of kings, councillors and princes in his central verses 14-15 in the first place represents power, rather than happiness. Job himself is completely powerless and suffers deeply from this. The contrast of power and impotence is covered by the contrast between the outside and inside verses in the ABBA pattern, but is at the same time reconciled by the argument. In his wishful thinking in strophes 4-5, Job now places himself next to these unworried potentates. As a result, the meaning of the preposition ʿim in 14a//15a fluctuates: it may be translated as 'with', but also as 'just like'.[38]

From a syntactical point of view, verses 14-15 are no more than complements. Sentence cores and main verbs only occur in the surrounding lines vv.13 + 16. They form the envelope and their syntax governs the strophe – the syntax of the counterfactual. After the bitter reproaches of strophe 3, in the centre of his poem the speaker indulges in wishful thinking and betrays this by using the counterfactual mode; strophe 5 which follows does contain 'facts' if taken literally, but is discursively speaking the extension of his wishing.

The five I-morphemes of the strophe are in the envelope. The two words 'for now' (כי עתה) mark the start of the new unit, and the wishing in v.13 becomes very intense on account of the increase in verbs. On either side of the caesura there are 2 + 2, a record within this chapter which will be deliberately matched

---

ductory 'why' is for me only acceptable in 3:20 and 10:18. See also Van der Lugt's figures on his p.495.

[36] In the Psalms, 'why' is strophe-initial in 82% of cases (11 as opposed to 2), according to Van der Lugt in his earlier book (Kampen 1980), *Strofische structuren in de bijbels-hebreeuwse poëzie*; see p.517 there for the relevant places.

[37] Moving v.16 to a position following v.12 is done by Dhorme, NEB and Van der Lugt (pp.50-51); to a position one line above that by Duhm, Skehan (CBQ 23, 1961), Pope (AB). Even worse: Fohrer deletes v.16.

[38] On p.65 Michel points out how this double עם is followed by the outright comparative preposition כ in 16a. Fohrer p.111 renders it by "so gut wie" and was followed by Dahood (see Michel p.63 note 129) who referred to the Ugaritic ʿm. Habel, JPS, Good and Hartley translate the preposition as 'with', as does Clines, who however on p.72 notes 'perhaps to be understood as 'like' ' and cites BDB 768a §2f.

in v.26. In both cola there is again the consecutive pattern *qtl* + *yqtl*, and אז echoes עתה. The anaphora on או in 15a//16a helps to keep v.16 inside the strophic unit.

Linguistically it is not really a problem to keep v.16a in its place, even though the exegetes who move the entire verse think so.[39] I prefer the following rendering: 'Or why was I not like a hidden stillbirth?'[40] The B-colon intensifies the sad image by putting these babies in the plural (עללים) and qualify them further by means of an asyndetic relative clause, 'that have not seen the light'. The words 'see' and 'light' are the chiastic continuation of the same words in v.9bc. The final verse of strophe 4 implies a perpetual darkness, and is thus a counterpart of the final verse of the previous L-strophe, v.9, which was also the end of stanza I. Here in strophe 4, the total darkness of strophe 2 is clearly that of not entering the world (alive, seeing).

Strophe 5 (vv.17-19).
The central strophe did not present parties as opposed to each other. Ultimately, this fifth unit does not do that either, as this strophe, too, says of Sheol that the fate of all people is the same there. However, the human resources employed here consist of four standard oppositions: the wicked versus the weary, prisoners versus taskmaster, small and great, slave and master. The selection of the very first pole (רשעים) is already judgmental. That Job does not want anything to do with 'the wicked' is confirmed by the double alliteration (r and sibilant) which puts *rogez* on their side, and by the positioning of the rest (*nuh) he so ardently wished for himself in v.13b on the side of the weary.

Through the four polarities shimmers the contrast between good and evil. In that order, it governs 18a + b, and the two pairs of 19a + b. Job is on the side of the prisoner, the little man, the slave. The beginning of the strophe, however, is a facer as it turns the order around and callously puts the wicked in front. Their word alliterates with the key word *šam* which dominates the strophe by itself being present in three cola, and being fully echoed in the other.[41] It is also the anaphora at colon level in v.17.

With this small deictic word 'there' the speaker pins us down on the one place where total equality obliterates the social differences and contrasts. In the service of such a message the spatial term is one of the most effective means to hold the strophe together.

---

[39] I see two ways to assimilate v.16a: either it is an unmarked question ('or would I not want to be like a buried stillbirth?'), or we suppose the three or four-fold 'why' of strophe 3 to be still active.
[40] A similar employment of *lmh* from vv.11-12 is also found with Habel as quoted here, and in the JPS, Clines, Good, Michel, Hartley and others.
[41] The adverb שם itself occurs in 17a, 17b and 19a. All its phonemes have been absorbed in *šamᵉʿu* in 18b, and the consonants shin and mem can also be found in immediately adjacent positions in 18a and 19b.

Verses 17 and 18 are connected by means of a chiasm. The ranting of the wicked (17a + 18b), which by the way comes to an end 'there', is contrasted with rest for the tormented (17b + 18a). There are connecting and separating alliterations. The phonetic similarity of $r^e\check{s}a^cim$ and $^{\jmath}asirim$ underlines the contrast in meaning, and the similarity of $\check{s}a^{\jmath a}nanu$ and $\check{s}am^{e c}u$ reinforces the relief of the harassed. In 18b, the wrong side is a singular for the first time. The taskmaster and his prisoners are for a moment reminiscent of the people in Ex.5 (a text whose concentric structure reflects the prevalent sense of confinement). Verses 17-18 have a verb as predicate in each colon. The four forms rhyme with each other on their -u endings, since they are plural forms. By way of the singular נגש we arrive at v.19 which is completely nominal and presents each party in the singular. Here, all movement or action is spent, so that the strophe has a tranquil ending. Nevertheless, there is an increase in intensity as the polarity strong/weak, which in vv.17-18 always occupied an entire verse, is now presented per colon.

The singular forms offer the suggestion that the strophe reflects Job's condition, be it in a very indirect manner. He himself is exhausted and has been shaken by *rogez*, as strophe 7 will make painfully clear to us. He himself is also a prisoner — of whom? And now he is small, while he used to be very great (i.e. rich).[42] He now feels a slave who yearns to be free from his master. The word *'adon* of v.19 catches the eye. Elsewhere it is often a title of the deity; here in the book of Job it is unique.[43] I interpret it as a dig at the person responsible for Job's misery and who has been covertly attacked by him earlier: God himself.[44]

Strophes 3-5 together form the long *stanza II*. This central part of the text derives its unity from two powerful factors: the counterfactual mode which determines Job's wishful dream, and death. In stanza I Job already wanted to strike out the day of his birth and the night of his conception, but at that point he had not got as far as speaking of death. There, he was cursing, usually in the form of commands and interdictions (marked or unmarked jussives and prohibitive forms). Here in the centre he is wishing and longing with great intensity. The first strophe of this stanza mentions death outright, the second translates this into rest and silence, and the third also speaks of rest, but particularly of all-embracing equality and liberation.

The three strophes show a certain concentricity. The central strophe of stanza and poem is the climax as regards modulating the counterfactual. This pivot contains few signals of space. Around it, however, there are two strophes which

---

[42] My interpretation of v.19a is as follows: '[whether somebody has been] great or small [here on earth]: it is there that he is now [i.e. in one and the same place]'. The rendering in the JPS is efficient: 'Small and great alike are there'.
[43] In Job 28:28 the word does occur one more time, but with a different application: as an equivalent of the tetragrammaton.
[44] Cf. Gerald Janzen, p.64, about Adonai as Job's taskmaster.

employ spatiality in a remarkable and prominent way. Strophe 3 concentrates strongly on the mother's body as the place where life and death clash, at the cost of the foetus. Strophe 5 completes the passionate combat against life by occupying itself exclusively with Sheol and placing the egalitarianism of death 'there'.

Finally, the strophe about the great desire for peace and quiet, the central strophe 4, has special and strong ties with the beginning and end of the entire song. There is a cross bond: the first verse of the pivot, v.13 with its four verbs of rest, is closely connected to the final strophe, which in v.26 ends in four verbs which destroy rest. The last verse of the central unit, v.16, however, is closely tied to the three previous strophes. Thanks to the first person there is a strong link with the opening verse (which is the only I-verse in the first stanza), while the motif of the stillborn child echoes strophe 3, and the notion of 'not seeing light' is a continuation of v.9 (the ending of strophe 2).

The first and second stanzas show a quantitative balance. Stanza I contains 10 four-word cola and 7 three-word cola, stanza II also has 10 cola consisting of four words and 7 cola consisting of three words.[45]

Stanza III = strophes 6-7 = vv.20-26.
The third stanza is the moment of truth for the speaker. Here, Job is no longer able to ward off his greatest pain with extensive verbal fireworks, and expresses his reality in very plain terms. The contours of the two strophes are not in doubt. Strophe 6 has four verses, strophe 7 three.

Strophe 6 is the third and last L-strophe, and its ABBA pattern is even more evident than in the previous L-strophes. Two verses which contain mainly singular forms again surround two verses full of plurals. From a syntactical point of view the two inside lines are mere appositions to the 'bitter in soul' of v.20b. As a pair, they are marked by the anaphora *ha-* + participle + ending *-im*, and the B-cola both continue the participles with *yqtl* forms, a well-known form of continuation. Even more remarkable in the syntax of the strophe is the fact that v.23a does not contain a main verb. We are expected to recognise its opening לגבר as an indirect object presupposing the predicate 'he gives', and we note that this predicate occurred in v.20a. So, this יתן is a crass – i.e., literally far-fetched – example of double duty!

The close syntactic relation between v.23 and v.20, bypassing the centre of vv.21-22, goes even deeper. In the same way that 'to the man' in 23a only makes sense when we use the verb from 20a, the subject of 20a can only be determined when our reading reaches the explicit 'God' of 23b. The crosswise movement we have to make here in order to grasp the syntax affects the outside verses of the strophe; it adapts itself to the concentric structure of the unit and confirms it.

---

[45] Besides that, stanza I contains one colon of five words, while stanza II contains three cola of five words (two of which always monosyllables).

Having noted all this, we may say that the deep structure of the entire L-strophe contains only one sentence core, 'Why does he give light/life to the bitter/wretched?'

We have not finished with the outside verses of strophe 6 yet. Their position is also important with respect to the poem as a whole. I recall that v.20 as the first verse of the final stanza has a chiastic relation with the first verse of the central stanza, v.10. We also saw that the end of strophe 6, v.23 (about the man hedged in by God), is closely connected to that same verse 10, that this connection is also chiastic, and that in this way we discover the true identity of the character who should have kept the womb locked. Its strategic position and semantic link with v.10 lend the envelope of strophe 6 great structural importance.

We now have a paradox. However subordinate the inside verses (vv.21-22) seem to be because of their syntactical dependence, from an emotional point of view they actually are the core of the strophe; it is here that Job most unequivocally reveals his utter despair. The envelope represents bitterness and accusing the deity, the core expresses exactly what is the greatest horror in a life such as Job's: craving death but being prevented from attaining it. People like Job, inundated by misery, are doomed to go on living. Job's grief is made even stronger as it mentions a word of happiness three times (שׂישׂ, גיל and שׂמח) – another type of paradox.

The relation between v.23 as a line referring to obstruction and v.10 not only leads us to the identity of the agent who in v.10 is the subject of 'not blocking' without receiving a vocable, but also to the identity of his victim. It is clear that 'the man' referred to in the envelope of strophe 6 is Job. If we now follow the thread tying this *laggeber* to the predicate of v.20a, the syntax will show, even in retrospect, that Job and 'the miserable' coincide; and of course he is also a member of the group called 'the bitter in soul' in 20b.

The word *geber* is apt for two reasons. Occupying the first position in its own verse, it is the immediate successor to the *qeber* on which the preceding verse ended. This form of contiguity is expressive.[46] We might use its two components to summarise the message of the poem as a whole: this is the *qeber-geber* song. The strength (an aspect of meaning present in many manifestations of the root *gbr*) has ebbed from this man who yearns for the grave, and who in that craving, too, is obstructed by the deity. In strophe 6 he is so taken up by his longing for death that his identity seeps away from it; not a single first-person morpheme is to be found. Around him he sees fellow-sufferers, and concedes them the heart of this strophe. In the last strophe, however, he will postulate his

---

[46] This contiguity is even stronger when exactly the same root is being repeated; an example of this we have seen in Deut.32:43b/c (נקם). Another example I mentioned is Is.45:1de (a doubled פתח on either side of a verse boundary).

battered 'I' with his last strength: suddenly, we have a cloud of -*ti* afformatives and -*i* suffixes, and the speaker refuses to avoid the full picture of his pain any longer or to avert it with rhetorical bombast. Strophe 7 is the foremost I-strophe of the song.

The second reason why the word גבר draws attention is the fact that it repeats the word from v.3b. The programmatic opening verse contains the sequence 'I ... man' and thus anticipates the sequence 'man ... I' which characterises the two parts of the final stanza. The quasi-anonymous singular of the indirect object in 20a//23ab flows over into, and is replaced by, the unique singular I-me-my of the climax (vv.24-26).

I will close this discussion of strophe 6 with two observations in v.21 and a conclusion drawn from these. The A-colon has the same structure and content as v.9b:
v.9b 'May it hope for light - but nope'
v.21a 'who wait for death - but nope'
This time, I have rendered the expressiveness of the outcome (w^e plus the telling *'ayin*) - if the reader will permit me - in a vulgar but unambiguous colloquialism.

My second observation regards the root *ṭmn*, which in 21b produces a broad nominal plural, 'hidden things', with the connotations of precious and sought after, but which in v.16a produces a gloomy passive Qal participle: the dead baby tucked away (such as I would like to be, says Job). We have hit upon a sad parallel: the central strophe ends in the longing for a death which precedes life, the sixth strophe has stricken people dig for the death which can deliver them from unbearable suffering. Both desires are frustrated. The connection between this strophe and v.16 is reinforced by a phonetic chiasm:

16a	*nefel* [dead]	16b	ʿ*llym* .. *'or*
20a	*lʿml 'or*	20b	life .. *nefeš*

These links between vv.20-21 with the 'night'-strophe and the strophe about the peace in Sheol point to the conclusion that the three long strophes are the pre-eminent area of darkness and concealment. The poet stresses this by means of a new paradox. The word 'light' occurs three times in this chapter, and always precisely in the L-strophes.

Strophe 7 is the climax in which Job faces his situation outright: sheer terror and pain. Verses 24-25 are marked by the anaphora *ki*, after which the final verse hammers home the terrible truth with a triple and ruthless *lo*, whose vowel is also active at the end: *wayyabo rogez*. The six cola contain 24 words, yielding an average per colon of four exactly. Each verse contains eight words: 5 + 3, 4 + 4 and 4 + 4. The first characteristic of the language is the fact that the ending (afformative or suffix) of the first person appears ten times. Together with the vowel of the doubled *ki* this makes twelve, rhyme as well as inner rhyme.[47] Here, it is the sound of fear and insignificance.

Up to this point, only the first two strophes had ten verbal predicates, the others had less. Strophe 7 returns to ten verbs. Their sequence shows a steep increase. The first verse distributes its predicates in the usual way: one verb per colon. The second verse contains twice this number, one of which occurs in a relative clause. The final verse shows a completely regular distribution of four verbs at one level, by means of a maintained syndesis.

What about the speaker? He does not waste time telling us, since the syntax of his very first colon shows an inversion putting the complement 'as my bread' in front, at the detriment of what is usually in front: the predicate or the subject. Among recent exegetes there is a growing consensus that the preposition לפני, counterbalancing the k^e of the B-colon, here means 'like' or even 'instead of'.[48] I myself detect in this syntactical upset the expressive force of an iconic relation. Job is the prisoner of the divine taskmaster; hence we expect water and bread to represent for him the most elementary, maybe even the only, necessities. But now he himself is telling us that there is something preceding even that: sighing and groaning (שאג and אנח) take precedence, which is why he places the complement in front. In this case, the word order is in itself an iconic sign.

While the second strophe contained a double prohibition of 'coming', the powerless Job admits by a fourfold 'coming' in his final strophe that pain and fear have engulfed him.[49] By means of a paronomasia he doubles the root *phd*. And in his final line he shows the honesty to repeat the series of verbs from his dream (v.13) and cross them out with the negation.[50] He replaces one of the four elements: 'sleep' is in v.26 converted to its opposite, agony. Note: the three verbs denoting rest and sleep (נוח, ישן and שקט) do not occur anywhere else.[51] In Job, they are characteristic and revealing for this chapter. The sounds r and g of this *rogez* have been foreshadowed in v.25b by *ygr*, the synonym of *phd*. The very last word is at the same time the courageous elimination of the illusion Job still had in v.17a: that the wicked would cease creating turmoil ($had^e lu\ rogez$). *In cauda venenum.*

---

[47] To be exact: nine times -*ti* or -*i* are used, at the end of v.24 there is -*ay* because of a plural noun, and finally there is *ki* twice.

[48] Thus in the past already Dhorme and the RSV; and recently the JPS, NEB, Clines (see his extensive discussion of the possibilities in his note on p.75), Habel p.99, Hartley p.97. Appeal is made to Job 4:19 and I Sam.1:16. What Good says (translating as '.. comes before my bread') comes close to my view: '*Lipney* can mean temporal precedence or spatial presence 'in front of', and I would accept either.' (p.56, note).

[49] This coming has three times been expressed by בוא, and once by אתה.

[50] While שקט and נוח remain the same, שכב has been changed to שלי, but the alliteration with the shin draws attention to their synonymy.

[51] Only *šqt* occurs further down in chs.34 and 37, but this is the Elihu section which by many is considered an interpolation.

No rest, v.26 says, which means that in v.24 there is no silence but groaning with pain. The sounds contrast *naḫti* with *ʾanḥati*, and *šaʾagotay* with *šalawti* \\ *šaqaṭṭi*. The message presented successively by the three verses can be summarised as: my groaning is all I have left - my fears have materialised - agony robs me of all rest.

§ 3. *Final remarks.*

First of all an observation relating to quantity. The great care with which the words have been chosen and the higher-level units have been constructed and connected in this poem is ruled by a considerable regularity in verse lengths. I am giving the relevant figures, grouped per strophe and stanza. E (for Excess) refers to the C-cola which make four verses of the first stanza protrude, S means short, L means long:

```
stanza I    S  16.15.15       L  17.17.17.14
     + E        +9 +9            +9       +9

stanza II   S  16.15.15       L  16.17.16.16      S  17.14.15

stanza III                    L  15.19.15.16      S  19.19.17
```

By separating the surplus consisting of the C-cola from the base (the A + B-cola) of the first two strophes, the striking similarities per strophe are once more revealed. The second S-strophe contains exactly the same sequence as the base of the first. The total for the three L-strophes is always 65, after subtracting the E in the first long strophe. Three of the four S-strophes contain 46 syllables (if we leave aside the E of strophe 1). The final strophe, also an S, deviates, but only by way of the significant nine.

The quantitative organisation of the seven strophes as regards S and L may be reduced to this diagram:

```
            S   L
            S   L   S
                L   S
```

Can we now move from the quantitative to the qualitative, from the prosodic aspect to the semantic or subject matter? Having arrived at this point after so much observation and analysis, we receive some assistance from the aspect of genre. In his strophes, the poet covered or touched on several genres. This flexibility may also be observed in other poems.[52] Here in Job 3 the first two stro-

---

[52] Rapid shifts in genre and hence in tone are frequent in the Song of Hannah, as I have described in NAPS IV, or in the Song of the Vineyard (Is.5:1-7; a clever mixture of misleading love poetry, narration, and the forms of an oracle of doom against the people, all this cast in the mould of a parable).

phes are a type of curse. Strophes 3 and 6 are complaints, and both have the significant interrogative *lámmah*. If we now try to catch the content or weight of the strophes in a formula, we may accommodate the first four strophes in a series ABAB and strophes 3-7 in a series AB-X-AB. These two sequences partly coincide as strophes 3 and 4 occur in both. This leads to the question whether in poetics we can and should attribute the phenomenon of double duty also to larger textual units than words.

Strophes 1-4 form the pattern ABA'B'. This labelling meshes with their alternation of S and L, but also requires a succinct defence as regards content or meaning. The ABA'B' structure is mainly based on the following data. In strophes 1 and 3 the speaker turns against his birth, first using the mode and tone of command sentences (with jussive and prohibitive predicates), next using the interrogative sentences of a complaint. In both strophes God occurs as subject.[53] Strophes 2 and 4 represent night and darkness, which first are the objects and then the subjects of negation and undoing. In their final verses they both contain the terms 'light' and 'see', but subject to the negation.

This parallel arrangement of four units may be summarised as follows:

A	cursing the day of birth	strophe 1
B	curse: the night of conception swallowed by greater, even infinite darkness	strophe 2
A'	complaint: I wish I had never been born, or had been stillborn	strophe 3
B'	result: the peace of death (wish, counterfactual) excludes the light of life: darkness again	strophe 4

The overview suggests that we may combine two spatial images and have them dissolve into one: the womb, usually conferring life but in this case death, melts into and is replaced by that other place of oceanic peace, Sheol.

Strophes 3-7 may be read according to the pattern ABXA'B'. Its middle strophe, i.e. unit 5, represents the much-desired peace and quiet which is so perfect that all earthly oppositions have been radically eliminated. This unity, however, is the eye of the storm: around it the full turbulence of desires and passions contra reality is raging. The correspondence A-A' is guaranteed by the following aspects: strophes 3 and 6 open with God as subject, their first verse contains the key word עמל, they are both turned into complaints by למה which poses a rhetorical question, and they both contain the significant vocable מות in their second A-colon (vv.11a and 21a). The relation between the God who tortures

---

[53] God is a fleeting but explicit subject in strophe 1 thanks to v.4b, and in strophe 3 he is the implied subject of both cola of v.10.

and his tortured victim is mentioned here, but not in strophes 4-5 and 7.

The correspondence B-B' is also based on several similarities. The quartet of verbs denoting rest and sleep within one verse appears in both strophes, 4 and 7. What was first a passionate wish (v.13) turns out at the end (v.26) to be utterly unattainable. Job has been robbed of it. Both strophes open with an asseverative כי and end with a repeated לא. Strophe 5 contains both terms for rest and for its opposite (the formidable word רגז which mercilessly concludes the poem). As the centre of the five-part series, this unit has links with both flanks.

The sequence of five strophes may be summarised as follows:

A'	complaint: I wish I had been born dead	strophe 3
B'	counterfactual: ardent desire for peace and quiet	strophe 4
X	silent centre:	
	in Sheol all differences will disappear	strophe 5
A"	complaint: the path to death has been closed to me	strophe 6
B"	reality: agony, no peace and quiet	strophe 7

The three strophes labelled A are the only places where God appears as subject. In the strophes sub B, which all contain four verses, the centres are always occupied by collectives of people: magicians, rulers, and the utterly powerless who vainly yearn for death.

As stated before, the sequence of four and the sequence of five strophes overlap.[54] Their labels may be written and combined as ABA'B'XA"B". The two arrangements may also be presented together with their prosodic quantity S or L:

A	(S)	strophe 1		
B	(L)	strophe 2		
A'	(S)	strophe 3	(S)	A'
B'	(L)	strophe 4	(L)	B'
		strophe 5	(S)	X
		strophe 6	(L)	A"
		strophe 7	(S)	B"

Job 3 is rather good at discussing things without mentioning them:
- strophe 4, the central unit, regards the realm of spirits and together with strophe 5 paints a vivid picture of it, without using the word Sheol;
- the corresponding verses 10 and 20 covertly accuse the deity without yielding up his name or any vocable for him;

---

[54] This arrangement of the strophes was suggested to me by the Rev. Aart Schippers (Amsterdam), after reading the rest of this chapter; I am greatly indebted to him.

- in strophe 6 Job speaks of his bitter fate and desperate longing without using 'I' or referring directly to himself.

Finally, a remark concerning interpretation. The thrust of this poem is the titanic struggle between the power of the death wish and the power which invites Job to come to terms with reality. Earlier, we saw how the speaker tried to get his dirty work done for him by the magical omnipotence of the frightening folks who can enlist the big sea monster in order to destroy life itself. The passion of Job's cursing is his own attempt to be magically omnipotent. At this stage of my analysis I would prefer to replace this term, which leans towards the psychiatric, with another: the verbal ability of (the poet, which he lends to) the speaker Job is so compact and powerful that we may call it poetically omnipotent. The paradox here is that this formidable power over the language is subservient to Job's total impotence. The poetical power refers to existential impotence.

In the domain of wish and counterfactual Job aims at omnipotence for two stanzas. His maledictions and his wishes articulated in the counterfactual mode are reminiscent of David's lament for Saul and Jonathan. That poet, too, maybe David himself, vainly tries to stave off reality and his immense sorrow by making a detour of two stanzas. In the third stanza - there as much as here - the bitter truth can no longer be avoided.[55]

---

[55] See my analysis of II Sam.1:19-27 in NAPS II *ad loc*. David opens (after the thematic sentence plus refrain which constitute v.19) with two or three unattainable wishes regarding messengers who should not bring joy to the Philistine home front, and then moves on to a curse which makes him the equal of God: as if he could personally withhold rain and dew from the flanks of the Gilboa. The central stanza is a form of escape by dwelling on the illustrious past of Saul and Jonathan.

Appendices

a) the Hebrew text of Ex.15
   plus two tables

b) the Hebrew text of Deut.32
   plus four tables

c) the Hebrew text of Job 3
   plus two tables

	strophe			line	verse
	9 = R	באלים יהוה	מי כמכה	21	11ab
		נאדר בקדש	מי כמכה	22	cd
		עשה פלא	נורא תהלת	23	ef
III	10	תבלעמו ארץ	נטית ימינך	24	12ab
		עם זו גאלת	נחית בחסדך	25	13ab
		אל נוה קדשך	נהלת בעזך	26	cd
	11	ירגזון	שמעו עמים	27	14ab
		ישבי פלשת	חיל אחז	28	cd
	12	אלופי אדום	אז נבהלו	29	15ab
		יאחזמו רעד	אילי מואב	30	cd
	13	ישבי כנען	נמגו כל	31	15ef
		אימתה ופחד	תפל עליהם	32	16ab
		ידמו כאבן	בגדל זרועך	33	cd
	14 = R	עמך יהוה	עד יעבר	34	16ef
		עם זו קנית	עד יעבר	35	gh
IV	15	בהר נחלתך	תבאמו ותטעמו	36	17ab
		פעלת יהוה	מכון לשבתך	37	cd
		כוננו ידיך	מקדש אדני	38	ef
	16	לעלם ועד	יהוה ימלך	39	18ab

Exodus 15 — The Song of Moses at the Reed Sea

	strophe			line	verse
I	1	כי גאה גאה	אשירה ליהוה	1	1ab
		רמה בים	סוס ורכבו	2	cd
	2	ויהי לי לישועה	עזי וזמרת יה	3	2ab
		אלהי אבי וארממנהו	זה אלי ואנוהו	4	cd
		יהוה שמו	יהוה איש מלחמה	5	3ab
	3	ירה בים	מרכבת פרעה וחילו	6	4ab
		טבעו בים סוף	ומבחר שלשיו	7	cd
		ירדו במצולת כמו אבן	תהמת יכסימו	8	5ab
	4 =R	נאדרי בכח	ימינך יהוה	9	6ab
		תרעץ אויב	ימינך יהוה	10	cd
II	5	תהרס קמיך	וברב גאונך	11	7ab
		יאכלמו כקש	תשלח חרנך	12	cd
	6	נערמו מים	וברוח אפיך	13	8ab
		נזלים	נצבו כמו נד	14	cd
		בלב ים	קפאו תהמת	15	ef
	7	ארדף אשיג	אמר אויב	16	9ab
		תמלאמו נפשי	אחלק שלל	17	cd
		תורישמו ידי	אריק חרבי	18	ef
	8	כסמו ים	נשפת ברוחך	19	10ab
		במים אדירים	צללו כעופרת	20	cd

Survey of Exodus 15: the figures for five levels

strophe #	1	2	3	4	5	6	7	8	9	10	11	12	13	14	15	16
S/L	S	L	L	S	S	L	L	S	L	L	S	S	L	S	L	S
verses	2	3	3	2	2	3	3	2	3	3	2	2	3	2	3	1
cola	4	6	6	4	4	6	6	4	6	6	4	4	6	4	6	2
words	9	17	16	8	8	12	12	8	12	14	7	8	12	9	12	4
beats	8	16	14	8	8	10	12	8	11	12	7	8	12	8	12	4
syllables	20	40	40	19	23	28	29	22	25	36	16	18	30	16	37	9
	stanza I			R_1		stanza II		R_2			stanza III		R_3		stanza IV	

Exodus 15: syllable counts

(numbers per word, colon, verse and strophe)

stanza		line			verse	strophe
I		1	3.3	/ 1.2.2	6+5 = 11	
		2	1.4	/ 2.2	5+4 = 9	20
		3	2.3.1	/ 2.1.3	6+6 = 12	
		4	1.2.4	/ 3.2.6	7+11= 18	
		5	2.1.3	/ 2.2	6+4 = 10	40
		6	3.2.3	/ 2.2	8+4 = 12	
		7	3.3	/ 3.2.1	6+6 = 12	
		8	3.4	/ 3.3.2.1	7+9 = 16	40
	R	9	3.2	/ 3.2	5+5 = 10	
		10	3.2	/ 2.2	5+4 = 9	19
II		11	3.3	/ 2.3	6+5 = 11	
		12	3.3	/ 4.2	6+6 = 12	23
		13	3.3	/ 3.1	6+4 = 10	
		14	3.2.1	/ 3	6+3 = 9	
		15	3.3	/ 2.1	6+3 = 9	28
		16	2.2	/ 2.2	4+4 = 8	
		17	3.2	/ 4.2	5+6 = 11	
		18	2.2	/ 4.2	4+6 = 10	29
		19	3.4	/ 3.1	7+4 = 11	
		20	3.3	/ 2.3	6+5 = 11	22
	R	21	1.3	/ 3.2	4+5 = 9	
		22	1.3	/ 2.2	4+4 = 8	
		23	2.3	/ 2.1	5+3 = 8	25

stanza	line	cola		verse	strophe
III	24	3.3	/ 4.1	6+5 = 11	
	25	3.4	/ 1.1.3	6+5 = 11	
	26	3.4	/ 1.2.3	7+6 = 13	36
	27	3.2	/ 3	5+3 = 8	
	28	1.2	/ 3.2	3+5 = 8	16
	29	1.3	/ 3.2	4+5 = 9	
	30	2.2	/ 4.1	4+5 = 9	18
	31	1.3	/ 3.2	4+5 = 9	
	32	2.3	/ 3.2	5+5 = 10	
	33	2.4	/ 3.2	6+5 = 11	30
R	34	1.2	/ 3.2	3+5 = 8	
	35	1.2	/ 1.1.3	3+5 = 8	16
IV	36	4.5	/ 2.4	9+6 = 15	
	37	2.4	/ 3.2	6+5 = 11	
	38	2.3	/ 3.3	5+6 = 11	37
	39	2.2	/ 3.2	4+5 = 9	9

Deuteronomium 32, the first section

exordium
1 האזינו השמים ואדברה
   ותשמע הארץ אמרי פי
2 יערף כמטר לקחי
   תזל כטל אמרתי
3 כשעירים עלי דשא
   וכרביבים עלי עשב

strophe 2
4 כי שם יהוה אקרא
   הבו גדל לאלהינו
5 הצור תמים פעלו
   כי כל דרכיו משפט
6 אל אמונה ואין עול
   צדיק וישר הוא

strophe 3
7 שחת לו לא בניו מומם
   דור עקש ופתלתל
8 הליהוה תגמלו זאת
   עם נבל ולא חכם
9 הלוא הוא אביך קנך
   הוא עשך ויכננך

second section, first half (=stanzas II and III)

strophe 4   10   זכר ימות עולם
                    בינו שנות דור ודור
             11   שאל אביך ויגדך
                    זקניך ויאמרו לך

strophe 5   12   בהנחל עליון גוים
                    בהפרידו בני אדם
             13   יצב גבלת עמים
                    למספר בני ישראל
             14   כי חלק יהוה עמו
                    יעקב חבל נחלתו

strophe 6   15   ימצאהו בארץ מדבר
                    ובתהו ילל ישמן
             16   יסבבנהו יבוננהו
                    יצרנהו כאישון עינו

strophe 7   17   כנשר יעיר קנו
                    על גוזליו ירחף
             18   יפרש כנפיו יקחהו
                    ישאהו על אברתו

second section, second half (=stanzas IV and V)

strophe 8

19 יהוה בדד ינחנו
ואין עמו אל נכר
20 ירכבהו על במותי ארץ
ויאכל תנובת שדי
21 וינקהו דבש מסלע
ושמן מחלמיש צור

strophe 9

22 חמאת בקר וחלב צאן
עם חלב כרים ואילים
23 בני בשן ועתודים
עם חלב כליות חטה
ודם ענב תשתה חמר

strophe 10

24 וישמן ישרון ויבעט
שמנת עבית כשית
25 ויטש אלוה עשהו
וינבל צור ישעתו
26 יקנאהו בזרים
בתועבת יכעיסהו

strophe 11

27 יזבחו לשדים לא אלה
אלהים לא ידעום
28 חדשים מקרב באו
לא שערום אבתיכם
29 צור ילדך תשי
ותשכח אל מחללך

third section, first half (stanzas VI and VII)

strophe 12   30 וירא יהוה וינאץ
                        מכעס בניו ובנתיו
                    31 ויאמר אסתירה פני מהם
                        אראה מה אחריתם
                    32 כי דור תהפכת המה
                        בנים לא אמן בם

strophe 13   33 הם קנאוני בלא אל
                        כעסוני בהבליהם
                    34 ואני אקניאם בלא עם
                        בגוי נבל אכעיסם

strophe 14   35 כי אש קדחה באפי
                        ותיקד עד שאול תחתית
                    36 ותאכל ארץ ויבלה
                        ותלהט מוסדי הרים

strophe 15   37 אספה עלימו רעות
                        חצי אכלה בם
                    38 מזי רעב ולחמי רשף
                        וקטב מרירי
                    39 ושן בהמות אשלח בם
                        עם חמת זחלי עפר

strophe 16   40 מחוץ תשכל חרב
                        ומחדרים אימה
                    41 גם בחור גם בתולה
                        יונק עם איש שיבה

third section, second half (stanzas VIII and IX)

strophe 17   42   אמרתי אפאיהם
                          אשביתה מאנוש זכרם
                43   לולי כעס אויב אגור
                          פן ינכרו צרימו
                44   פן יאמרו ידינו רמה
                          ולא יהוה פעל כל זאת

strophe 18   45   כי גוי אבד עצות המה
                          ואין בהם תבונה
                46   לו חכמו ישכילו זאת
                          יבינו לאחריתם

strophe 19   47   איכה ירדף אחד אלף
                          ושנים יניסו רבבה
                48   אם לא כי צורם מכרם
                          ויהוה הסגירם
                49   כי לא כצורנו צורם
                          ואיבינו פלילים

strophe 20   50   כי מגפן סדם גפנם
                          ומשדמת עמרה
                51   ענבמו ענבי רוש
                          אשכלת מררת למו
                52   חמת תנינם יינם
                          וראש פתנים אכזר

strophe 21   53   הלא הוא כמס עמדי
                          חתם באוצרתי
                54   לי נקם ושלם
                          לעת תמוט רגלם
                55   כי קרוב יום אידם
                          וחש עתדת למו

fourth section (stanzas X and XI)

strophe 22	56	כי ידין יהוה עמו
		ועל עבדיו יתנחם
	57	כי יראה כי אזלת יד
		ואפס עצור ועזוב
strophe 23	58	ואמר אי אלהימו
		צור חסיו בו
	59	אשר חלב זבחימו יאכלו
		ישתו יין נסיכם
	60	יקומו ויעזרכם
		יהי עליכם סתרה
strophe 24	61	ראו עתה כי אני אני הוא
		ואין אלהים עמדי
	62	אני אמית ואחיה
		מחצתי ואני ארפא
		ואין מידי מציל
strophe 25	63	כי אשא אל שמים ידי
		ואמרתי חי אנכי לעלם
	64	אם שנותי ברק חרבי
		ותאחז במשפט ידי
strophe 26	65	אשיב נקם לצרי
		ולמשנאי אשלם
	66	אשכיר חצי מדם
		וחרבי תאכל בשר
	67	מדם חלל ושביה
		מראש פרעות אויב
strophe 27	68	הרנינו גוים עמו
		כי דם עבדיו יקום
	69	ונקם ישיב לצריו
		וכפר אדמתו עמו

size of the STANZAS, in six rows of figures

NUMBERS

STANZA	STROPHES	VERSES	COLA	WORDS	BEATS	SYLLABLES
I	3	9	18	62	53	134
II	2	5	10	32	30	73
III	2	4	8	23	21	65
IV	2	5	11	39	32	82
V	2	6	12	35	34	97
VI	2	5	10	34	30	77
VII	3	7	14	47	39	103
VIII	3	8	16	55	48	122
IX	2	6	12	37	33	83
X	3	7	15	51	47	115
XI	3	7	14	46	42	106

The range (of the numbers of syllables) is, from small to big:

65 - 73 - 77 - 82 - 83 - 97 - 103 - 106 - 115 - 122 - 134

figures for the 27 **strophes** in Deut.32, in five rows

	STROPHE	verses	cola	words	beats	syllables
	1	3	6	19	16	46
I	2	3	6	21	18	39
	3	3	6	22	19	49
II	4	2	4	13	12	31
	5	3	6	19	18	42
III	6	2	4	11	11	35
	7	2	4	12	10	30
IV	8	3	6	20	18	46
	9	2	5!	19	14	36
V	10	3	6	16	16	50
	11	3	6	19	18	47
VI	12	3	6	21	19	45
	13	2	4	13	11	32
	14	2	4	14	12	32
VII	15	3	6	20	17	45
	16	2	4	13	10	26
	17	3	6	21	19	46
VIII	18	2	4	14	13	30
	19	3	6	20	16	46
IX	20	3	6	18	16	43
	21	3	6	19	17	40
	22	2	4	15	12	30
X	23	3	6	18	17	44
	24	2	5!	18	16	41
	25	2	4	16	13	35
XI	26	3	6	17	17	41
	27	2	4	13	12	30

The stanzas and their beats, the strophes and their lengths

I) L + L + L

    3+3   3+3   4+3
    3+3   3+3   3+3
    2+2   3+3   3+3

———————————

II) S + L

    3+3   3+3
    3+3   3+3
             3+3

III) S + S

    3+3   3+2
    2+3   3+2

IV) L + S⁺

    3+3   3+3
    3+3   3+3+3
    3+3

V) L + L

    3+3   3+3
    3+3   3+3
    2+2   3+3

———————————

VI) L + S

    3+3   3+2
    4+3   3+3
    3+3

VII) S + L + S

    3+3   3+2   3+2
    3+3   4+2   2+3
             3+3

VIII) L + S + L

    2+3   4+3   3+3
    3+3   4+2   3+2
    4+4   3+2

IX) L + L

    3+2   3+2
    2+3   3+3
    3+3   3+3

———————————

X) S + L + S⁺

    3+3   3+3   4+3
    3+3   3+3   3+3+3
             2+3

XI) S + L + S

    3+4   3+2   3+3
    3+3   3+3   3+3
             3+3

syllables in Deut.32, counted per colon, verse and strophe

section					
I	*str.1*	*str.2*	*str.3*		
	11+8=19	6+7=13	8+7 =15		
	7+7=14	6+7=13	8+7 =15		
	6+7=13	7+6=13	9+10=19		
	$\overline{46}$+	$\overline{39}$+	$\overline{49}$+		
IIA	*str.4*	*str.5*	*str.6*	*str.7*	
	6+7=13	7+8=15	8+8=16	6+7=13	
	9+9=18	7+8=15	10+9=19	9+8=17	
		6+6=12			
	$\overline{31}$+	$\overline{42}$+	$\overline{35}$+	$\overline{30}$+	
IIB	*str.8*	*str.9*	*str.10*	*str.11*	
	7+7=14	8+7=15	9+9=18	9+7=16	
	9+8=17	8+6+7=21	8+9=17	8+8=16	
	9+6=15		7+8=15	6+9=15	
	$\overline{46}$+	$\overline{36}$+	$\overline{50}$+	$\overline{47}$+	
IIIA	*str.12*	*str.13*	*str.14*	*str.15*	*str.16*
	8+8=16	8+8=16	8+8=16	8+6=14	6+7=13
	10+6=16	9+7=16	7+9=16	9+5=14	7+6=13
	7+6=13			9+8=17	
	$\overline{45}$+	$\overline{32}$+	$\overline{32}$+	$\overline{45}$+	$\overline{26}$+
IIIB	*str.17*	*str.18*	*str.19*	*str.20*	*str.21*
	6+8=14	8+7=15	7+9=16	7+7=14	8+7=15
	7+8=15	8+7=15	8+6=14	7+8=15	6+6=12
	9+8=17		8+8=16	7+7=14	6+7=13
	$\overline{46}$+	$\overline{30}$+	$\overline{46}$+	$\overline{43}$+	$\overline{40}$+
IV	*str.22*	*str.23*	*str.24*	*str.25*	*str.26*	*str.27*
	7+8=15	8+5=13	10+8=18	8+11=19	7+8=15	7+7=14
	8+7=15	10+6=16	8+8+7=23	8+8 =16	6+7=13	8+8=16
		8+7=15			7+6=13	
	$\overline{30}$+	$\overline{44}$+	$\overline{41}$+	$\overline{35}$+	$\overline{41}$+	$\overline{30}$+

The Hebrew text of Job 3

	אחרי כן פתח איוב את פיהו ויקלל את יומו	1
	ויען איוב ויאמר	2
	והלילה אמר הרה גבר	יאבד יום אולד בו	3
אל תופע עליו נהרה	אל ידרשהו אלוה ממעל	היום ההוא יהי חשך	4
יבעתהו כמרירי יום	תשכן עליו עננה	יגאלהו חשך וצלמות	5
במספר ירחים אל יבא	אל יחד בימי שנה	הלילה ההוא יקחהו אפל	6
	אל תבא רננה בו	הנה הלילה ההוא יהי גלמוד	7
	העתידים ערר לויתן	יקבהו אררי יום	8
ואל יראה בעפעפי שחר	יקו לאור ואין	יחשכו כוכבי נשפו	9
	ויסתר עמל מעיני	כי לא סגר דלתי בטני	10
	מבטן יצאתי ואגוע	למה לא מרחם אמות	11
	ומה שדים כי אינק	מדוע קדמוני ברכים	12
	ישנתי אז ינוח לי	כי עתה שכבתי ואשקוט	13
	הבנים חרבות למו	עם מלכים ויעצי ארץ	14
	הממלאים בתיהם כסף	או עם שרים זהב להם	15
	כעללים לא ראו אור	או כנפל טמון לא אהיה	16
	ושם ינוחו יגיעי כח	שם רשעים חדלו רגז	17
	לא שמעו קול נגש	יחד אסירים שאננו	18
	ועבד חפשי מאדניו	קטן וגדול שם הוא	19
	וחיים למרי נפש	למה יתן לעמל אור	20
	ויחפרהו ממטמונים	המחכים למות ואיננו	21
	ישישו כי ימצאו קבר	השמחים אלי גיל	22
	ויסך אלוה בעדו	לגבר אשר דרכו נסתרה	23
	ויתכו כמים שאגתי	כי לפני לחמי אנחתי תבא	24
	ואשר יגרתי יבא לי	כי פחד פחדתי ויאתיני	25
	ולא נחתי ויבא רגז	לא שלותי ולא שקטתי	26

JOB 3: PROPORTIONS

STROPHE #	1	2	3	4	5	6	7	totals
S/L	S	L	S	L	S	L	S	
verses	3	4	3	4	3	4	3	24
cola	8	10	6	8	6	8	6	52
words	29	37	22	32	22	26	24	192
beats ±	26	31	20	25	19	23	20	164
syllables	64	83	46	65	46	65	55	424

STANZA #	I	II	III
verses	7	10	7
cola	18	20	14
words	66	76	50
beats ±	57	64	43
syllables	147	157	120

S-strophes (numbers 1, 3, 5, and 7)   totals

syllables	64	46	46	55	211
accents	26/7	20	19	20	85/6
words	29	22	22	24	97

L-strophes (numbers 2, 4, and 6)

syllables	83	65	65	213
accents ±	31/2	25	23	79/80
words	37	32	26	95

Words (scale from low to high)

22	22	24	26	29	32	37
S	S	S	L!	S!	L	L

Job 3: syllables (cola, verses, strophes)

	verse						
	3	2.1.3.1 / 4.2.2.1		= 7+9	= 16	46+**18**
8 cola	4	2.2.1.1 / 1.4.2.2 /	2.2.2.3	= 6+9+**9**	= 24	=
	5	4.1.3 / 2.2.3 /	5.3.1	= 8+7+**9**	= 24	64
	6	3.2.4.1 / 1.2.2.2 /	3.3.1.2	=10+7+**9**	= 26	
	7	2.3.2.1.2 / 1.2.3.1		=10+7	= 17	65+**18**
10 cola	8	4.3.1 / 4.2.3		= 8+9	= 17	=
	9	3.3.2 / 2.2.2 /	2.2.4.1	= 8+6+**9**	= 23	83

	10	1.1.2.2.2 / 3.2.3		= 8+8	= 16	
6 cola	11	2.1.2.2 / 2.3.3	= 7+8	= 15		46
	12	2.4.2 / 2.2.1.2	= 8+7	= 15		
	13	1.2.3.3 / 3.1.2.1	= 9+7	= 16		
8 cola	14	1.3.4.1 / 3.3.2	= 9+8	= 17		65
	15	1.1.2.2.2 / 4.3.1	= 8+8	= 16		
	16	1.2.2.1.2 / 4.1.2.1	= 8+8	= 16		
	17	1.3.3.1 / 2.3.3.1	= 8+9	= 17		
6 cola	18	1.3.3 / 1.3.1.2	= 7+7	= 14		46
	19	2.3.1.1 / 2.2.4	= 7+8	= 15		

	20	2.2.3.1 / 3.3.1	= 8+7	= 15		
8 cola	21	4.2.4 / 5.4	=10+9	= 19		65
	22	4.2.1 / 3.1.3.1	= 7+8	= 15		
	23	2.2.2.3 / 3.2.2	= 9+7	= 16		
	24	1.2.2.3.2 / 4.2.3		=10+9	= 19	
6 cola	25	1.1.3.5 / 3.3.2.1	=10+9	= 19		55
	26	1.3.2.3 / 2.2.3.1	= 9+8	= 17		

Abbreviations

AB	The Anchor Bible, New York
BDB	Francis Brown, S.R. Driver & Charles A. Briggs, A Hebrew and English Lexicon of the Old Testament, reprint Oxford 1976 (first ed. 1907)
BEThL	Bibliotheca Ephemeridum Theologicarum Lovaniensium
BHS	K. Elliger, W. Rudolph (eds.), Biblia Hebraica Stuttgartensia, 1967-77
BZ	Biblische Zeitschrift
BZAW	Beihefte zur ZAW
CBQ	Catholic Biblical Quarterly
CTAT	D. Barthélemy et al., Critique Textuelle de l'Ancien Testament, Orbis Biblicus et Orientalis 50/1, Göttingen 1982
EThL	Ephemerides Theologicae Lovanienses
GK	Wilhelm Gesenius & E. Kautzsch, Hebräische Grammatik, 28. Auflage, Leipzig 1909
HAL	L. Köhler, W. Baumgartner, J.J. Stamm, Hebräisches und aramäisches Lexicon zum Alten Testament, 3. Auflage, Leiden 1967-95
HKAT	Handkommentar zum alten Testament
HThR	Harvard Theological Review
JPS	The Jewish Publication Society of America: Tanakh translation, 2nd ed., 1985
JSOT(S)	Journal for the Study of the Old Testament (Supplements), Sheffield
KAT	Kommentar zum Alten Testament
NAG	J.P. Fokkelman, Narrative Art in Genesis, Specimens of Stylistic and Structural Analysis, Van Gorcum, Assen 1975; second edition: JSOT Press, Sheffield (The Biblical Seminar, 12) 1991
NAPS	J.P. Fokkelman, Narrative Art and Poetry in the Books of Samuel, A Full Interpretation based on Stylistic and Structural Analyses, four volumes, Assen 1981-1993

NBE	Nueva Biblia Española
NEB	New English Bible
NICOT	The New International Commentary on the Old Testament
OTS	Oudtestamentische Studiën
PPP	D.N. Freedman, Pottery, Poetry, and Prophecy, Winona Lake IN (1980)
RB	Revue Biblique
RSR	Revue de Science Religieuse
VT	Vetus Testamentum
VTS	Supplements to VT
ZAW	Zeitschrift der alttestamentlichen Wissenschaft
ZBK	Zürcher Bibelkommentare

Selected Bibliography

Alonso Schökel, L.	A Manual of Hebrew Poetics, Subsidia Biblica #11, Roma 1988
Alonso Schökel, L. & J.L. Sicre Diaz	Job, Comentario teológico y literario, NBE, Madrid 1983
Barré, M.	'My Strength and My Song' in Exodus 15:2, CBQ 54 (1992) pp.623-637
Beaucamp, E.	Structure strophique des Psaumes, RSR 56 (1968), 199-223
Berlin, Adele	On the Meaning of *pll* in the Bible, RB 96 (1989), pp.345-351
Bogaert, P.-M.	Les trois rédactions conservées et la forme originale de l'envoi du Cantique de Moïse (Dt 32,43), *in:* N. Lohfink, Das Deuteronomium, BEThL lxviii (1985) pp.329-340
Brenner, M.L.	The Song of the Sea, BZAW 195, Berlin 1991
S. Carrillo Alday	Género literario del Cántico de Moisés (Dt. 32), Estudios Bíblicos, xxvi (1967) pp.69-76
S. Carrillo Alday	El Cántico de Moisés (Dt. 32), Estudios Bíblicos, xxvi (1967),pp.143-185, 227-248, 327-352
S. Carrillo Alday	Contexto redaccional del Cántico de Moisés (Dt. 31, 1-32, 47), Estudios Bíblicos, xxvi (1967), pp.383-394
Cassuto, U.A.	Commentary on the Book of Exodus, Jerusalem 1967
Clines, D.J.A.	Job 1-20 (Word Biblical Commentary, 17), Dallas, Texas, 1989
Collins, Terence	Line-Forms in Hebrew Poetry, A grammatical approach to the stylistic study of the Hebrew Prophets, Rome 1978
Craigie, P.C.	Deuteronomy, NICOT 1976, Grand Rapids
Delitzsch, Franz	Das Buch Iob, Leipzig 1864, part IV.2 of Keil-Delitzsch, Biblischer Kommentar.
Duhm, B.	Die Psalmen, KHK XIV, 2nd ed. Tübingen 1922
Ehrlich, A.B.	Randglossen zur hebräischen Bibel, II, Leipzig 1909

Eissfeldt, Otto	Das Lied Moses Deuteronomium 32 1-43 und das Lehrgedicht Asaphs Psalm 78 samt einer Analyse der Umgebung des Mose-Liedes, *in:* Berichte über die Verhandlungen der sächsischen Akademie der Wissenschaften zu Leipzig, Philologisch-historische Klasse, Band 104, Heft 5 (Berlin 1958).
Fischer, Georg	Das Schilfmeerlied Exodus 15 in seinem Kontext, Biblica 77 (1996), pp.33-47
Fohrer, Georg	Das Buch Hiob (KAT 16), Gütersloh 1963
Fokkelman, J.P.	The Structure of Psalm 68, OTS xxvi, 1990, pp.72-83.
idem	The Song of Deborah and Barak: Its Prosodic Levels and Structure, pp.595-628 of *Pomegranates and Golden Bells*, Studies in Biblical, Jewish, and Near Eastern Ritual, Law, and Literature in Honor of Jacob Milgrom (edited by David P. Wright, David Noel Freedman, and Avi Hurvitz), Winona Lake IN, 1995
Freedman, David Noel	Pottery, Poetry and Prophecy, Winona Lake IN 1980
Geller, Stephen A.	The Dynamics of Parallel Verse. A Poetic Analysis of Deut 32:6-12, HTR 75 (1982) pp.35-56
Good, Edwin M.	In Turns of Tempest. A Reading of Job, with a translation, Stanford CA, 1990
Gosse, B.	Le texte d'Exode 15,1-21 dans la rédaction biblique, BZ 37 (1993), pp. 264-271.
Habel, Norman C.	The Book of Job, A Commentary, Old Testament Library, London, 1985
Hartley, John E.	The Book of Job (NICOT) Grand Rapids, 1988
Howell, M.	Exodus 15,1b-18: A Poetic Analysis, ETL 65 (1989) pp.5-42
Janzen, J. Gerald	The Root pr^c in Judges V 2 and Deuteronomy xxxii 42, VT xxxix (1989) pp.393-406
idem	Job, Interpretation, Atlanta, 1985
Joüon P. - Muraoka T.	A Grammar of Biblical Hebrew, Rome 1991, 2 vols.
Knowles, Michael P.	"The Rock, His Work is Perfect": Unusual Imagery for God in Deuteronomy xxxii, VT xxxix (1989) pp.307-322
van der Kooy, Arie	The Ending of the Song of Moses: On the Pre-Masoretic Version of 32:43, pp.93-100 in F. García Martínez, *et al.* (eds.), Studies in Deuteronomy (= Festschrift for C. Labuschagne), VTS 53, Leiden 1994
Kugel, James L.	The Idea of Biblical Poetry, Parallelism and Its History, Yale UP 1981

Labuschagne, C.	The Song of Moses: Its Framework and Structure, *in:* De Fructu Oris Sui (Festschrift A. van Selms, eds. I.H. Eybers *et al.*), pp.85-98, Leiden 1971
Ley, J.	Grundzüge des Rhythmus, des Vers- und Strophenbaues in der hebräischen Poesie, Halle 1875
Lohfink, N. (ed.)	Das Deuteronomium, Entstehung, Gestalt und Botschaft, Leuven 1985 (= BEThL LXVIII)
van der Lugt, Pieter	Strofische structuren in de Bijbels-Hebreeuwse poëzie, Kampen 1980
van der Lugt, Pieter	Rhetorical Criticism and the Poetry of the Book of Job, OTS xxxii, Leiden 1995
van der Meer, W. & de Moor, J.C.	The Structural Analysis of Biblical and Canaanite Poetry, JSOTS 74, Sheffield 1988
Michel, Walter M.	Job in the light of Northwest Semitic, volume I, Biblica et Orientalia 42, Rome 1987
Mowinckel, S.	Real and Apparent Tricola in Hebrew Psalm Poetry, *in:* Avhandlinger utgitt av Det Norske Videnskaps-Akademi i Oslo, 2, 1957
Nigosian, S.A.	The Song of Moses (Dt 32), A Structural Analysis, ETL LXXII (1996) pp.5-22
O'Connor, Michael	Hebrew Verse Structure, Winona Lake IN 1980
Pope, Marvin H.	Job (AB 15), New York 1979
Robertson, David A.	Linguistic Evidence in Dating Early Hebrew Poetry, SBL Dissertation Series #3, Missoula, Montana, 1972
Rose, M.	5. Mose, ZBK (AT) 1994
Skehan, P.W.	The Structure of the Song of Moses in Deuteronomy (Deut.32:1-43),CBQ 13 (1951), pp.153-163
Steuernagel, C.	Das Deuteronomium, HKAT, Göttingen 1898
Tur-Sinai, N.H.	The Book of Job, a New Commentary, Jerusalem 1967
Waltke, B.K. & M. O'Connor	An Introduction to Biblical Hebrew Syntax, Winona Lake IN, 1990
Watson, Wilfred G.E.	Classical Hebrew Poetry: A Guide to its Techniques, JSOTS 26, Sheffield 1984 (2nd ed. 1986)
Weitzman, Steven	Lessons from the Dying: The Role of Deuteronomy 32 in its Narrative Setting, HTR 87 (1994) p.377-393
Winter, P.	Der Begriff "Sohne Gottes" im Moselied Dt.32:1-43, ZAW 67 (1955) pp.40-48
Wright, G.E.	The Lawsuit of God: A Form-Critical study of Deuteronomy 32, *in:* B.W. Anderson & W. Harrelson (eds.), Israel's Prophetic Heritage (Festschrift J. Muilenburg), New York 1962

Subject Index

This index concentrates on the pertinent literary terms, disregards the footnotes, and skips words which are too frequent, such as strophe, colon, or common grammatical terms.

entry	*page number*
alliteration	7, 8, 9, 12, 13, 15, 31, 40, 43, 44, 47, 64, 67, 89, 90, 92, 93, 99, 100-102, 107, 115, 122, 125, 129, 161, 168, 169
ambiguity	98, 124
anaphora	9, 27, 28, 32, 38, 41, 47, 64, 72, 89, 90, 92, 121, 122, 129, 134, 147, 163, 167, 168, 170, 172
anticlimax	91, 94, 96
antithesis, antithetic	74, 80, 110, 113, 125, 130
antonymy	74
argument(ative structure)	22, 23, 58, 73, 75, 107, 111, 133, 138, 141, 142
assonance	9, 13, 38, 45, 64, 86, 87, 99, 103, 107, 115, 125
axis	15, 39, 52, 78, 101, 111, 130, 145, 147
balance	7, 11, 15, 17, 43, 48, 50, 60, 71, 77, 82, 85, 88, 99, 101, 105, 109, 145-147, 155, 164
binary	1, 13, 32, 50, 103, 147
boundary (of textual units)	41, 52, 74, 75, 79, 82, 87, 91, 93, 96, 98, 100, 133, 140, 164, 165
caesura	12, 15, 27, 32, 48, 82, 93, 99, 101, 115, 167
centripetal	29, 33, 41, 48, 51, 66
chain	9-11, 14, 15, 49, 79, 86, 93, 94, 98, 101, 103, 154, 157 (compare 'string')
chiasm, chiastic	6, 9, 12, 13, 32, 33, 39, 43-45, 47, 69, 70, 84, 85, 87, 88, 92-96, 99, 100, 109, 123, 125, 129, 147, 163, 165, 168, 169, 171, 172

chronology	6, 28, 43-45, 49, 51, 161, 166
circular	46, 47, 111, 112
climax	38, 89, 91, 96, 124, 128, 140, 154, 156, 157, 169, 172
closure	7, 8
coda	48, 50, 51, 130, 141
cohortative	37, 69, 98, 102, 108
communication	2, 6, 112, 142
concentric	33, 42, 50, 101, 134, 145, 148, 155, 169, 170
connotation	70, 99, 102, 161
contiguity	130, 171
counterfactual (mode, *irrealis*)	59, 107-113, 134, 141, 147, 153, 154, 159, 167, 169, 176, 177
deictic	39, 77, 168
density	5, 66, 85
diagonal	6, 12, 14, 28, 43, 82, 83, 99, 108, 115, 116, 125, 128, 130, 134, 147
dialectic(s)	75, 109, 112
difference (versus similarity)	9, 75, 77, 83, 91, 110
direct discourse	59, 106, 108, 121, 127, 130, 131, 134, 148
discourse, discursive	22, 41, 58, 59, 61, 75, 97, 111, 112, 118, 120, 141, 142, 152
double duty	33, 48, 164, 166, 170, 175
doubling	15, 60, 71-73, 76, 117
ellipsis	101, 165
embedding	31, 43, 58-61, 68, 75, 106, 108, 112, 120, 140, 149
enjambment	15, 27, 30, 33, 37, 41, 72, 82, 83, 90, 98, 117, 128, 134, 164
enumeration	47, 89, 90, 103, 124, 133, 147
factual (actual, versus counterfactual, unreal)	107, 109, 111, 134, 147
figura etymologica	6
hendiadys	117, 122
hyperbola	89, 111
iconic	100, 173
image	22, 43, 63, 66, 78, 86, 120, 124, 129, 141, 168, 175
imaginary	59, 112, 113
inclusio	7, 8, 30, 46, 50, 78, 94, 96, 98, 117, 121, 127, 130, 133, 134, 140, 141, 145
intracolon parallelism	76, 90, 98
isotopy	66
jussive	12, 76, 160-162, 169, 175
key word	41, 97, 99, 110, 117, 119, 134, 168

linguistic	2, 4, 5
litotes	70, 77, 81
merism	7, 12-14, 63, 66, 98, 103, 104, 124, 125, 147, 158, 161, 164
metaphor	67, 80, 86, 89, 90, 92, 95, 116, 123, 128, 133, 163, 165
metonymy	63, 66, 79, 80, 102, 103, 117, 122, 128, 129, 141
monologue	106, 127
narration, narrator, narrative section	58, 61, 67, 68, 74, 75, 78, 79, 84, 91, 94, 96, 97, 104, 112, 120, 133, 148, 165
opposition	61, 66, 80, 99, 109, 117, 119, 129, 168, 175
oral/auditory	80
oxymoron	166
paradox(ical)	98, 110, 112, 1133, 171, 172, 177
parallelism	17, 29, 63, 64, 69, 76, 81, 90, 98, 106, 108, 117, 119, 121, 122, 125, 162
parallelismus membrorum	8, 14, 22, 63, 69, 71, 82, 98, 129, 159, 161
paronomasia	6, 38, 173
pivot(al)	10, 102, 108, 123, 129, 166, 170
polar(ity)	15, 47, 106, 107, 112, 145, 159, 169
proleptic	109, 117
prosody, prosodical	8, 9, 12, 16, 17, 23, 29, 30, 33, 44, 46, 50, 62, 67, 76, 77, 85, 114, 116, 174, 176
quotation	58, 112, 120
quotation formula	9, 44, 59-61, 97, 98, 106, 111, 113, 121, 127
real, reality (versus the counterfactual)	110, 112, 113, 141, 154, 159, 176, 177
refrain strophe	29, 30, 33, 41, 42, 45, 48, 51, 52
regular(ity)	16, 18, 41, 52, 76-78, 85, 94, 99, 105, 114, 126, 131, 148, 152, 155, 173, 174
reversal	7, 91, 95, 122, 134, 141
rhetoric(al)	11, 22, 41, 110, 112, 117, 138, 142, 166, 172
rhetorical question	10, 28, 45, 59, 72, 73, 76, 164, 175
rhyme	9, 13, 39, 40, 42, 47, 49, 63, 64, 86, 87, 92, 102, 103, 117, 119, 128, 130, 147, 169, 173
rhythm	31, 44, 86, 148
ring (structure)	46, 48, 96, 99, 118, 120, 129, 131, 132, 140, 163
semiotic	7, 67
sensory	9, 65, 85
similarity (versus difference)	9, 75, 83
soliloquy	59, 98, 106, 108, 112, 120, 121
staircase parallelism	26-28, 30, 32, 41, 48, 50
string	74, 75, 92

strophe boundary	9, 12, 13, 22, 90, 122, 128, 129
symmetry	9, 17-19, 50, 51, 63, 77, 85, 94, 96, 99, 101, 126, 131, 134, 145, 146, 155, 164
syndesis	173
synecdoche	129
synonymy	12, 46, 49, 92, 130, 143, 148, 160, 162
ternary	94
triad, trio, threesome	39, 63, 81, 83, 92, 115, 116, 119-122, 143, 157
vocal/auditory	7
word pair	14, 15, 63, 69, 80, 81, 98, 102, 103, 107, 123, 128-130, 159
word play	99, 102, 109, 130

Published in the series STUDIA SEMITICA NEERLANDICA

1   C. van Leeuwen, Le développement du sens social en Israel avant l' ère chrétienne*
2   M. Reisel, The mysterious Name of Y.H.W.H. The Tetragrammation in connection with the names of EHYEH ašer EYHEH - Huhā - and Šem Hamm^{e}phôraš*
3   A.S. van der Woude, Die messianischen Vorstellungen der Gemeinde von Qumrân*
4   B. Jongeling, Le rouleau de la guerre des manuscrits de Qumrân*
5   N.A. van Uchelen, Abraham de Hebreeër. Een literair- en historisch-kritische studie naar aanleiding van Genesis 14:13*
6   H.J.W. Drijvers, Bardaisan of Edessa*
7   J.H. Meesters, Op zoek naar de oorsprong van de Sabbat*
8   A.G. van Daalen, Simson. Een onderzoek naar de plaats, de opbouw en de funktie van het Simsonverhaal in het kader van de Oudtestamentische geschiedschrijving*
9   Leon A. Feldman, R. ABRAHAM b. ISAAC ha-LEVI TaMaKH. Commentary on the Song of Songs. Based on MSS and Early Printings with an Introduction, Notes, Variants and Comments*
10 W.A.M. Beuken, Haggai-Sacharja I-8. Studien zur Überlieferungsgeschichte der frühnachexilischen Prophetie
11 Curt Leviant, King Artus, a Hebrew Arthurian Romance of 1279*
12 Gabriel H. Cohn, Das Buch Jona. Im lichte der Biblischen Erzählkunst*
13 G. van Driel, The Cult of Aššur*
14 H. Jagersma, Leviticus 19, Identiteit - Bevrijding - Gemeenschap
15 Wilhelm Th. In der Smitten, ESRA. Quellen, Überlieferung und Geschichte*
16 Travels in the World of the Old Testament. Studies presented to prof. M.A. Beek, on the occasion of his 65th birthday*
17 J.P. Fokkelman, Narrative Art in Genesis. Specimens of Stylistic and Structural Analysis*
18 M.D. Koster, The Peshitta of Exodus. The Development of its Text in the Course of Fifteen Centuries
19 C.H.J. de Geus, The Tribes of Israel. An Investigation into some of the Presuppositions of Martin Noth's Amphictyony Hypothesis*
20 J.P. Fokkelman, Narrative Art and Poetry in the Books of Samuel. A full interpretation based on stylistic and structural analyses. Volume I: King David (II Sam. 9-20 & I Kings, 1-2)
21 J. Hoftijzer, The Function and Use of the Imperfect Forms with Nun Paragogicum in Classical Hebrew
22 K. van der Toorn, Sin and Sanction in Israel and Mesopotamia. A Comparative Study*
23 J.P. Fokkelman, Narrative Art and Poetry in the Books of Samuel. A full interpretation based on stylistic and structural analyses. Volume II: The Crossing Fates (I Sam. 13-31 & II Sam. 1)
24 L.J. de Regt, A Parametric Model for Syntactic Studies of a Textual Corpus, Demonstrated on the Hebrew of Deuteronomy 1-30
25 E.J. van Wolde, A Semiotic Analysis of Genesis 2-3. A Semiotic Theory and Method of Analysis Applied to the Story of the Garden of Eden
26 T.A.M. Fontaine, In Defence of Judaism: Abraham Ibn Daud. Sources and Structures of ha-Emunah ha-Ramah

27	*J.P. Fokkelman*, Narrative Art and Poetry in the Books of Samuel. A full interpretation based on stylistic and structural analyses. Volume III: Throne and City (II Sam. 2-8 & 21-24)
28	*A.J.C. Verheij*, Verbs and Numbers. A Study of the Frequencies of the Hebrew Verbal Tense Forms in the Books of Samuel, Kings, and Chronicles
29	*P.J. Siebesma*, The function of the niph'al in Biblical Hebrew. In relationship to other passive-reflexive verbal stems and to the pu'al and hoph'al in particular
30	*Y. Gitay*, Isaiah and His Audience. The Structure and Meaning of Isaiah 1-12
31	*J.P. Fokkelman*, Narrative Art and Poetry in the Books of Samuel. A full interpretation based on stylistic and structural analyses. Volume IV: Vow and Desire (I Sam. 1-12)
32	*Y. Endo*, The verbal System of Classical Hebrew in the Joseph Story. An Approach from Discourse Analysis
33	*N.J.C. Kouwenberg*, Gemination in the Akkadian Verb
34	*Rodriques Pereira*, Studies in Aramaic Poetry (c. 100 B.C.E. - c. 600 C.E.). Selected Jewish, Christian and Samaritan Poems
35	*Johnson Teng Kok Lim*, The Sin of Moses and the Staff of God. A Narrative Approach
36	*M. Rosenbaum*, Word-Order Variation in Isaiah 40-55. A Functional Perspective
37	*J.P. Fokkelman*, Major Poems of the Hebrew Bible. At the Interface of Hermeneutics and Structural Analysis Volume I: Ex. 15, Deut. 32, and Job 3.

* *Out of print*

BS
1405.2
.F65
1998